OXFORD WORLD'S CLASSICS

MEMOIRS OF EMMA COURTNEY

MARY HAYS was born in 1760 in Southwark, near London. At 17, she fell in love with John Eccles, but was at first forbidden to marry him. Although their families eventually relented, Eccles died from a fever just before the marriage in 1780. Hays was inconsolable. Thereafter she turned to intellectual pursuits, corresponding with men such as Robert Robinson, George Dyer, William Godwin, and Henry Crabb Robinson, who became her mentors. An ardent admirer of Mary Wollstonecraft, Hays published *Letters and Essays, Moral and Miscellaneous* (1793) which discussed female education, friendship, and the doctrines of materialism and necessity. She became friends with the circle of London radicals, including Thomas Holcroft, associated with the publisher Joseph Johnson, and fell in love with a Cambridge mathematician, William Frend, writing a series of passionate though unreciprocated love letters to him. On Godwin's advice this unrequited romance became her first novel, *Memoirs of Emma Courtney* (1796). Towards the end of the 1790s she associated with Charles Lamb, Samuel Taylor Coleridge, and Robert Southey, and was satirized by other reactionary anti-Jacobins, who depicted her as a 'modern philosopher' because of her public confession of love for Frend and her outspoken feminist and revolutionary sympathies. Her second novel, *The Victim of Prejudice* (1799), describes abuses of male power in a society which victimizes women without fortune or family. After 1800, Hays lived a quieter life and produced works which were less critical of authority and institutions. She published two biographical works, *Female Biography* (1803) and *Memoirs of Queens* (1821), and wrote a number of didactic novels and historical narratives for young readers. She corresponded with Eliza Fenwick and Henry Crabb Robinson until her death in 1843.

ELEANOR TY is Professor of English at Wilfrid Laurier University in Waterloo, Ontario. She is the author of *Empowering the Feminine: The Narratives of Mary Robinson, Jane West, and Amelia Opie, 1796–1812* (1998), *Unsex'd Revolutionaries: Five Women Novelists of the 1790s* (1993) and the editor of *The Victim of Prejudice* (1994) by Mary Hays.

OXFORD WORLD'S CLASSICS

*For over 100 years Oxford World's Classics have brought
readers closer to the world's great literature. Now with over 700
titles—from the 4,000-year-old myths of Mesopotamia to the
twentieth century's greatest novels—the series makes available
lesser-known as well as celebrated writing.*

*The pocket-sized hardbacks of the early years contained
introductions by Virginia Woolf, T. S. Eliot, Graham Greene,
and other literary figures which enriched the experience of reading.
Today the series is recognized for its fine scholarship and
reliability in texts that span world literature, drama and poetry,
religion, philosophy and politics. Each edition includes perceptive
commentary and essential background information to meet the
changing needs of readers.*

OXFORD WORLD'S CLASSICS

═

MARY HAYS

Memoirs of
Emma Courtney

═

Edited with an Introduction and Notes by
ELEANOR TY

OXFORD
UNIVERSITY PRESS

OXFORD
UNIVERSITY PRESS

Great Clarendon Street, Oxford OX2 6DP

Oxford University Press is a department of the University of Oxford.
It furthers the University's objective of excellence in research, scholarship,
and education by publishing worldwide in

Oxford New York

Athens Auckland Bangkok Bogotá Buenos Aires Calcutta
Cape Town Chennai Dar es Salaam Delhi Florence Hong Kong Istanbul
Karachi Kuala Lumpur Madrid Melbourne Mexico City Mumbai
Nairobi Paris São Paulo Shanghai Singapore Taipei Tokyo Toronto Warsaw

with associated companies in Berlin Ibadan

Oxford is a registered trade mark of Oxford University Press
in the UK and in certain other countries

Published in the United States
by Oxford University Press Inc., New York

Editorial matter © Eleanor Ty 1996

The moral rights of the author have been asserted
Database right Oxford University Press (maker)

First published as a World's Classics paperback 1996
Reissued as an Oxford World's Classics paperback 2000

British Library Cataloguing in Publication Data

Data available

Library of Congress Cataloging in Publication Data
Hays, Mary, 1759 or 60–1843.
Memoirs of Emma Courtney/Mary Hays; edited with an introduction
by Eleanor Ty.
p. cm.—(Oxford world's classics)
Includes bibliographical references.
1. England—Social life and customs—18th century—Fiction.
2. Man–woman relationships—England—Fiction. 3. Feminism—England—
Fiction. 4. Sex role—England—Fiction. 5. Women—England—
Fiction I. Ty, Eleanor Rose, 1958– . II. Title. III. Series.
[PR4769.H6M4 1996] 823'.7—dc20 95–17356

ISBN–13: 978–0–19–283729–5
ISBN–10: 0–19–283729–X

4

Printed in Great Britain by
Clays Ltd, St Ives plc

CONTENTS

ACKNOWLEDGEMENTS

In preparing this book, I have used the printed materials and manuscript resources of the British Library; Dr Williams's Library in London; the Carl Pforzheimer Collection in the New York Public Library; the McMaster University Library, and the University of Toronto Library. I am grateful to these institutions and to their courteous and efficient librarians and staff. Thanks are due to the Social Sciences and Humanities Research Council of Canada for financial support, and to Wilfrid Laurier University for awarding me a generous Book Preparation Grant and a Course Remission Grant for the fall of 1994.

I am indebted to several individuals who assisted me in various ways: Anthony W. Shipps, for amazing and quick help with identifying about a dozen quotations; Gary Kelly and Peter Sabor, for discussions about editing and eighteenth-century novels; Jason Koskela, for enthusiastic and intelligent research assistance; Pat Elliot, Lorette Clement-Smith, and Paul Bleton, for stimulating conversations about the nature of desire. I owe much to my students, and to my colleagues in the English Department at Wilfrid Laurier University for making work such a pleasure. Finally, I thank my family, whose support and love have been constant.

INTRODUCTION

I love action, but I have but little to employ myself in; I love society, but my sex and acquired delicacy, and still more the narrowness of my fortune, deprives me of this resource. I would travel, I would change the scene, I would put myself in the way of receiving new impressions, I would sluice of my thoughts into various channels, I would place myself in new situations, I would propose to myself new labours, and engage with ardor in new pursuits—all this I should prescribe to another in my circumstances, but all this is, to me, unattainable. Ah! how impotent is *mere* reasoning against reiterated feeling!

Impassioned, intimate, emotional, and eloquent—this passage, from a letter written to William Godwin dated 13 October 1795,[1] shows many typical traits of the writings of Mary Hays. *Memoirs of Emma Courtney*, published in 1796, is an extraordinary literary work precisely because of the author's characteristic intensity and energy. It is one of the most articulate and detailed expressions of the yearnings and frustrations of a woman living in late-eighteenth-century English society. Though primarily a sentimental novel, it is indebted to various genres such as life writing, the epistle, and the philosophical essay. What distinguishes this work from others in the period is its attempt to fuse or break down traditional opposites: reason and passion, public and private, autobiography and fiction, freedom and restraint, female and male. Hays's insistence that there be no boundaries is one of the reasons why the novel is so powerful. For her, the private and the personal world—her loneliness, heartbreak, ambition, desires, and disappointments—provided the best materials for political and intellectual analysis in the public sphere.

---

[1] Twenty-seven letters written by Mary Hays to William Godwin between 1794 and 1796 are at the Carl Pforzheimer Library in New York.

Mary Hays was born in 1760 in Southwark, London, and grew up in a large middle-class Dissenting family.[2] Around 1777 she met and fell in love with another Dissenter, John Eccles, who lived close by on Gainsford Street. Her widowed mother disapproved of Eccles because she thought him socially inferior, while Eccles's father wished him to join in the family business before he would agree to his son's marriage. John Eccles refused, and the couple was admonished by their families not to see each other again. Over the next year or so, Hays and Eccles met and corresponded secretly with the help of her sister, Elizabeth. Their letters are sweet, romantic, and full of youthful enthusiasm. For example, in a letter dated 12 February 1779, John Eccles wrote:

Miss Hays, I have loved you; I adore you, and the greater discouragements I have met with, the more firmly has my heart been attached to you![3]

Mary Hays's commitment was equally fervent:

It has been a fatal attachment, a source of distress from its commencement!—My heart bleeds for you. If it will give you any satisfaction, I here promise never to be the wife of any other, while you remain single,—a promise which I owe to your sufferings.[4]

---

[2] Protestant Dissenters, like Roman Catholics, were barred from public office by the Test Act of 1673. Marilyn Butler notes that 'throughout the eighteenth century the Dissenters provided an element of pacific dissidence in English society, a tradition of individualism and "levelling" that went back to the Civil War.' They 'played down religion's magical and liturgical aspects, and stressed instead the moral and the rational', *Romantics, Rebels and Reactionaries: English Literature and its Background 1760–1830* (Oxford, Oxford Univ. Press, 1972), 13–14. Biographical information is found in A. F. Wedd, *The Love-Letters of Mary Hays (1779–80)* (London, Methuen, 1925); Gina Luria, 'Mary Hays: A Critical Biography', Ph.D. thesis (New York University, 1972); Janet Todd, ed. *A Dictionary of British and American Women Writers 1660–1800* (Totowa, NJ, Rowman & Littlefield, 1987); Virginia Blain, Patricia Clements, and Isobel Grundy (eds.), *The Feminist Companion to Literature in English* (New Haven, Yale Univ. Press, 1990), and Gary Kelly, *Women, Writing, and Revolution 1790–1827* (Oxford, Clarendon, 1993).

[3] Wedd, *Love-Letters*, 16.   [4] Ibid. 23.

They felt that they shared mutual interests. Hays explained to Eccles, ''tis your sensibility, your sentiments, your understanding that claim my tenderest esteem'.[5] But her passion for him did not make her forget social expectations of herself as a 'proper lady'.[6] She reminded him on 10 September 1779:

Endeavor not to take advantage of my partiality in your favor, by freedoms which I dare not allow, and that are not consistent with the delicacy I owe to my sex and character, and which I am sure you expect in the woman you wish to be united.[7]

The correspondence not only provided Hays with romance; it was also her avenue to intellectual growth. Eccles, like the fictional Augustus Harley in *Emma Courtney*, was her mentor as well as her lover. Writing often in a desultory fashion, at other times in the style of Samuel Johnson's essays, she would discuss in her letters subjects ranging from the pleasures of the city versus those of nature; to female propriety or Prudence; to differences between male and female upbringing. Hays recognized early on that women and men had dissimilar capacities because of their education. To Eccles she observed, 'I concluded that your education being different, gave a different turn to your pursuits, and your ideas also.'[8] This epistolary exchange with a male intellectual figure was the first of many in the life of Mary Hays. She later corresponded in the same way with the radical nonconformist Robert Robinson (1735–1790); with Robinson's biographer, George Dyer (1755–1841); with the Cambridge mathematician William Frend (1757–1841); and with the Romantic chronicler Henry Crabb Robinson (1775–1867). The epistolary mode became the basic form which structures *Emma Courtney*.

Consent for the long-wished-for union between the

---

[5] Ibid. 118.

[6] See Mary Poovey, *The Proper Lady and the Woman Writer: Ideology as Style in the Works of Mary Wollstonecraft, Mary Shelley, and Jane Austen* (Chicago, Univ. of Chicago Press, 1984), ch. 1.

[7] Wedd, *Love-Letters,* 79.   [8] Ibid. 29.

lovers was finally obtained in 1780. Just before they were to
be married, however, John Eccles became ill and died on
23 August 1780. Mary Hays was inconsolable, and to
Eccles's sister she wrote on 29 August 1780:

Your loss is not to be compared with mine; mine is irreparable,
unspeakable! he was the friend of my heart; the best beloved of
my soul! all my happiness—all my pleasure—and every opening
prospect are buried with him! He was all I saw in the creation; I
had not a hope but what was centered in him; buried with him—
and at a time so interesting! . . . Instead of those scenes of social
and domestic bliss which my imagination had pictured to itself, I
am involved in misery—left desolate in a world which cannot
afford me one satisfying idea![9]

For Hays this loss was to remain one of the defining moments of her life, an incident to which she ascribed much
of her subsequent character and actions. In a letter to
William Godwin of 13 October 1795 she explained,

I was an enthusiast in friendship, an enthusiast in love, an enthusiast in my desire and knowledge! The result was, that my
heart was pierced through with many sorrows, and my understanding, alternately, harrassed with doubt and bewilder'd in
error. The spring of life is now past, and it has been worn in
anguish.[10]

Eccles's death meant that the 'social and domestic bliss' of
becoming wife and mother, the most common subject
positions open to women at the time, was no longer available to Hays.

This early tragedy, along with the more immediate experience of frustrated desire in Hays's second failed *amour*,
provided the real-life materials for *Memoirs of Emma
Courtney*. When Hays fell in love the second time, it was
with William Frend, a man who evidently did not recipro-
cate her romantic feelings for him. Once again the relationship was based on mutual interests and was partly
epistolary in nature. Their friendship began on 16 April
1792 when William Frend wrote to Mary Hays from

[9] Wedd, *Love-Letters*, 203–4.
[10] Letter in the Pforzheimer Collection.

Jesus College, Cambridge, expressing his admiration for 'Eusebia'. Hays had published a pamphlet, 'Cursory Remarks on an Enquiry into the Expediency and Propriety of Public or Social Worship: Inscribed to Gilbert Wakefield', under the name of Eusebia in 1791. In this work, which she felt was rather bold coming from 'a woman, young, unlearned, unacquainted with language but her own; possessing no other merit than a love of truth and virtue, an ardent desire of knowledge', she refutes Wakefield's argument that public worship should be abolished because it was hypocritical and ostentatious.[11] Hays demonstrated her ability to write a well-constructed and convincing argument based on biblical evidence as well as her own experience. Citing numerous instances of social prayer in the gospels and her own sense of 'satisfaction, intellectual entertainment, and improvement, from an attendance on the public ordinances of religion', she maintained that 'the world is not yet ripe for a religion purely mental and contemplative'.[12]

Frend was eager to meet Eusebia and was excited by her 'freedom of candor' and 'sound reasoning'.[13] The actual circumstances of their initial meetings are unknown. However, he did encourage Hays as a writer, making marginal comments in late 1792 on the manuscript version of her *Letters and Essays, Moral and Miscellaneous*, a work influenced by Mary Wollstonecraft's *A Vindication of the Rights of Woman* (1792). By 1794 Hays and Frend were corresponding with each other, and they met in London frequently in the company of Rational Dissenters and radicals such as Theophilus Lindsey, John Disney, George Dyer, and later, Thomas Holcroft and William Godwin. That Hays saw Frend as a Rousseauistic Abelard or tutor figure in the way that her heroine saw Augustus can be seen by her eager-

[11] Eusebia, *Cursory Remarks on an Enquiry into the Expediency and Propriety of Public or Social Worship: Inscribed to Gilbert Wakefield* (2nd edn., with a postscript; London, T. Knott, 1792), 3; Gilbert Wakefield, *An Enquiry into the Expediency and Propriety of Public or Social Worship*, a New Edition (London, J. Deighton, 1792).
[12] Eusebia, *Cursory Remarks*, 15, 13.
[13] See Wedd, *Love-Letters*, 220–2.

ness to study what Frend was interested in, to read what he endorsed. She was studying mathematics under the direction of Hugh Worthington in 1794, and mentioned that she must consult her 'Euclid' in a letter to Godwin in December 1795. On Frend's high recommendation of *An Enquiry Concerning Political Justice*, Hays wrote to William Godwin on 14 October 1794 to ask him if he would lend her his copy of the book.

At this time, Hays was increasingly moving towards the radicalism inspired by the French Revolution of 1789.[14] In the early years of the 1790s many English intellectuals, including Richard Price, Tom Paine, and Mary Wollstonecraft, saw the abolition of the monarchy in France as a sign of the dawning of a new age of equality and freedom. Writers like William Godwin, Robert Bage, and Thomas Holcroft were referred to by contemporary critics as 'Jacobin' novelists because of their opposition to tyranny and oppression, and their belief, as Gary Kelly puts it, that 'reason should decide the issue in human affairs and human government, not power based on money, age, rank, sex, or physical strength'.[15] Edmund Burke, whose *Reflections on the Revolution in France* (1790) passionately attacked the French Revolution on behalf of English aristocratic and monarchic order, quickly became the target of the radicals. Unlike Burke, the sympathizers of the Revolution were in favour of a system of government based not on heredity and property, but one based on liberty, rational judgement, and individual merit. Many of these reformers, including Dr Joseph Priestley, Thomas Holcroft, the philologist John Horne Tooke, and the shoemaker Thomas Hardy, were later branded as traitors. Some of them were arrested for high treason in 1794.

While Hays was not directly involved in the debates

[14] For a more detailed study of the way women writers were inspired by the French Revolution, see the Introduction to my book, *Unsex'd Revolutionaries: Five Women Writers of the 1790s* (Toronto, Univ. of Toronto Press, 1993), 3–30.
[15] Gary Kelly, *The English Jacobin Novel 1780–1805* (Oxford, Oxford Univ. Press, 1976), 8.

about the French Revolution, she was an active member of
the circle of middle-class artists, writers, and intellectuals
who clustered around the bookseller and publisher Joseph
Johnson. In addition to Godwin and Wollstonecraft, this
group included Henry Fuseli, Anna Laetitia Barbauld,
William Blake, Maria Edgeworth, Elizabeth Inchbald, and
Helen Maria Williams. The publication of her *Letters and
Essays, Moral and Miscellaneous* in 1793[16] allied her with this
politically subversive group. As its title suggests, the book
was a collection of essays in the form of epistles on a variety
of topics such as civil liberty, female education, the
dangers of novel reading, the doctrines of materialism and
necessity, friendship, and human nature. As Katharine
Rogers notes, 'through concrete examples, carrying the
authenticity of familiar experience, Hays has made her
case for encouraging women to form ideas and think out
rational and moral principles . . . She makes her case in a
plain, colloquial style appropriate to showing that it is
perfectly evident to common sense.'[17] Thus, by the time
she came to write her letters to William Frend and William
Godwin between 1794 and 1796, she was not just any
romantic thirty-something young woman, but a published
author who had read widely, albeit rather eclectically, on
religious, political, historical, and philosophical subjects.
Like her heroine, Emma, Hays was familiar with the
works of William Shakespeare, Alexander Pope, Samuel
Johnson, and James Thomson, and with the novels of
Samuel Richardson, Laurence Sterne, and Jean-Jacques
Rousseau, as well as those of her contemporaries, William
Godwin, Elizabeth Inchbald, and Thomas Holcroft.

Memoirs of Emma Courtney was a direct result of Hays's love
and romantic pursuit of William Frend. It is not clear how
one-sided the romance was, since all we have are second-
hand accounts from Henry Crabb Robinson's diary, and a

[16] Her sister Elizabeth Hays contributed two essays (X, XI) to this
collection.
[17] Katharine M. Rogers, 'The Contribution of Mary Hays', *Prose Studies*,
10/2 (Sept. 1987), 137.

caricatured version of Hays's life and philosophy in the parodic novel *Memoirs of Modern Philosophers* (1800) by Elizabeth Hamilton. Hays was also featured as Lady Gertrude Sinclair, 'a woman of warm affections, strong passions, and energetic intellect, yielding herself to . . . loose and declamatory principles, yet at the same time uncorrupted in her intentions, unfortunate from error, and not from deliberate vice', in Charles Lloyd's anti-Jacobin, anti-Coleridge novel, *Edmund Oliver* (1798).[18] At one point Crabb Robinson noted that Frend professed an attachment for Hays, but at another point suggested that 'the love-making was all on the lady's side'.[19] Hamilton's novel has a heroine named Bridgetina Botherim based on Hays, who misapplies or takes Godwin's precepts literally. She becomes an object of ridicule because of her exaggerated belief in the 'perfectibility of humankind', and her comedic and rash pursuit of a man who was clearly in love with another woman.[20] From Hays's correspondence with Godwin, we know that Hays wrote long, passionate letters to Frend explaining her desire for him. According to Gina Luria, 'in the months between May, 1795, and March, 1796, she passed through a "crisis" of confrontation with Frend which ended in the "blasting" of her hopes for marriage'.[21] Hays then wrote to Godwin, the Mr Francis figure in the novel, for advice and for consolation.

Since many of the letters to Godwin are replicated *verbatim* in *Emma Courtney*, we can assume that as many of the letters Emma writes to Augustus were originally Hays's love letters to Frend. But *Emma Courtney* is nevertheless very much a novel, though it has strong autobiographical elements. Tilottama Rajan prefers to use the term

[18] Charles Lloyd, *Edmund Oliver* (2 vols.; Bristol, J. Cottle, 1798) vol. i. p. ix.

[19] Henry Crabb Robinson, *On Books and Their Writers*, ed. Edith J. Morley (London, 1938), 235, as quoted by Gina Luria, 'Mary Hays: A Critical Biography', 228.

[20] For a study of the effects of parody in *Memoirs of Modern Philosophers*, see my 'Female Philosophy Refunctioned: Elizabeth Hamilton's Parodic Novel', *Ariel: A Review of International English Literature*, 22/4 (Oct. 1991), 111–29.   [21] Gina Luria, 'Mary Hays: A Critical Biography', 228.

'autonarration', as it 'is a textually self-conscious work that draws upon personal experience as part of its rhetoric, so as to position experience within textuality and relate textuality to experience'.[22] Hays had written to Godwin asking him for advice as to what she might do to occupy herself after having failed to find happiness through love. He had apparently suggested that she attempt to set down her thoughts in the form of a novel.[23] In a letter of February 1796 she asked Godwin, 'What then am I to do? I want a substitute for the mind must have an object—but where am I to gain it?'[24] Hays saw that the problem for women was that society did not allow them enough scope to exercise their talents constructively. It was a problem that was to face her heroines in *Emma Courtney* and in her second novel, *The Victim of Prejudice*. Hays complained,

I can think, write, reason, converse with men and scholars, and despise many petty, feminine, prejudices. But I have not the talents for a legislator or a reformer of the world, I have still many shrinking delicacies and female foibles, that unfit me for rising to arduous heights ... Where, then, shall I find this object to call forth my exertions, and preserve me from languour and apathy?[25]

Reworking the recent events of her life into a fictional form was not only to serve the function of preserving her from her dejected spirits, but also that of giving her a sense of identity, providing her with a purpose in life, and channelling her intellectual energies.

In the Preface to the novel, Hays states that the 'most interesting and the most useful fictions' are those that

[22] Tilottama Rajan, 'Autonarration and Genotext in Mary Hays' *Memoirs of Emma Courtney'*, *Studies in Romanticism*, 32/2 (Summer 1993), 149–76. Rajan defines autonarration as 'a genre characterized by its transgressive miscegenation of private and public spaces. Autonarration is part of a larger discursive formation characteristic of romanticism, in which writers bring details from their personal lives into their texts, speaking in a voice that is recognizably their own or through a persona whose relation to the biographical author is obvious', 158–9.

[23] Luria, 'Mary Hays', 229.

[24] Letter 14, Pforzheimer Collection.   [25] Ibid.

examine the 'consequences of one strong indulged passion or prejudice'. Influenced by Claude Adrien Helvétius as well as by William Godwin, Hays believed that it was possible to determine the way the human mind worked by detailing and analysing the circumstances that lead to important human actions. In his *A Treatise on Man, His Intellectual Faculties and His Education*, Helvétius asserts that 'the character of a man is the immediate effect of his passions, and his passions are often the immediate effects of his situations.'[26] Hays was then determined to explore the origins and effects of a woman's passion through her novel, an ambitious task as it meant a frank assessment and revelation of her thoughts and feelings. It may have seemed a self-indulgent act, but Hays had Jean-Jacques Rousseau as a model. In his *Confessions*, Rousseau stated that he 'was resolved on an enterprise which has no precedent'. His purpose was to display 'a portrait in every way true to nature' using himself as a model.[27] In the June 1796 issue of *The Monthly Magazine*, Hays wrote:

But were every great man to become his own biographer, and to examine and state impartially, to the best of his recollection, the incidents of his life, the course of his studies, the causes by which he was led into them, the reflections and habits to which they gave birth, the rise, the change, the progress of his opinions, with the consequences produced by them on his affections and conduct, great light might be thrown in the most interesting of all studies, that of moral causes and the human mind.[28]

Hays, then, was interested in displaying a portrait of a woman, and hoped to study the causes and consequences

---

[26] [Claude Adrien] Helvétius, *A Treatise on Man, His Intellectual Faculties and His Education*, transl. W. Hooper (2 vols.; London, B. Law & G. Robinson, 1777), 27.

[27] Jean-Jacques Rousseau, *The Confessions*, transl. J. M. Cohen (Harmondsworth, Penguin, 1954), i. 17.

[28] M. H. [Mary Hays], 'Reply to J. T. on Helvétius', *The Monthly Magazine and British Register*, 1 (Feb.–June 1796), (London, R. Phillips, 1796), 387.

of the 'universal sentiment' of love with some 'degree of originality' (Preface). Her aim was not to depict an ideal character, but one 'liable to the mistakes and weaknesses of our fragile nature' (Preface).

While Hays herself saw a difference between the writing of fiction and the composition of letters based on events in her life, twentieth-century theorists of autobiography remind us that distinctions between the factual and the fictive are more tenuous. For example, Sidonie Smith argues that 'the autobiographer is the self-historian, auto-biography representation. Purporting to reflect upon or recreate the past through the processes of memory, auto-biography is always, multiply, storytelling: memory leaves only a trace of an earlier experience that we adjust into story; experience itself is mediated by the ways we describe and interpret it to others and ourselves; cultural tropes and metaphors which structure autobiographical nar-rative are themselves fictive; and narrative is driven by its own fictive conventions about beginnings, middles, and ends.'[29] According to Smith's theories, even Hays's ac-counts of Frend's rejection of her love would already be implicated in the fictional realm because of its use of narrative conventions. In her letters Hays constructs her-self, albeit unintentionally, as the sentimental heroine, as a victim of sensibility. Rajan contends that what she calls 'autonarration' is a 'specific form of self-writing, in which the author writes her life as a fictional narrative, and thus *consciously* raises the question of the relationship between experience and its narrativization.'[30] What is important here is that by the conscious presentation of these letters as a work of fiction for public eyes, Hays was staking her place in the literary and philosophical world. Feminist Monique Wittig writes, 'For each time I say "I," I reorgan-ize the world from my point of view and through abstrac-

[29] Sidonie Smith, 'Construing Truths in Lying Mouths: Truthtelling in Women's Autobiography', *Studies in the Literary Imagination*, 23/2 (Fall 1990), 145.
[30] Rajan, 'Autonarration and Genotext', 160.

tion I lay claim to universality. This fact holds true for every locutor.'[31]

In the same year that Hays was preparing *Memoirs of Emma Courtney*, Mary Wollstonecraft's *Letters Written During a Short Residence in Sweden, Norway, and Denmark* appeared. Wollstonecraft's letters, like Hays's, were written to an actual person, but became a means whereby the author examines larger questions about human life, art, nature, happiness, gender, and national differences.[32] Hays had read Wollstonecraft's work, of which William Godwin had written: 'If ever there was a book calculated to make a man fall in love with its author, this appears to me to be the book.'[33] Wollstonecraft's *Letters Written . . . in Sweden* showed how the desiring subject in the private sphere could become the subject of desire through an articulation of female subjectivity in the public realm. Its form was one that would have appealed to Hays; as she had remarked earlier to Godwin, 'the epistolary form I conceived the most adapted to my style and habits of composition, . . . fictitious correspondence affords me not the stimulus which I ever feel when addressing my friends.'[34] Like Wollstonecraft, Hays was attempting to grapple with the vexed relation between feminist politics, individual autonomy, and romantic love. Wollstonecraft's inability to fully control and rationalize her yearning for her lover, Gilbert Imlay, creates much of the tension in the work, and adds a hint of poignancy and pathos to the

[31] Monique Wittig, 'The Mark of Gender', *The Straight Mind and Other Essays* (Boston, Beacon Press, 1992), 81.

[32] For a study of the way in which gender, genre, and language function in the work, see my essay, 'Writing as a Daughter: Autobiography in Wollstonecraft's Travelogue', Marlene Kadar (ed.) *Essays on Life Writing: From Genre to Critical Practice* (Toronto, Univ. of Toronto Press, 1992), 61–77.

[33] William Godwin (ed.), *Memoirs of the Author of a Vindication of the Rights of Woman* (London, J. Johnson, G. G. & J. Robinson, 1798), 129. Shortly after the publication of *Letters* Godwin and Wollstonecraft began seeing each other. They got married on 29 March 1797 after she became pregnant.

[34] Letter 9 to William Godwin dated 20 Nov. 1795, Pforzheimer Collection.

Letters in much the same way as Hays's struggle with her unreciprocated passion for Frend does. Both women were intellectuals, followers of Enlightenment thinking, but were at the same time animated by strong feelings and sensibility which come through in their writing.

For Hays, strong feelings and passions were not necessarily flaws or signs of weakness in an individual, but could be an indication of the strength of one's character. She did not subscribe to the binary world-view which tends to divide systems into hierarchical opposites such as male/female, sun/moon, reason/passion.[35] As a disciple of Helvétius, Hays believed that 'strong mental powers appear to be connected with acute and lively sensation, or the capacity of receiving forcible impressions'.[36] In his *De L'esprit: or, Essays on the Mind*, Helvétius stated that 'passions are in the moral, what motion is in the natural world. If motion creates, destroys, preserves, animates the whole, that without it everything is dead; so the passions animate the moral world.' For him, strong passion need not be confined to the sensual realm; rather, the term refers to a 'passion, the object of which is so necessary to our happiness that without the possession of it life would be insupportable'.[37] In *Memoirs of Emma Courtney* the belief in her passion, or in the object necessary to her happiness, is what motivates the heroine, what propels her to continue her quest of Augustus Harley despite his seeming lack of interest. After Emma decides that '*the desire of being beloved*, of inspiring sympathy, is congenial to the human heart,' (i. Ch. XXV), she resolves to do what she can to attain the object of her affection for both his sake and hers. The

[35] This system of 'dual, hierarchical oppositions' which links woman with the inferior term permeates 'literature, philosophy, criticism, centuries of representation and reflection', according to Hélène Cixous and Catherine Clément in 'Sorties: Out and Out: Attacks/Ways Out/Forays', *The Newly Born Woman*, transl. Betsy Wing (Minneapolis, Univ. of Minnesota Press, 1985), 63–132.

[36] M. H. [Mary Hays], 'Are Mental Talents Productive of Happiness?', *The Monthly Magazine*, 3 (May 1797), 358.

[37] Helvétius, *De L'esprit: or, Essays on the Mind, and Its Several Faculties* (London, 1759), 149, 150.

pursuit of Augustus may seem rather egotistical, but Emma believes that the union would benefit them both. For her, 'philosophy' does not 'regulate the feelings, but it has added fervor' to her passion (i. Ch. XXVI).

Influenced by Helvétius, Hays's heroine reasons, 'What are passions, but another name for powers? The mind capable of receiving the most forcible impressions is the sublimely improveable mind!' (i. Ch. XXVI). The argument equates superiority of the mind with strength of passions. Helvétius had cited figures like Alexander, Pericles, Zamolxis, Zaleuxus, and others as examples of how 'in reality great passions only can produce great men'.[38] Implicitly, Emma is comparing herself to these heroes by her echoing of Helvétius's language. At another point, she tells Augustus, 'You may suspect me of wanting resolution, but strong, persevering affections, are no mark of a weak mind' (ii. Ch. IV). To Godwin, Hays had compared her love for Frend to that of Petrarch for Laura:

I am by no means convinced, that a hopeless, persevering, and unrequited attachment, is *in itself* uninteresting—it is a proof of a lively and strong imagination, of a sanguine, an enterprising, an ardent, an unconquerable, spirit—It is strength, tho' ill-directed![39]

Hays views Emma's passion therefore not as the sentimental, weak, tearful, and pining sort, but one that is indicative of a potent and fiery force.

In fact, Emma's analysis of her feelings leads her to conclude that 'contradictions' and 'oppositions' rouse the energy of her mind (ii. Ch. XII) rather than dampen it. She tells Francis, the Godwinian character in the novel, 'my reason was the auxiliary of my passion, or rather my passion the generative principle of my reason' (ii. Ch. XII). Emma's thinking about passion comes from the philosophical traditions of Helvétius and Rousseau which were espoused in the 1790s by novelists such as Godwin

[38] Helvétius, *De L'esprit*, 153.
[39] Letter 25 dated May 1796, to William Godwin, Pforzheimer Collection.

and Thomas Holcroft. In his *Treatise on Man*, Helvétius had noted that 'love is a powerful principle of activity in man. It has often changed the face of empires.'[40] In the same work, he acknowledged that 'desire is the motive principal of the soul, without desire it stagnates! We must desire to act, and act to be happy.'[41] From Rousseau's *Émile*, Emma picks up the idea of natural relations, what she describes as the 'union between mind and mind', irrespective of class and social differences (ii. Ch. II). In addition, in his *Héloïse*, which Emma reads with 'transport' and 'enthusiasm' (i. Ch. VIII), are romantic assertions such as 'true love is the chastest of all human connexions; and [that] its sacred flame should purify our natural inclinations, by concentring them in one object.'[42] The notion of love based on mutual feelings, interests, and intellectual compatibility rather than on possessions and class is one of the central themes of Holcroft's novel *Anna St. Ives* (1795).

Both Rousseau's *Julie ou La Nouvelle Héloïse* and Holcroft's *Anna St. Ives*, from which Hays quotes extensively in *Emma Courtney*, are epistolary novels about transgression and forbidden love. Linda Kauffman has suggested that the letter constantly reiterates an equation of writing with sexual freedom, transgression, and seduction.[43] Even though *Emma Courtney* is not a sustained epistolary work, it is framed by letters to the young Augustus Harley in crucial moments: at the beginning, middle, and end. Its genesis as actual letters by Hays and its use of these letters also locate it as a kind of epistolary fiction, a popular form in the eighteenth century. Rousseau's *La Nouvelle Héloïse*, as Nicola Watson has pointed out, 'plays out a contest between female sexuality/textuality'. Watson examines the influence of Rousseau's *La Nouvelle Héloïse* on sentimental fiction written in Britain

---

[40] Helvétius, *A Treatise on Man*, ii. 74.   [41] Ibid. 254.

[42] J. J. Rousseau, *Eloisa: Or, A Series of Original Letters*, transl. William Kendrick (4 vols.; London, T. Beckett, 1776), i. 167.

[43] See Linda S. Kauffman, *Discourses of Desire: Gender, Genre, and Epistolary Fictions* (Ithaca, NY, Cornell Univ. Press, 1986), 64.

after the French Revolution, and argues that 'the woman's letter, exemplified in Julie's last missive, . . . concentrates in the most heady and potent form the complex of desire and transgression upon which the narrative of revolution, in the 1790s and thereafter, is founded'.[44] What is significant about this woman's letter is its articulation of female desire in spite of patriarchal injunctions that attempt to efface it with claims of duty and honour to the family.

That Emma (and Hays herself) should express desire through the writing of letters is appropriate, as letters are midway between the private form of a diary and the more public realm of fiction. By nature, letter-writing depends on both presence and absence. The writer needs the absence of the addressee in order for her to come into being as a correspondent. At the same time the presence of the absent or lost object can be evoked through the materiality of epistles—ink, paper, words on a page. Though grounded in the factual, letters are always part-fantasy, detailing scenes from an unrecoverable past, or articulating a yet unattainable future. Kauffman asserts that a 'letter to the beloved is also a self-address', and that letter writing involves 'self-creation, self-invention'.[45] Unlike those of Richardson's Clarissa or Rousseau's Julie, most of Emma's letters are never answered. The result is that *Emma Courtney* has a monologic rather than dialogic effect.[46] Emma inscribes herself through her letters, and her desire is willed into being through her insistent repetition. With its interest in causes and effects, Hays's novel reveals the complex origins of female desire, one which is 'transcribable, yet ultimately elusive'.[47] This

---

[44] Nicola J. Watson, *Revolution and the Form of the British Novel, 1790–1825: Intercepted Letters, Interrupted Seductions* (Oxford, Clarendon, 1994), 14, 15.

[45] Kauffman, *Discourses of Desire*, 25.

[46] M. M. Bakhtin, in *The Dialogic Imagination: Four Essays*, transl. Caryl Emerson and Michael Holquist (Austin, Tex., Univ. of Texas Press, 1981), suggests that the novel has a dialogic quality as it contains 'a diversity of social speech types . . . and a diversity of individual voices, artistically organized', 262.

[47] Kauffman, *Discourses of Desire*, 24.

desire, ostensibly for Augustus Harley, has its roots in various sources which can be explained through literary models, as well as socio-historical and psychoanalytical theories.

As Emma insists on telling young Augustus her story from her infancy, in order to demonstrate Godwin's belief in the 'irresistible power of circumstances, modifying and controuling our characters, and introducing, mechanically, those associations and habits which makes us what we are' (i. Ch. I), the novel can be categorized as a *Bildungsroman*, or a novel of formation, much like George Eliot's *The Mill on the Floss* (1860). In these types of novels, the main subject is the development of the protagonist's mind and character from childhood, through a spiritual or physical crisis, to maturity and the recognition of her identity and role in the world. Emma's pursuit of Augustus Harley can be read as her attempt to fulfil the socially acceptable role of wife and mother. But Harley's rejection of her prevents her from taking on this role. To complicate matters, as a woman, Emma cannot pursue other options or careers in the public sphere as a man could in late-eighteenth-century Britain. Hays's novel does not conclude, as James Joyce's *A Portrait of the Artist as a Young Man* (1914) does, with the protagonist's realization of his role as an artist. One wonders whether it is possible for a female *Bildungsroman* to end without marriage and still end happily, given the limitations for women socially and historically.

Through Emma's account of her childhood, Hays raises questions about the efficacy of female education. The novel does not enter into a full-fledged discussion about education, as Mary Wollstonecraft's *Thoughts on the Education of Daughters* (1787) and *A Vindication of the Rights of Woman* (1792) do. However, Hays does analyse the growth of her heroine's mind in the same way as a Romantic writer like William Wordsworth does with his *Prelude*, which was started in the same decade, though published much later. Emma's character owes much to her reading of literature. As a child, her maternal aunt, Mrs Melmoth, entertains her and her cousins with 'stories from the Arabian Nights, Turkish Tales, and other works of like marvellous import' (i. Ch. III). At 6, Emma learns to recite verses from 'Pope's Homer, and Thomson's Seasons' (i. Ch. III). Literature fires her imagination, 'stories were still my passion, and I sighed for a romance that would never end. In my sports with my companions, I acted over what I had read: I was alternately the valiant knight—the gentle damsel—the adventurous mariner—the daring robber—the courteous lover—and the airy coquet' (i. Ch. III). At 14 she subscribes to a circulating library and devours 'ten to fourteen novels in a week' (i. Ch. V), which leads Mr Courtney to fear that her 'fancy requires a *rein* rather than a *spur*' (i. Ch. VII). Her aunt's dying words echo this fear: 'I dread, lest the illusions of imagination should render those powers, which would give force to truth and virtue, the auxiliaries of passion' (i. Ch. IX).

The freedom with which Emma pursues literature is contrasted with the restrictive nature of her formal education. At boarding school, Emma says, 'my actions were all constrained;—I was obliged to sit poring over needlework, and forbidden to prate;—my body was tortured into forms, my mind coerced, and tasks imposed upon me, grammar and French, mere words, that conveyed to me no ideas' (i. Ch. IV). While her own random reading leads her to a Quixote-like apprehension of reality, boarding-school education is reductive and limiting. Its purpose is to create the male fantasy of a feminine and sexualized woman with superficial ornamental skills. It does not provide a woman with practical or useful skills. At Morton Park, Emma offers to teach the children 'music, drawing, French, or any other accomplishment' with which her education had equipped her (i. Ch. XII). However, Mrs Morton calls them '*elegant* accomplishments' which might 'unfit' her children 'for their future, probable stations' (i. Ch. XII). On the subject of female education, Hays agreed with Mary Wollstonecraft and with the conservative moralist, Hannah More, both of whom criticized Rousseau for his creation of the beautiful, soft, and submissive Sophie as an ideal woman for his Emile.[48]

In *A Vindication of the Rights of Woman*, Wollstonecraft argued that women must be better educated if men want them to be good wives and mothers. 'Women, whose minds are not enlarged by cultivation, or the natural selfishness of sensibility expanded by reflection, are very unfit to manage a family.'[49] She was critical of social practices which make women 'entirely dependent on their senses for employment and amusement', and felt that women 'have been stripped of the virtues that should clothe humanity, they have been decked with artificial graces that enable them to exercise a short-lived tyranny'.[50] In order to teach women virtues such as 'modesty, temperance, and self-denial', it was necessary to change the system of education: 'give their activity of mind a wider range, and nobler passions and motives will govern their appetites and sentiments'.[51] In an essay called 'Improvements Suggested in Female Education' published in *The Monthly Magazine*, Hays echoed Wollstonecraft in spirit, but focused the problem slightly differently. She writes:

Female education, as at present conducted, is a complete system of artifice and despotism; all the little luxuriances and exuberances of character which individualise the being, which give promise of and lay foundation for future powers are so carefully lopped and pruned away; sincerity and candour are repressed with solicitude, the terrors of opinion are set in array, and suspended over the victim, till the enfeebled and broken

[48] For a study of the ways in which Wollstonecraft and More sought 'to endow woman's role with more competence, dignity, and consequence', see Mitzi Myers, 'Reform or Ruin: "A Revolution in Female Manners" ', *Studies in Eighteenth-Century Culture*, 11 (1982), 199–216. Both Wollstonecraft and More criticized Rousseau's views of women as creatures who charm and please men, but who have limited intellectual and physical capabilities.

[49] Mary Wollstonecraft, *A Vindication of the Rights of Woman*, ed. Carol Poston (New York, Norton Critical Edn., 1975), 66.

[50] Wollstonecraft, *Rights of Woman*, 29, 37.   [51] Ibid. 82.

xxvi *Introduction*

spirit submits to the trammels, and passive, tame and docile, is stretched or shortened . . . to the universal standard.[52]

Hays valued the exuberances, the idiosyncratic and the unconventional characteristics that make each person slightly different from the other.[53] Like Godwin, she did not believe that society should make all human beings, 'however different', subscribe to 'a precise, general rule' (ii. Ch. II). Distinctive characteristics or passions, particularly in females, were often suppressed in order that women might conform to the ideal of the proper lady.

However, Hays did share Wollstonecraft's concern that women were being given a frivolous education. She observes:

One of the principal causes which seems to have given rise to the present dissolute and venal motives by which the intercourse of the sexes is influenced, is perhaps the *dependence* for which women are uniformly educated. . . . The greater proportion of young women are trained up by thoughtless parents; in ease and luxury, with no other dependence for their future support than the precarious chance of establishing themselves by marriage: for this purpose . . . elaborate attention is paid to external attractions and accomplishments, to the neglect of more useful and solid acquirements.[54]

In *Emma Courtney* the theme of dependence is echoed by the heroine, who uses the imagery of the magic circle and the adamantine chain to talk of women's entrapment, professionally, physically, and socially (i. Ch. XI).[55] The

[52] M. H. [Mary Hays], 'Improvements Suggested in Female Education', *The Monthly Magazine*, 3 (March 1797), 193–5.
[53] Hays's interest in the individual coincides with what Lawrence Stone has termed the 'growth of affective individualism', the 'desire for personal self-expression in the late seventeenth and the eighteenth centuries', as well as John Locke's theory that the individual preceded society. See Stone, *The Family, Sex and Marriage In England 1500–1800* (New York, Harper & Row, 1977), 230.
[54] Hays, 'Improvements Suggested in Female Education', 194.
[55] For a more detailed discussion of entrapment, see ch. 2, 'Breaking the "Magic Circle": From Repression to Effusion in *Memoirs of Emma Courtney*', in Ty, *Unsex'd Revolutionaries*.

philosopher's wisdom and metaphysical advice seem to be impractical for a woman. Francis tells Emma: 'You have talents, cultivate them, and learn to rest on your own powers' (i. Ch. XII), and, 'the first lesson of enlightened reason, the great fountain of heroism and virtue, the principle by which alone man can become what man is capable of being, is *independence*' (ii. Ch. XI). However, Emma finds that 'the customs of society, . . . have enslaved, enervated, and degraded woman' (i. Ch. XIII). Francis's male-centred discourse reflects the androcentric world of late-eighteenth-century society. In practice, she discovers that most professions and trades are not available to her: 'Active, industrious, willing to employ my faculties in any way, by which I might procure an honest independence, I beheld no path open to me, but that to which my spirit could not submit—the degradation of servitude' (ii. Ch. XVII). Her only other alternative is to marry, even though she does not have 'a heart to bestow' to Montague (ii. Ch. XVIII).

In *Emma Courtney*, Hays shows the difference between marriages based on love, or what historian Lawrence Stone calls 'the companionate marriage', and those made for convenience. By the end of the eighteenth century, as Stone and Randolph Trumbach have pointed out, marriage for companionship and affection was becoming increasingly more widespread.[56] Emma's parents, who married for ambition, vanity, and material gain, have an unhappy, short marriage with unsatisfactory social results (i. Ch. I). Mr Courtney, 'little moved by . . . domestic distresses', is unable and unwilling to take responsibilities as parent after his wife's death. In her late adolescence, Emma realizes that he is a 'man of pleasure, . . . inaccessible to those kindlings of the affections', and her heart revolts at the thought of calling him 'father' (i. Ch. X). This family situation is contrasted in the novel with the

---

[56] See Stone, *Family, Sex and Marriage*, pt. 4, ch. 6–8, and Randolph Trumbach, *The Rise of the Egalitarian Family: Aristocratic Kinship and Domestic Relations in Eighteenth-Century England* (New York, Academic Press, 1978), ch. 2 and 3.

Melmoths, who married 'from motives of affection' (i. Ch. II). Unlike Mr Courtney, Mr Melmoth, who has an 'affectionate heart', views his family as a 'source of joy, . . . his hours of relaxation were devoted to his family and social enjoyment' (i. Ch. II). His home is the ideal example of the new style of domesticity which, Trumbach argues, replaced patriarchy in the eighteenth century.[57]

These contrasting circumstances are important because in seeking a union with Augustus Harley based on 'nature, reason, and virtue', Emma believed that she would be replicating the harmonious domestic environment of the Melmoths (i. Ch. XXV). One difficulty, though, is that Augustus Harley, as Margaret Anne Doody has pointed out, is a descendant of Henry Mackenzie's Harley, the original *Man of Feeling* (1771).[58] MacKenzie's hero is an impulsive and emotionally excitable man, full of delicacy and sensibility. He has 'an acute capacity to feel deeply and to put himself in another's place' which are necessary qualities for benevolent human actions.[59] Hays, like other female novelists of the 1790s such as Wollstonecraft, in *Wrongs of Woman; or Maria* (1797); Elizabeth Inchbald, in *Nature and Art* (1796); Charlotte Smith, in *Desmond* (1792) and *The Young Philosopher* (1798); and Frances Burney, in *The Wanderer; or, Female Difficulties*, was experimenting with depictions of the sensitive male protagonists who possessed refined judgement, generosity, and sympathy. However, as Doody notes, this ideal man 'was perpetually attractive and puzzling to women writers, as they tried to construct what a man of real feeling and sensitivity might be like'.[60]

Part of the problem stems from an Enlightenment tradition where reason is set in opposition to passion and/or

[57] Trumbach argues that 'domesticity', which was 'based on the friendship of husband and wife', gradually replaced patriarchy, and that 'romantic rather than arranged marriages became the ideal and the practice', *Rise of the Egalitarian Family*, 97, 123, 3, and ch. 3.

[58] Margaret Anne Doody, Introduction to *The Wanderer; or, Female Difficulties* by Frances Burney (Oxford, World's Classics, 1991), pp. xxv–xxvi.

[59] Gerard A. Barker, *Henry Mackenzie* (Boston, Twayne, 1975), 30.

[60] Doody, Introduction to *The Wanderer*, p. xxvi.

feeling; where restraint and authority are the markers of
masculinity and order. The Man of Feeling and the husband of the new-style domesticity tend not to conform
strictly to these fundamental divisions. Hays and the other
women novelists saw that there was something wrong with
the old paradigm, but were not yet sure of what a new
conception of male and female subjectivities and the relationship between them would be like. Hence, there were
some uneven and awkward resolutions to plots by these
writers.[61] The ending of *Emma Courtney* has been criticized
by readers of the eighteenth as well as of the twentieth
century. Many are disconcerted by the fact that even
though the bulk of the novel consists of Emma's concentrated pursuit of Augustus, in the last few chapters of the
novel a number of improbable incidents occur: Emma
marries the insipid Mr Montague, has a brief reunion with
Augustus, who dies in her home, and then discovers her
husband's infidelity. The husband's subsequent suicide
seems to be too contrived for some readers. In a letter to
Hays dated January 1797, Mary Wollstonecraft informed
Hays that the poet and novelist Mary Robinson had read
Emma Courtney and thought 'the death of Augustus the end
of the story and that the husband should have been suffered to die a natural death'. Wollstonecraft remarked that
her 'sympathy ceased at the same place'.[62] Feminist critic
Janet Todd regrets that in Hays's novel, 'what the heroine
wants is the conventional romantic ending albeit brought
about by unromantic means: marriage to Harley proposed
by herself'.[63] I would argue that what Hays wants for
her heroine, and for herself, perhaps, may be found, not
in the melodramatic and somewhat artificial ending, but
in the novel's interesting middle section, particularly in

[61] For example, Wollstonecraft had a difficult time with the ending of
Wrongs of Woman, while Inchbald defers novelistic closure to the next
generation.
[62] Mary Wollstonecraft, *Collected Letters of Mary Wollstonecraft*, ed. Ralph
M. Wardle (Ithaca, NY, Cornell Univ. Press, 1979), 376.
[63] Janet Todd, *The Sign of Angellica: Women, Writing and Fiction, 1660–
1800* (New York, Columbia Univ. Press, 1989), 245.

Hays's attempt to explore the enigmatic nature of female desire.

Hays's desire for Augustus, whom she believes to be the embodiment of a man of refined sensibility, is linked to her search for her mother and her wish for the power that comes with knowledge. According to Jacques Lacan's psychoanalytic theory, there is almost always a gap between what one demands and what one desires. Desire is 'an element necessarily lacking, unsatisfied, impossible, mis-construed'.[64] As the object of desire is 'only a partial representation of something beyond it', Tilottama Rajan suggests that 'Emma's desire for Augustus' is about 'something else that is signified by that desire'.[65] For Emma's love for Augustus does not start with their meeting but begins before that, with her friendship with his mother, Mrs Harley. When Mrs Harley talks about Augustus, Emma is so 'affected by her maternal love' that she sheds a tear, as 'tender remembrances, and painful comparisons crouded into' her mind (i. Ch. XVI). Mrs Harley's maternal discourse evokes for Emma her own regrets and losses. Emma lost her mother at birth, and subsequently lost her aunt, whom she calls 'my more than mother' at that 'critical period of life, when the harmless sports and occupations of childhood gave place to the pursuits, the passions, and the errors of youth' (i. Ch. IX). It is not surprising that, in such a psychically vulnerable position, Emma's 'grateful love for Mrs Harley . . . transferred itself to her son' (i. ch. XVIII). Emma's desire, which could be for any number of things, such as maternal solicitude, approbation, companionship, sex, intellectual and artistic stimulation, becomes focused on Augustus because this desire 'can express itself only in the socially prescribed form of heterosexual love'.[66]

Part of Augustus's attraction for Emma is his mystique. Emma creates him in her imagination as the Rousseauvian

---

[64] Jacques Lacan, *The Four Fundamental Concepts of Psycho-Analysis*, transl. Alan Sheridan (New York, Norton, 1981), 154.

[65] Rajan, 'Autonarration and Genotext', 154.

[66] Ibid. 155.

'St. Preux, the Emilius' of her sleeping and waking reveries
(i. Ch. XVIII). Her first encounter with him looks forward
to the well-known scene in Charlotte Brontë's *Jane Eyre*
(1847) where the young and inexperienced Jane sees Mr
Rochester for the first time, half-believing him to be a
mythical spirit or a Gytrash.[67] The meetings in both novels
take place in the month of January on a cold, moonlit
night in an isolated road. In both cases an accident occurs
and the man is injured, which makes him temporarily
dependent on the heroine. The parallels may be coin-
cidental, but they reveal much about female fantasy and
the complicated expression of desire. As both Hays and
Brontë were writing at a time when decorum and propriety
did not allow single women and men to have much physical contact with each other, especially at the initial stages
of courtship, an injury becomes an acceptable and oppor-
tune occasion for a demonstration of sympathy and affection. The presence of the moon, the secluded, if not
romantic setting, the turbulent night, contribute to the
enchantment of the moment. Both Jane Eyre and Emma
Courtney are forlorn orphans, both are outcasts who see
themselves at a kind of crossroads. As Jane Eyre remarked:
'it was an incident of no moment, no romance, no interest
in a sense; yet it marked with change one single hour of a
monotonous life'.[68] In Hays's scene, Emma literally comes
in with one man, the mundane Montague, and exits
with another, the dark, mysterious stranger. In the wind-
swept heath, Emma unconsciously 'clasped the stranger'
to her 'throbbing bosom' (i. Ch. XX). Her actions are
indicative of her internal agitations and her suppressed
desires.

For Emma, Augustus represents many things she lacks.
He is associated with the maternal, with the state of pleni-
tude, with being loved and idolized. She notes his resemblance 'to his mother', and weeps, 'tears half delicious,
half agonizing' (i. Ch. XX). Her tears are not simply for

[67] Charlotte Brontë, *Jane Eyre* (Oxford, World's Classics, 1981), i.
ch. 12.
[68] Ibid.

him, but for all the things she sees in him that could have
been in her own life. It is by nursing Augustus that Emma
becomes Mrs Harley's 'beloved daughter' (i. Ch. XXI). As
her 'new *brother*', Augustus assists Emma 'in the pursuit of
learning and sciences', in astronomy, philosophy, and
languages (i. Ch. XXII). He becomes her tutor, her
Abelard, who is identified not only with learning, but also
with sexual transgression and the prohibition of desire.
She is attracted to him because he has access to those
'truths divine' which, as a woman, Emma felt she did not
have.

   Twentieth-century philosopher and historian Michel
Foucault has examined the links between power, knowledge, and sexuality in a number of his works. Foucault
notes that 'knowledge and power are integrated with one
another, . . . it is not possible for power to be exercised
without knowledge, it is impossible for knowledge not to
engender power'.[69] In part, Emma's desire for Augustus
stems from her yearning not only to possess the knowledge
he offers, but also the power that constitutes that knowledge. In *The History of Sexuality* Foucault shows the ways in
which 'power and desire are joined to one another', argu-
ing that 'where there is desire, the power relation is already present'.[70] As one critic puts it, 'sexuality and
identity can be only understood . . . in terms of the complicated and often paradoxical ways in which pleasures,
knowledges, and power are produced and disciplined in
language, and institutionalized across multiple social
fields.'[71] In *Emma Courtney*, when the heroine says, 'I feel,
that I am neither a philosopher, nor a heroine—but a
woman, to whom education has given a sexual character' (ii. Ch.
VI), she is making the connection between the acquisition

[69] Michel Foucault, *Power/Knowledge: Selected Interviews and Other Writings 1972–1977*, ed. Colin Gordon (Brighton, Harvester, 1980), 52.
[70] Michel Foucault, *The History of Sexuality: An Introduction*, transl.
Robert Hurley (New York, Vintage, 1990), 81.
[71] Biddy Martin, 'Feminism, Criticism, and Foucault', in Irene Dia-
mond and Lee Quinby (eds.), *Feminism and Foucault: Reflections on Resist-
ance* (Boston, Northeastern Univ. Press, 1988), 9.

of knowledge and the development of her sexuality. Her efforts to understand her 'sexual character', or how she became a sexualized female, are a kind of genealogical analysis of how women were produced, defined, and categorized in late-eighteenth-century society.

Because of the complicated nature of Emma's desire for Augustus, it is not surprising that her quest for him should end in an unsatisfactory manner. As the embodiment of her many unfulfilled wishes, Augustus cannot be the simple solution to Emma's many needs, social dissatisfactions, and desires. The narrative ends in the way that it had begun—with yet another woman who has lost her child accepting the responsibility of bringing up the offspring of a man who cannot adequately be a parent. What Shawn Maurer says of Mary Wollstonecraft applies to Hays: 'motherhood serves literally to dis-place, in the sense of seeking a different place for, female desire that could find no room in the oppressive system she so cogently analyzed. As a culturally sanctioned biological function, motherhood could thus provide for the fullest, because the only available, development of women's capacities, both emotional and intellectual.'[72] Hays reconfigures female desire in her fiction, allowing Emma to take maternity as a subject position, an alternative which was not possible in her own life.

Of the ending, Nicola Watson says, 'this improbably rapid *débâcle* seems to be directed at re-establishing the much-desired dyad of Emma and Harley, albeit at one remove'.[73] Watson observes,

Her efforts to transmute the unstable relation of the lovers into the mother–son relationship can be seen as a restructuring of the original disastrous love-affair. In the act of writing her memoirs her powerless letters are embedded within, and thereby transformed into, a powerful monologic discourse.[74]

[72] Shawn Lisa Maurer, 'The Female (As) Reader: Sex, Sensibility, and the Maternal in Wollstonecraft's Fictions', *Essays in Literature*, 19/1 (Spring, 1992), 39.
[73] Watson, *Revolution and the Form of the British Novel*, 48.
[74] Ibid. 48–9.

As a mother, Emma can fruitfully make use of her intelligence, her experience, and her sensibilities in an avenue acceptable to society. The ending seems at once to be a tribute to maternity and an elegy on romantic love and the potentials of woman. Emma's comment towards the end, that 'there seems to have been something strangely wrong in the constitutions of society' suggests that much reformation is needed before one sees the dawning of the world that she had envisioned, a world of freedom, of 'true dignity and virtue' for women and men (ii. Ch. XXVII).

After *Memoirs of Emma Courtney*, which was received favourably by contemporary reviewers, Mary Hays published nine more books in her lifetime.[75] However, her most radical and original works were those published in the decade of the 1790s. *Appeal to the Men of Great Britain in Behalf of Women* appeared anonymously in 1798, though it has been subsequently attributed to Hays. In this book, Hays calls on the 'fathers, brothers, husbands, sons, and lovers' of Britain to 'consider of what importance it is to society, to improve the understandings, the talents, and the hearts' of women.[76] Through an analysis based on reason, she attempts to correct 'the erroneous ideas which men have formed, of the characters and abilities of women' and posits some possibilities regarding 'what women ought to be'.[77] Hays uses the revolutionary language of the decade to describe the positive effects of such a change: 'the consequences then reasonably to be expected, are, such as seldom fail to ensue, when any individuals, or societies, or classes of mankind are restored to their natural rights, . . . when they find themselves at ease in their proper places; not degraded nor fettered by unnecessary confinement.'[78]

[75] For extracts of some of these reviews, see Gary Kelly, *Women, Writing, and Revolution 1790–1827* (Oxford, Clarendon, 1993), 107–8.
[76] *Appeal to the Men of Great Britain in Behalf of Women* (New York, Garland Facsimile, 1974), p. iii.
[77] Ibid. 31, 125.   [78] Ibid. 290.

Her second novel, *The Victim of Prejudice* (1799), is much darker in tone than her first. It reveals the sombre and serious mood of the radicals by the end of the century. After Wollstonecraft's death in 1797 and Godwin's publication of *Memoirs of the Author of a Vindication of the Rights of Woman* (1798)—which offers accounts of her suicide attempts, her illegitimate daughter, and her love affairs— there was an increasing wave of antifeminist sentiment in England. At the same time, the atrocities of Maximilien Robespierre and the Reign of Terror in France made the supporters of the Revolution extremely unpopular. Along with Anna Laetitia Barbauld, Mary Robinson, Charlotte Smith, Helen Maria Williams, and others, Hays is cited in the Reverend Richard Polwhele's poem *The Unsex'd Females* (1798) among Wollstonecraft's female band of rebels who despise 'Nature's law'.[79] With Wollstonecraft gone, Hays bore the brunt of the anti-Jacobin attacks, which weakened her spirits and changed the tone of her writing. There is a quality of despair in *The Victim of Prejudice* which is not present in *Emma Courtney*. Continuing the arguments about the need to place women on a more equitable position with men which she raised in *Emma Courtney*, Hays depicts a Gothic-like world where male power and wealth are set in opposition to, and eventually overcome, female virtue. The notions of female entrapment and marginalization become horribly real in the novel as the heroine is slowly driven out of social existence, every means of survival taken away from her. The heroine concludes,

The vigorous promise of my youth has failed. The victim of a barbarous prejudice, society has cast me out from its bosom. The sensibilities of my heart have been turned to bitterness, the powers of my mind wasted, my projects rendered abortive, my virtues and my suffering alike unrewarded.[80]

---

[79] See Richard Polwhele, *The Unsex'd Females* (New York, Garland Facsimile, 1974).

[80] Mary Hays, *The Victim of Prejudice*, ed. Eleanor Ty (Peterborough, Ont., Broadview Press, 1994), 174.

The novel, a mournful lament on the waste of female powers and potentials, remains one of the most powerful critiques of patriarchy written at that time.

After the turn of the century, Mary Hays continued to support herself through literary writing. The novels she wrote became more didactic and conservative. She was influenced in her latter years by the works of Hannah More, Elizabeth Hamilton, and Maria Edgeworth. However, her commitment to feminism manifests itself in two biographical works devoted exclusively to women. She produced *Female Biography; or, Memoirs of Illustrious and Celebrated Women, Of All Ages and Countries* (1803) and *Memoirs of Queens, Illustrious and Celebrated* (1821), both collections and compilations of lives of important women. Implicitly, these projects reinforce her belief that an examination of the causes and effects of one's actions was a worthwhile human endeavour. Though the works are not as critical of society or of institutions as her earlier books were, by focusing on females, Hays was making a political statement about the significant, though often unacknowledged, role women have played in historical, social, and cultural spheres.

Hays spent much of the second half of her life in retirement, taking refuge in correspondence mostly with Henry Crabb Robinson and Eliza Fenwick, who remained devoted friends through her later years. She seemed to have made up her mind about a change of direction of her life and adhered to it. In a letter to Henry Crabb Robinson dated 27 February 1802, Hays wrote:

I no longer care for authors except for reading their books, which is always my dear delight, and I have done with systems. I am a complete and an indifferent sceptic. Nothing appears to me of importance but as it is connected with individual happiness, and all human happiness must have a physical foundation.[81]

Her wish was to seek for a finer balance between the spiritual and the physical in order that 'the mind and body' might be 'preserved in their just and equal tempera-

[81] Letter dated 27 Feb. 1802, in Dr Williams's Library, London.

ment'; therefore, she banished 'all intense studies and pursuits, all excess in sedentary occupation, all unnatural institutions and pernicious restraints'.[82] Her revolutionary ideas and her forthrightness earned her much criticism in the late 1790s, which took its toll on her sensibilities. Though she was only in her mid-forties, she told Robinson in 1804, 'that energy of mind on which you compliment me, if I ever possessed it, is nearly extinguished'.[83] Like the heroines of her first two novels, she felt that the world had not comprehended her.

Mine has been a singular and romantic life, its incidents arising out of a singular and romantic mind: I am not suited to the times and the persons among which I have fallen, and I will say—that I have deserved a better fate.[84]

Hays expressed much regret over her extravagances, yet these were what distinguished her as a woman and as writer. Her intensity, her ardour, and her ability to articulate her passionate feelings remain the most striking qualities about her. Looking back on her life, she justly observed,

With Petrarch, I sometimes feel inclined to say—My short pleasures have been like the light breezes of summer, that refresh the air but for a moment. Yet my satisfactions, like my pains, are of a vivid nature, and exquisitely felt. . . . I sought and made to myself an extraordinary destiny.[85]

[82] Ibid.
[83] Letter to Henry Crabb Robinson dated 10 Sept. 1804, Dr Williams's Library, London.
[84] Ibid.
[85] Letter to Henry Crabb Robinson, dated 14 Feb. 1806, Dr Williams's Library, London.

NOTE ON THE TEXT

THIS edition is based on the text of *Memoirs of Emma Courtney*, published in two volumes by G. G. and J. Robinson in November 1796 and reprinted in facsimile form by Garland Publishing, Inc. in 1974. The long 's' has been modernized, and the running quotation marks on the left-hand margin have been eliminated. The original text uses at least three different lengths of the dash. The most common kind, the short dash, is used interchangeably with the medium dash to replace or reinforce a full point, set off parenthetical material that Hays wished to emphasize, and to direct attention to a quotation. I have distinguished between the first two types and the long dash, which is used to indicate material absent from the text, such as a name omitted or abbreviated, or to suggest inarticulate, intense emotion. At some points in Volume II, the distinctions between the long and the medium break down, necessitating some changes.

Obvious misprints have been silently corrected, but idiosyncrasies of punctuation and grammar, and inconsistencies in spelling have been left untouched as they conform to acceptable eighteenth-century usage. I have noted original spelling which might confuse modern readers, such as 'wave' for 'waive', 'dose' for 'doze', 'sooth' for 'soothe', 'desert' for 'dessert', 'desart' for 'desert', and 'confident' for 'confidante', the first time these words occur. Other examples of variants in spelling include the following:

Apostrophes in possessive forms: 'your's' and 'her's'.
Substituting -ce for -se: 'expence', 'suspence', 'recompence'.
An extra -e- or an extra consonant: 'developement', 'groupe', 'fanatice', 'atchieved', 'alledge'.
Phonetic spelling: 'blythsome', 'doggrel', 'sopha', 'farewel', 'pourtrayed', 'accesary', 'controuling',

'ideots', 'crouded', 'shrowd', 'synonimous', 'choaked', 'encrease', 'chearful', 'faultering', 'Shakespear', 'Woolstonecraft'.

Hays's notes, indicated by numbers in superscript, are retained at the foot of the page; editorial notes, indicated by asterisks, are placed at the end of the text.

SELECT BIBLIOGRAPHY

BOOKS BY MARY HAYS

Cursory Remarks on an Enquiry into the Expediency and Propriety of Public or Social Worship: Inscribed to Gilbert Wakefield, as Eusebia (London, T. Knott 1791).

Letters and Essays, Moral and Miscellaneous, by Mary and Elizabeth Hays (London, T. Knott, 1793; facsimile, New York, Garland, 1974).

Memoirs of Emma Courtney (2 vols., London, G. G. & J. Robinson, 1796; New York, Hugh M. Griffith, 1802; facsimile, New York, Garland, 1974).

Memoirs of Emma Courtney, ed. Marilyn L. Brooks (Peterborough, Ont., Broadview Press, 2000).

Appeal to the Men of Great Britain in Behalf of Women, anonymous (London, J. Johnson, 1798; facsimile, New York, Garland, 1974).

The Victim of Prejudice (2 vols., London, J. Johnson, 1799; facsimile, Delmar, NY Scholars' Facsimiles & Reprints, 1990).

The Victim of Prejudice, ed. Eleanor Ty (Peterborough, Ont., Broadview Press, 1994).

Female Biography; or, Memoirs of Illustrious and Celebrated Women, of all Ages and Countries (6 vols., London, Richard Phillips, 1803; 3 vols., Philadelphia, Byrch & Small, 1807).

Harry Clinton: A Tale of Youth (London, J. Johnson for T. Bensley, 1804).

History of England, from the Earliest Records to the Peace of Amiens: in a Series of Letters to a Young Lady at School (3 vols.; vols. i & ii by Charlotte Smith, vol. iii by Hays, London, J. G. Barnard for Richard Phillips, 1806).

Historical Dialogues for Young Persons (3 vols., London, J. Johnson with J. Mawman, 1806–8).

The Brothers; or Consequences: A Story of What Happens Every Day; Addressed to that Most Useful Part of the Community, the Labouring Poor (Bristol, Prudent Man's Friend Society, 1815).

Family Annals; or the Sisters (London, Simpkin & Marshall, 1817).

Memoirs of Queens, Illustrious and Celebrated (London, T. & J. Allman, 1821).

Other (Selected)

'Mary Wollstonecraft', in *The Annual Necrology for 1797–8; Including Also, Various Articles of Neglected Biography* (London, Richard Phillips, 1800).

'Life of Charlotte Smith', with Charlotte Smith, unsigned, in *Public Characters of 1800–1801* (London, Richard Phillips, 1807).

Selected Periodical Publications—Uncollected

'A Sonnet' [Ah let not Hope], *Universal Magazine*, 77 (Dec. 1785), 329.

'Ode to her Bullfinch', *Universal Magazine*, 77 (Dec. 1785), 329.

'The Hermit: An Oriental Tale', *The Universal Magazine of Knowledge and Pleasure*, 78 (Apr. 1786), 204–8; (May 1786), 234–8.

'Reply to J.T. on Helvetius', as M.H., *The Monthly Magazine*, 1 (June 1796), 385–7.

'Remarks on A. B. Strictures on the Talents of Women', as A Woman, *The Monthly Magazine*, 2 (July 1796), 469–70.

'The Talents of Women', *The Monthly Magazine*, 2 (Nov. 1796), 784–7.

'Defence of Helvetius', as M.H., *The Monthly Magazine*, 3 (Jan. 1797), 26–8.

'Improvements Suggested in Female Education', as M.H., *The Monthly Magazine*, 3 (Mar. 1797) 1935.

'Are Mental Talents Productive of Happiness?', as M.H., *The Monthly Magazine*, 3 (May 1797), 358–60.

'On Novel Writing', as M.H., *The Monthly Magazine*, 4 (Sept 1797), 180–1.

Obituary of Mary Wollstonecraft, anonymous, *The Monthly Magazine*, 4 (Sept. 1797), 232–3.

'Remarks on Dr Reid on Insanity', *The Monthly Magazine*, 9 (1800), 523–4.

Letters

The Love-Letters of Mary Hays (1779–1780), ed. A. F. Wedd (London: Methuen, 1925).

Selected Letters of Mary Hays (1779–1843), ed. Marilyn L. Brooks (forthcoming).

BIOGRAPHICAL AND CRITICAL STUDIES

Barker-Benfield, G. J., *The Culture of Sensibility: Sex and Society in Eighteenth-Century Britain* (Chicago, University of Chicago Press, 1992).

Blain, Virginia, Grundy, Isobel, & Clements, Patricia (eds.), *The Feminist Companion to Literature in English: Women Writers from the Middle Ages to the Present* (New Haven, Yale Univ. Press, 1990).

Butler, Marilyn, *Jane Austen and the War of Ideas* (Oxford, Clarendon, 1975; repr. 1989).

Doody, Margaret Anne, 'English Women Novelists and the French Revolution', *La Femme en Angleterre et dans les colonies américaines aux XVIIe et XVIIIe siècles* (Paris, Actes du Colloque tenu à Paris Université de Lille, iii. 1975), 176–98.

Hoagwood, Terence Allan, Introduction to *Victim of Prejudice* by Mary Hays (Delmar, NY, Scholars' Facsimiles & Reprints, 1990).

Johnson, Claudia L., *Jane Austen: Women, Politics, and the Novel* (Chicago, Univ. of Chicago Press, 1988).

Jones, Vivien, 'Placing Jemima: Women Writers of the 1790s and the Eighteenth-Century Prostitution Narrative', *Women's Writing*, 4/2 (1997), 201–20.

—— ' "The Tyranny of Passions": Feminism and Heterosexuality in the Fiction of Wollstonecraft and Hays', *Political Gender: Texts and Contexts*, eds. Sally Ledger, Josephine McDonagh and Jane Spencer (London, Harvester Wheatsheaf, 1994), 173–88.

Kelly, Gary, *English Fiction of the Romantic Period 1789–1830* (London, Longman Literature in English Series, 1989).

—— *Women, Writing, and Revolution 1790–1827* (Oxford, Clarendon Press, 1993).

Logan, P. Melville, *Nerves and Narratives: A Cultural History of Hysteria in 19th Century British Prose* (University of California Press, 1996).

Luria, Gina, 'Mary Hays: A Critical Biography', Ph.D. thesis (New York Univ., 1972).

—— 'Mary Hays's Letters & Manuscripts', *Signs: Journal of Women in Culture and Society*, 3/2 (Winter 1977), 524–30.

Mellor, Anne K., *Mothers of the Nation: Women's Political Writing in England, 1780–1830* (Bloomington, Indiana University Press, 2000).

—— *Romanticism and Gender* (New York, Routledge, 1993).

Pollin Burton R., 'Mary Hays on Women's Rights in the *Monthly Magazine*', *Études Anglaises*, 24/3 (1971), 271–82.

Rajan, Tilottama, 'Autonarration and Genotext in Mary Hays' *Memoirs of Emma Courtney*', *Studies in Romanticism*, 32/2 (Summer 1993), 149–76.

Rogers, Katharine M., 'The Contribution of Mary Hays', *Prose Studies*, 10/2 (Sept. 1987), 131–42.

Sherman, Sandra, 'The Feminization of "Reason" in Hays's *The Victim of Prejudice*', *The Centennial Review*, 41/1 (Winter 1997), 143–72.

—— 'The Law, Confinement, and Disruptive Excess in Hays's *The Victim of Prejudice*', *1650–1850: Ideas, Aesthetics, and Inquiries in the Early Modern Era*, 5 (New York, AMS Press, 1998).

Spencer, Jane, *The Rise of the Woman Novelist: From Aphra Behn to Jane Austen* (Oxford, Blackwell, 1986).

Spender, Dale, *Mothers of the Novel: 100 Good Women Writers before Jane Austen* (New York, Pandora, 1986).

Todd, Janet (ed.), *A Dictionary of British and American Women Writers 1660–1800* (Totowa, NJ, Rowman & Littlefield, 1987).

—— *The Sign of Angellica: Women, Writing and Fiction, 1660–1800* (London, Virago, 1989).

Tompkins, J. M. S., *The Popular Novel in England 1770–1800* (London, Constable, 1932).

Ty, Eleanor, 'Female Philosophy Refunctioned: Elizabeth Hamilton's Parodic Novel', *Ariel: A Review of International English Literature*, 22/4 (Oct. 1991), 111–29.

—— 'Mary Hays', *Dictionary of Literary Biography*, 142: *Eighteenth-Century British Literary Biographers*, ed. Steven Serafin (Detroit, Bruccoli Clark Layman, 1994), 152–60.

—— *Unsex'd Revolutionaries: Five Women Novelists of the 1790s* (Toronto, Univ. of Toronto Press, 1993).

—— 'The Imprisoned Female Body in Mary Hays's *The Victim of Prejudice*', *Women, Revolution, and the Novels of the 1790s*, ed. Linda Lang-Peralta (East Lansing, MI, Michigan State UP, 1999), 133–53.

Watson, Nicola J., *Revolution and the Form of the British Novel, 1790–1825: Intercepted Letters, Interrupted Seductions* (Oxford, Clarendon, 1994).

A CHRONOLOGY OF MARY HAYS

1760   Born into large Dissenting family in Southwark, near London.

1777   Meets and falls in love with John Eccles. Relationship disapproved by both families.

1778–80 Intimate correspondence with Eccles, her lover and 'mentor'.

1780   Engagement meets approval of the families. Death of John Eccles from fever on 23 August.

1782   Begins correspondence with rational Dissenter and opponent of the slave trade, Robert Robinson, about Deism and other theological subjects.

1786   'The Hermit: An Oriental Tale' published in the *Universal Magazine*.

1791   *Cursory Remarks on an Enquiry into the Expediency and Propriety of Public or Social Worship: Inscribed to Gilbert Wakefield*.

1792   Reads Mary Wollstonecraft's *A Vindication of the Rights of Woman*. Meets Wollstonecraft at Joseph Johnson's.

1793   *Letters and Essays, Moral and Miscellaneous*. Writes to William Godwin to borrow his copy of *Enquiry Concerning Political Justice*. Six-year friendship with Godwin begins.

1796   Invites William Godwin, Mary Wollstonecraft, and Thomas Holcroft to tea at her home in January. Confesses to William Frend about her secret love for him. *Memoirs of Emma Courtney* published in November.

1796–7 Contributor to *The Monthly Magazine*. Begins to review novels for the *Analytical Review*.

1797   Publishes unsigned obituary of Mary Wollstonecraft in the September issue of *The Monthly Magazine*.

1798   *Appeal to the Men of Great Britain in Behalf of Women* published anonymously by Joseph Johnson.

1799   *The Victim of Prejudice*. Close association with Romantic writers—Robert Southey, Samuel Taylor Coleridge, and Charles Lloyd.

1800   Second obituary of Wollstonecraft published in *Annual Necrology, 1797–1798*. Friendship with Eliza Fenwick and Henry Crabb Robinson.

1803   *Female Biography; or, Memoirs of Illustrious and Celebrated Women, of All Ages and Countries.*

1804   *Harry Clinton: A Tale for Youth.* Moves out of London to a small house in Camberwell, Surrey.

1806   *The History of England, from the Earliest Records to the Peace of Amiens; in a Series of Letters to a Young Lady at School.* Written with Charlotte Smith. Moves back to London (Islington). Complains of headaches, pains, and depressions.

1806–8   *Historical Dialogues for Young Persons.*

1807   Co-authors 'Life' of Charlotte Smith with Smith for Richard Phillips's *Public Characters of 1800–1801*.

1808   Marriage of William Frend to Sara Blackburne. Crabb Robinson and Coleridge note Hays's distress.

1813   Visited often by Henry Crabb Robinson. Employed for a year as schoolmistress at a school for girls in Oundle.

1814   Stays in Hot Wells, Clifton with Mrs Penelope Weston Pennington. Influenced by works of Hannah More and Maria Edgeworth.

1815   *The Brothers; or, Consequences: A Story of What Happens Every Day; Addressed to that Most Useful Part of the Community, the Labouring Poor.*

1817   *Family Annals; or the Sisters.*

1819   Lives in Pentonville.

1821   *Memoirs of Queens, Illustrious and Celebrated.*

1843   Dies at 83 years old. At her own request is buried in Newington Cemetery with the simple memorial 'Mary Hays' engraved on the headstone.

MEMOIRS OF
EMMA COURTNEY

'The perceptions of persons in retirement are very different from those of people in the great world: their passions, being differently modified, are differently expressed; their imaginations, constantly impressed by the same objects, are more violently affected. The same small number of images continually return, mix with every idea, and create those strange and false notions, so remarkable in people who spend their lives in solitude.'*

ROUSSEAU

PREFACE

THE most interesting, and the most useful, fictions, are, perhaps, such, as delineating the progress, and tracing the consequences, of one strong, indulged, passion, or prejudice, afford materials, by which the philosopher may calculate the powers of the human mind, and learn the springs which set it in motion*—'Understanding, and talents,' says Helvetius, 'being nothing more, in men, than the produce of their desires, and particular situations.'* Of the passion of terror Mrs Radcliffe* has made admirable use in her ingenious romances.—In the novel of Caleb Williams,* curiosity in the hero, and the love of reputation in the soul-moving character of Falkland, fostered into ruling passions, are drawn with a masterly hand.

For the subject of these Memoirs, a more universal sentiment* is chosen—a sentiment hackneyed in this species of composition, consequently more difficult to treat with any degree of originality;—yet, to accomplish this, has been the aim of the author; with what success, the public will, probably, determine.

Every writer who advances principles, whether true or false, that have a tendency to set the mind in motion, does good. Innumerable mistakes have been made, both moral and philosophical:—while covered with a sacred and mysterious veil, how are they to be detected? From various combinations and multiplied experiments, truth, only, can result. Free thinking, and free speaking, are the virtue and the characteristics of a rational being:—there can be no argument which militates against them in one instance, but what equally militates against them in all; every principle must be doubted, before it will be examined and proved.

It has commonly been the business of fiction to pourtray characters, not as they really exist, but, as, we are told, they ought to be—a sort of *ideal perfection*,* in which nature and passion are melted away, and jarring attributes wonderfully combined.

In delineating the character of Emma Courtney, I had not in view these fantastic models: I meant to represent her, as a human being, loving virtue while enslaved by passion, liable to the mistakes and weaknesses of our fragile nature.—Let those readers, who feel inclined to judge with severity the extravagance and eccentricity of her conduct, look into their own hearts; and should they there find no record, traced by an accusing spirit, to soften the asperity of their censures—yet, let them bear in mind, that the errors of my heroine were the offspring of sensibility; and that the result of her hazardous experiment is calculated to operate as a *warning*, rather than as an example.—The philosopher—who is not ignorant, that light and shade are more powerfully contrasted in minds rising above the common level; that, as rank weeds take strong root in a fertile soil, vigorous powers not unfrequently produce fatal mistakes and pernicious exertions; that character is the produce of a lively and constant affection—may, possibly, discover in these Memoirs traces of reflection, and of some attention to the phænomena of the human mind.

Whether the incidents, or the characters, are copied from life, is of little importance—The only question is, if the *circumstances*, and situations, are altogether improbable? If not—whether the consequences *might* not have followed from the circumstances?—This is a grand question, applicable to all the purposes of education, morals, and legislation—*and on this I rest my moral*—'Do men gather figs of thorns, or grapes of thistles?'* asked a moralist and a reformer.

Every *possible* incident, in works of this nature, might, perhaps, be rendered *probable*, were a sufficient regard paid to the more minute, delicate, and connecting links of the chain.* Under this impression, I chose, as the least arduous, a simple story*—and, even in that, the fear of repetition, of prolixity, added, it may be, to a portion of indolence, made me, in some parts, neglectful of this rule:—yet, in tracing the character of my heroine from her birth, I had it in view. For the conduct of my hero, I consider myself less responsible—it was not *his* memoirs that I professed to write.

I am not sanguine respecting the success of this little publication. It is truly observed, by the writer of a late popular novel[1]—'That an author, whether good or bad, or between both, is an animal whom every body is privileged to attack; for, though all are not able to write books, all conceive themselves able to judge them. A bad composition carries with it its own punishment—contempt and ridicule:—a good one excites envy, and (frequently) entails upon its author a thousand mortifications.'*

To the feeling and the thinking few, this production of an active mind, in a season of impression, rather than of leisure, is presented.

[1] The Monk.

VOLUME I

RASH young man!—why do you tear from my heart the affecting narrative, which I had hoped no cruel necessity would ever have forced me to review?—Why do you oblige me to recall the bitterness of my past life, and to renew images, the remembrance of which, even at this distant period, harrows up my soul* with inconceivable misery?—But your happiness is at stake, and every selfish consideration vanishes.—Dear and sacred deposit of an adored and lost friend!—for whose sake I have consented to hold down, with struggling, suffocating reluctance, the loathed and bitter portion of existence;—shall I expose your ardent mind to the incessant conflict between truth and error—shall I practise the disingenuousness, by which my peace has been blasted—shall I suffer you to run the wild career of passion—shall I keep back the recital, written upon my own mind in characters of blood, which may preserve the child of my affections from destruction?

Ah! why have you deceived me?—Has a six months' absence obliterated from your remembrance the precept I so earnestly and incessantly laboured to inculcate—the value and importance of unequivocal sincerity? A precept, which I now take shame to myself for not having more implicitly observed! Had I supposed your affection for Joanna more than a boyish partiality; had I not believed that a few months' absence would entirely erase it from your remembrance; had I not been assured that her heart was devoted to another object, a circumstance of which she had herself frankly informed you; I should not now have distrusted your fortitude, when obliged to wound your feelings with the intelligence—that the woman, whom you have so wildly persecuted, was, yesterday, united to another.

TO THE SAME

I resume my pen. Your letter, which Joanna a few days
since put into my hands, has cost me——Ah! my Augustus,
my friend, my son—what has it not cost me, and what
impressions has it not renewed? I perceive the vigour of
your mind with terror and exultation. But you are mistaken! Were it not for the insuperable barrier that separates you, for ever, from your hopes, perseverance itself,
however active, however incessant, may fail in attaining its
object. Your ardent reasoning, my interesting and philosophic young friend, though not unconsequential, is a
finely proportioned structure, resting on an airy foundation. The science of morals is not incapable of demonstration, but we want a more extensive knowledge of
particular facts, on which, in any given circumstance,
firmly to establish our data.—Yet, be not discouraged; exercise your understanding, think freely, investigate every
opinion, disdain the rust of antiquity, raise systems, invent
hypotheses, and, by the absurdities, they involve, seize on
the clue of truth. Rouse the nobler energies of your
mind; be not the slave of your passions, neither dream of
eradicating them.* Sensation generates interest, interest
passion, passion forces attention, attention supplies the
powers, and affords the means of attaining its end: in
proportion to the degree of interest, will be that of attention and power. Thus are talents produced. Every man is
born with sensation, with the aptitude of receiving impressions; the force of those impressions depends on a thousand circumstances, over which he has little power; these
circumstances form the mind, and determine the future
character.* We are all the creatures of education; but in
that education, what we call chance, or accident, has so
great a share, that the wisest preceptor, after all his cares,
has reason to tremble: one strong affection, one ardent
incitement, will turn, in an instant, the whole current of
our thoughts, and introduce a new train of ideas and
associations.

  You may perceive that I admit the general truths of your
reasoning; but I would warn you to be careful in their

particular application; a long train of patient and laborious experiments must precede our deductions and conclusions. The science of mind is not less demonstrative, and far more important, than the science of Newton; but we must proceed on similar principles. The term *metaphysics* has been, perhaps, justly defined—*the first principles of arts and sciences.*[1]* Every discovery of genius, resulting from a fortunate combination of circumstances, may be resolved into simple facts: but in this investigation we must be patient, attentive, indefatigable; we must be content to arrive at truth through many painful mistakes and consequent sufferings.—Such appears to be the constitution of man!

To shorten and meliorate your way, I have determined to sacrifice every inferior consideration. I have studied your character: I perceive, with joy, that its errors are the ardent excesses of a generous mind. I loved your father with a fatal and unutterable tenderness: time has softened the remembrance of his faults.—Our noblest qualities, without incessant watchfulness, are liable insensibly to shade into vices—but his virtues and *misfortunes*, in which my own were so intimately blended, are indelibly engraven on my heart.

A mystery has hitherto hung over your birth. The victim of my own ardent passions, and the errors of one whose memory will ever be dear to me, I prepare to withdraw the veil—a veil, spread by an importunate, but, I fear, a mistaken tenderness. Learn, then, from the incidents of my life, entangled with those of his to whom you owe your existence, a more striking and affecting lesson than abstract philosophy can ever afford.

CHAPTER I

THE events of my life have been few, and have in them nothing very uncommon, but the effects which they have produced on my mind; yet, that mind they have helped to

[1] Helvetius.

form, and this in the eye of philosophy, or affection, may render them not wholly uninteresting. While I trace them, they convince me of the irresistible power of circumstances, modifying and controuling our characters, and introducing, mechanically, those associations and habits which make us what we are; for without outward impressions we should be nothing.

I know not how far to go back, nor where to begin; for in many cases, it may be in all, a foundation is laid for the operations of our minds, years—nay, ages—previous to our birth. I wish to be brief, yet to omit no one connecting link in the chain of causes, however minute, that I conceive had any important consequences in the formation of my mind, or that may, probably, be useful to your's.

My father was a man of some talents, and of a superior rank in life, but dissipated, extravagant, and profligate. My mother, the daughter of a rich trader, and the sole heiress of his fortunes, allured by the specious address and fashionable manners of my father, sacrificed to empty shew the prospect of rational and dignified happiness. My father courted her hand to make himself master of her ample possessions: dazzled by vanity, and misled by self-love, she married him;—found, when too late, her error; bitterly repented, and died in child-bed the twelfth month of her marriage, after having given birth to a daughter, and commended it, with her dying breath, to the care of a sister (the daughter of her mother by a former marriage), an amiable, sensible, and worthy woman, who had, a few days before, lost a lovely and promising infant at the breast, and received the little Emma, as a gift from heaven, to supply its place.

My father, plunged in expence and debauchery, was little moved by these domestic distresses. He held the infant a moment in his arms, kissed it, and willingly consigned it to the guardianship of its maternal aunt.

It will here be necessary to give a sketch of the character, situation, and family, of this excellent woman; each of which had an important share in forming the mind of her charge to those dispositions, and feelings, which irresistibly led to the subsequent events.

CHAPTER II

M R and Mrs Melmoth, my uncle and aunt, married young, purely from motives of affection. Mr Melmoth had an active, ardent, mind, great benevolence of heart, a sweet and chearful temper, and a liberal manner of thinking, though with few advantages of education: he possessed, also, a sanguine disposition, a warm heart, a generous spirit, and an integrity which was never called in question. Mrs Melmoth's frame was delicate and fragile; she had great sensibility, quickness of perception, some anxiety of temper, and a refined and romantic manner of thinking, acquired from the perusal of the old romances, a large quantity of which, belonging to a relation, had, in the early periods of her youth, been accidentally deposited in a spare room in her father's house. These qualities were mingled with a devotional spirit, a little bordering on fanaticism. My uncle did not exactly resemble an Orlando, or an Oroondates,* but he was fond of reading; and having the command of a ship in the West India trade,* had, during his voyages in fine weather, time to indulge in this propensity; by which means he was a tolerable proficient in the belles lettres, and could, on occasion, quote Shakespeare, scribble poetry, and even philosophize with Pope and Bolingbroke.*

Mr Melmoth was one-and-twenty, his bride nineteen, when they were united. They possessed little property; but the one was enterprizing and industrious, the other careful and œconomical; and both, with hearts glowing with affection for each other, saw cheering hope and fairy prospects dancing before their eyes. Every thing succeeded beyond their most sanguine expectations. My uncle's cheerful and social temper, with the fairness and liberality of his dealings, conciliated the favour of the merchants. His understanding was superior, and his manners more courteous, than the generality of persons in his line of life: his company was eagerly courted, and no vessel stood a chance of being freighted till his had its full cargo.

His voyages were not long, and frequent absences and meetings kept alive between him and my aunt, the hopes, the fears, the anxieties, and the transports of love. Their family soon increased, but this was a new source of joy to Mr Melmoth's affectionate heart. A walk or a ride in the country, with his wife and little ones, he accounted his highest relaxation:—on these occasions he gave himself up to a sweet and lively pleasure; would clasp them alternately to his breast, and, with eyes overflowing with tears of delight, repeat Thomson's charming description of the joys of virtuous love—

> 'Where nothing strikes the eye but sights of bliss,
> All various nature pressing on the heart!'*

This was the first picture that struck my young imagination, for I was, in all respects, considered as the adopted child of the family.

This prosperity received little other interruption than from my uncle's frequent absences, and the pains and cares of my aunt in bringing into the world, and nursing, a family of children. Mr Melmoth's successful voyages, at rather earlier than forty years of age, enabled him to leave the sea, and to carry on an extensive mercantile employment in the metropolis.—At this period his health began to be injured by the progress of a threatening internal disorder; but it had little effect either on his spirits or activity. His business every day became wider, and his attention to it was unremitted, methodical, and indefatigable. His hours of relaxation were devoted to his family and social enjoyment; at these times he never suffered the cares of the counting house* to intrude;—he was the life of every company, and the soul of every pleasure.

He at length assumed a more expensive style of living; took a house in the country (for the charms of which he had ever a peculiar taste) as a summer residence; set up an equipage,* increased the number of his servants, and kept an open and hospitable, though not a luxurious, table.

The hours fled on downy pinions; his wife rested on him, his children caught sunshine from his smiles; his domestics adored him, and his acquaintance vied with each other in paying him respect. His life, he frequently repeated, had been a series of unbroken success. His religion, for he laid no stress on forms, was a sentiment of grateful and fervent love.—'*God is love,*' he would say, 'and the affectionate, benevolent heart is his temple.'

CHAPTER III

I T will now be necessary, for the developement of my own particular character, again to revert to earlier periods.—A few days before my birth, my aunt had lost (as already related) a lovely female infant, about four months old, and she received me, from the hands of my dying mother, as a substitute.—From these tender and affecting circumstances I was nursed and attended with peculiar care. My uncle's ship (it being war time)* was then waiting for a convoy at Portsmouth,* where he was joined by his wife: she carried me with her, and, tenderly watchful over my safety, took me on all their little excursions, whether by sea or land: I hung at her breast, or rested in her arms, and her husband, or attendant, alternately relieved her.— Plump, smiling, placid, happy, I never disturbed her rest, and the little Emma was the darling of her kind guardians, and the plaything of the company.

At the age at which it was thought necessary to wean me, I was sent from my tender nurse* for that purpose, and consigned to the care of a stranger, with whom I quickly pined myself into a jaundice and bilious fever. My aunt dared not visit me during this short separation, she was unable to bear my piercing cries of anguish at her departure. If a momentary sensation, at that infantine period, deserve the appellation, I might call this my first affectionate sorrow. I have frequently thought that the tenderness of this worthy woman generated in my infant disposition that susceptibility, that lively propensity to attachment, to which I have through life been a martyr. On my return to my friends, I quickly regained my health and spirits; was active, blythsome, ran, bounded, sported, romped; always light, gay, alert, and full of glee. At church, (whither on Sunday I was accustomed to accompany the family) I offended all the pious ladies in our vicinity by my gamesome tricks, and avoided the reprimands of my indulgent guardians by the drollery and good humour which accompanied them.

When myself and my little cousins had wearied ourselves with play, their mother, to keep us quiet in an evening, while her husband wrote letters in an adjoining apartment, was accustomed to relate (for our entertainment) stories from the Arabian Nights, Turkish Tales, and other works of like marvellous import.* She recited them circumstantially, and these I listened to with ever new delight: the more they excited vivid emotions, the more wonderful they were, the greater was my transport: they became my favourite amusement, and produced, in my young mind, a strong desire of learning to read the books which contained such enchanting stores of entertainment.

Thus stimulated, I learned to read quickly, and with facility. My uncle took pleasure in assisting me; and, with parental partiality, thought he discovered, in the ardour and promptitude with which I received his instructions, the dawn of future talents. At six years old I read aloud before company, with great applause, my uncle's favourite authors, Pope's Homer, and Thomson's Seasons,* little comprehending either. Emulation was roused, and vanity fostered: I learned to recite verses, to modulate my tones of voice, and began to think myself a wonderful scholar.

Thus, in peace and gaiety, glided the days of my childhood. Caressed by my aunt, flattered by her husband, I grew vain and self-willed; my desires were impetuous, and brooked no delay; my affections were warm, and my temper irascible; but it was the glow of a moment, instantly subsiding on conviction, and, when conscious of having committed injustice, I was ever eager to repair it, by a profusion of caresses and acknowledgements. Opposition would always make me vehement, and coercion irritated me to violence; but a kind look, a gentle word, a cool expostulation—softened, melted, arrested, me, in the full career of passion. Never, but once, do I recollect having received a blow; but the boiling rage, the cruel tempest, the deadly vengeance it excited, in my mind, I now remember with shuddering.

Every day I became more attached to my books; yet, not less fond of active play; stories were still my passion, and I sighed for a romance that would never end. In my sports with my companions, I acted over what I had read: I was alternately the valiant knight—the gentle damsel—the adventurous mariner—the daring robber—the courteous lover—and the airy coquet. Ever inventive, my young friends took their tone from me. I hated the needle:—my aunt was indulgent, and not an hour passed unamused:— my resources were various, fantastic, and endless. Thus, for the first twelve years of my life, fleeted my days in joy and innocence. I ran like the hind, frisked like the kid, sang like the lark,* was full of vivacity, health, and animation; and, excepting some momentary bursts of passion and impatience, awoke every day to new enjoyment, and retired to rest fatigued with pleasure.

CHAPTER IV

AT this period, by the command of my father, I was sent to boarding school.*—Ah! never shall I forget the contrast I experienced. I was an alien and a stranger;—no one loved, caressed, nor cared for me;—my actions were all constrained;—I was obliged to sit poring over needle-work,* and forbidden to prate;—my body was tortured into forms, my mind coerced, and tasks imposed upon me, grammar and French, mere words, that conveyed to me no ideas. I

loved my guardians with passion—my tastes were all
passions—they tore themselves from my embraces with
difficulty. I sat down, after their departure, and wept—
bitter tears—sobbed convulsively—my griefs were un-
heeded, and my sensibility ridiculed—I neither gave nor
received pleasure. After the rude stare of curiosity, ever
wounding to my feelings, was gratified, I was left to sob
alone.

At length, one young lady, with a fair face and a gentle
demeanour, came and seated herself beside me. She
spoke, in a soft voice, words of sympathy—my desolate
heart fluttered at the sound. I looked at her—her features
were mild and sweet; I dried my tears, and determined that
she should be my friend.—My spirits became calmer, and
for a short time I indulged in this relief; but, on enquiry, I
found my fair companion had already a selected favourite,
and that their amity was the admiration of the school.—
Proud, jealous, romantic—I could not submit to be the
second in her esteem—I shunned her, and returned her
caresses with coldness.

The only mitigation I now felt to the anguish that had
seized my spirits, was in the hours of business. I was soon
distinguished for attention and capacity; but my governess
being with-held, by an infirm constitution, from the duties
of her office, I was consigned, with my companions, to
ignorant, splenetic, teachers, who encouraged not my
emulation, and who sported with the acuteness of my
sensations. In the intervals from school hours I sought and
procured books.—These were often wantonly taken from
me, as a punishment for the most trivial offence; and,
when my indignant spirit broke out into murmurs and
remonstrance, I was constrained to learn, by way of pen-
ance, chapters in the Proverbs of Solomon, or verses from
the French testament.* To revenge myself, I satirized my
tyrants in doggrel rhymes: my writing master also came in
for a share of this little malice; and my productions,
wretched enough, were handed round the school with
infinite applause. Sunk in sullen melancholy, in the hours
of play I crept into corners, and disdained to be amused:—

home appeared to me to be the Eden from which I was driven, and there my heart and thoughts incessantly recurred.

My uncle from time to time addressed to me—with little presents—kind, pleasant, affectionate notes—and these I treasured up as sacred relics. A visit of my guardians was a yet more tumultuous pleasure; but it always left me in increased anguish. Some robberies had been committed on the road to town.—After parting with my friends, I have laid awake the whole night, conjuring up in my imagination all the tragic accidents I had ever heard or read of, and persuading myself some of them must have happened to these darling objects of my affections.

Thus passed the first twelvemonth of my exile from all I loved; during which time it was reported, by my schoolfellows, that I had never been seen to smile. After the vacations, I was carried back to my prison with agonizing reluctance, to which in the second year I became, however, from habit, better reconciled. I learned music, was praised and encouraged by my master, and grew fond of it; I contracted friendships, and regained my vivacity; from a forlorn, unsocial, being, I became, once more, lively, active, enterprising,—the soul of all amusement, and the leader of every innocently mischievous frolic. At the close of another year I left school. I kept up a correspondence for some time with a few of my young friends, and my effusions were improved and polished by my paternal uncle.

CHAPTER V

THIS period, which I had anticipated with rapture, was soon clouded by the gradual decay, and premature death, of my revered and excellent guardian. He sustained a painful and tedious sickness with unshaken fortitude;— with more, with chearfulness. I knelt by his bedside on the day of his decease; and, while I bathed his hand with my tears, caught hope from the sweet, the placid, serenity of

his countenance, and could not believe the terrors of dissolution near.

'The last sentiment of my heart,' said he, 'is gratitude to
the Being who has given me so large a portion of good;
and I resign my family into his hands with confidence.'

He awoke from a short slumber a few minutes before his
death.——'Emma,' said he, in a faint voice, (as I grasped
his cold hand between both mine) turning upon me a
mild, yet dying, eye, 'I have had a pleasant sleep—Be a
good girl, and comfort your aunt!'—

He expired without a groan, or a struggle—'His death
was the serene evening of a beautiful day!'* I gazed on his
lifeless remains, the day before their interment, and the
features still wore the same placid, smiling benignity. I was
then about fourteen years of age,—this first emotion of
real sorrow rent my heart asunder!

The sensations of Mrs Melmoth were those of agonizing,
suffocating anguish:——the fair prospect of domestic felicity was veiled for ever! This was the second strong impression which struck my opening mind. Many losses
occurred, in consequence of foreign connections, in the
settlement of Mr Melmoth's affairs.—The family found
their fortunes scanty, and their expectations limited:—
their numerous fair-professing acquaintance gradually
deserted them, and they sunk into œconomical retirement; but they continued to be respectable, because they
knew how to contract their wants, and to preserve their
independence.

My aunt, oppressed with sorrow, could be roused only by
settling the necessary plans for the future provision of her
family. Occupied with these concerns, or absorbed in
grief, we were left for some time to run wild. Months
revolved ere the tender sorrows of Mrs Melmoth admitted
of any mitigation: they at length yielded only to tender
melancholy. My wonted amusements were no more; a
deep gloom was spread over our once cheerful residence;
my avidity for books daily increased: I subscribed to a
circulating library,* and frequently read, or rather devoured—little careful in the selection—from ten to fourteen novels in a week.

CHAPTER VI

M Y father satisfied himself, after the death of my beloved
uncle, with making a short and formal visit of condolence
to the family, and proposing either my return to school, or
to pay an annual stipend (which Mr and Mrs Melmoth had
hitherto invariably refused) for defraying the expences of
my continuance and board with the amiable family by
which I had been so kindly nurtured. I shrunk from the
cold and careless air of a man whom I had never been able
to teach my heart either to love or honour; and, throwing
my arms round the neck of my maternal aunt, murmured
a supplication, mingled with convulsive sobs, that she
would not desert me. She returned my caresses affectionately, and entreated my father to permit me to remain with
her; adding, that it was her determination to endeavour to
rouse and strengthen her mind, for the performance of
those pressing duties—the education of her beloved children, among whom she had ever accounted her Emma—
which now devolved wholly upon her.

My father made no objection to this request; but observed, that notwithstanding he had a very favourable
opinion of her heart and understanding, and considered
himself indebted to her, and to her deceased husband, for
their goodness to Emma, he was nevertheless apprehensive that the girl had been weakened and spoiled by their
indulgence;—that his own health was at present considerably injured;—that it was probable he might not survive
many years;—in which case, he frankly confessed, he had
enjoyed life too freely to be able to make much provision
for his daughter. It would therefore, he conceived, be
more judicious to prepare and strengthen my mind to
encounter, with fortitude, some hardships and rude
shocks, to which I might be exposed, than to foster a
sensibility, which he already perceived, with regret, was but
too acute. For which purpose, he desired I might spend
one day in every week at his house in Berkley-square,*
when he should put such books into my hands (he had
been informed I had a tolerable capacity) as he judged

would be useful to me; and, in the intervals of his various occupations and amusements, assist me himself with occasional remarks and reflections. Any little accomplishments which Mrs Melmoth might judge necessary for, and suitable to, a young woman with a small fortune, and which required the assistance of a master, he would be obliged to her if she would procure for me, and call upon him to defray the additional expence.

He then, looking on his watch, and declaring he had already missed an appointment, took his leave, after naming Monday as the day on which he should constantly expect my attendance in Berkley-square.

Till he left the room I had not courage to raise my eyes from the ground—my feelings were harrowed up—the tone of his voice was discordant to my ears. The only idea that alleviated the horror of my weekly punishment (for so I considered the visits to Berkley-square) was the hope of reading new books, and of being suffered to range uncontrouled through an extensive and valuable library, for such I had been assured was Mr Courtney's. I still retained my passion for adventurous tales, which, even while at school, I was enabled to gratify by means of one of the day-boarders, who procured for me romances from a neighbouring library, which at every interval of leisure I perused with inconceivable avidity.

CHAPTER VII

THE following Monday I prepared to attend Mr Courtney. On arriving at his house, and announcing my name, a servant conducted me into his master's dressing-room. I appeared before him with trembling steps, downcast eyes, and an averted face.

'Look up, child!' said my father, in an imperious tone. 'If you are conscious of no crime, why all this ridiculous confusion?'

I struggled with my feelings: the tone and manner in which I was addressed gave me an indignant sensation:—

a deeper suffusion than that of modesty, the glow of wounded pride, burnt in my cheeks:—I turned quick, gazed in the face of Mr Courtney with a steady eye, and spoke a few words, in a firm voice, importing—that I attended by his desire, and waited his direction.

He regarded me with somewhat less *hauteur*;* and, while he finished dressing, interrogated me respecting the books I had read, and the impression they had left on my mind. I replied with simplicity, and without evasion. He soon discovered that my imagination had been left to wander unrestrained in the fairy fields of fiction; but that, of historical facts, and the science of the world, I was entirely ignorant.

'It is as I apprehended,' said he:—'your fancy requires a *rein* rather than a *spur*. Your studies, for the future, must be of a soberer nature, or I shall have you mistake my valet for a prince in disguise, my house for a haunted castle,* and my rational care for your future welfare for barbarous tyranny.'

I felt a poignant and suffocating sensation, too complicated to bear analyzing, and followed Mr Courtney in silence to the library. My heart bounded when, on entering a spacious room, I perceived on either side a large and elegant assortment of books, regularly arranged in glass cases, and I longed to be left alone, to expatiate freely in these treasures of entertainment. But I soon discovered, to my inexpressible mortification, that the cases were locked, and that in this intellectual feast I was not to be my own purveyor. My father, after putting into my hands the lives of Plutarch,* left me to my meditations; informing me, that he should probably dine at home with a few friends, at five o'clock, when he should expect my attendance at the table.

I opened my book languidly, after having examined through the glass doors the titles of those which were withheld from me. I felt a kind of disgust to what I considered as a task imposed, and read a few pages carelessly, gazing at intervals through the windows into the square.—But my attention, as I proceeded, was soon forcibly arrested, my

curiosity excited, and my enthusiasm awakened. The
hours passed rapidly—I perceived not their flight—and at
five o'clock, when summoned to dinner, I went down into
the dining-room, my mind pervaded with republican ardour, my sentiments elevated by a high-toned philosophy,
and my bosom glowing with the virtues of patriotism.

I found with Mr Courtney company of both sexes, to
whom he presented me on my entrance. Their easy compliments disconcerted me, and I shrunk, abashed, from
the bold and curious eyes of the gentlemen. During the
repast I ate little, but listened in silence to every thing that
passed.

The theatres were the first topic of conversation, Venice
Preserved* had been acted the preceding evening, and
from discussing the play, the conversation took a political
turn. A gentleman that happened to be seated next me,
who spoke fluently, looking around him every moment for
approbation, with apparent self-applause, gave the discourse a tone of gallantry, declaring—'Pierre to be a noble
fellow, and that the loss of a mistress was a sufficient excuse
for treason and conspiracy, even though the country had
been deluged in blood and involved in conflagration.'

'And the mistresses of all his fellow citizens destroyed of
course;'—said a gentleman coolly, on the opposite side of
the table.

Oh! that was not a consideration, every thing must give
place when put in competition with certain feelings.
'What, young lady, (suddenly turning to me) do you think
a lover would not risque, who was in fear of losing you?'

Good God! what a question to an admirer of the
grecian heroes! I started, and absolutely shuddered. I
would have replied, but my words died away upon my lips
in inarticulate murmurs. My father observed and enjoyed
my distress.

'The worthies of whom you have been reading, Emma,
lived in ancient times: Aristides the just,* would have made
but a poor figure among our modern men of fashion!'

'This lady reads, then'—said our accomplished coxcomb—'Heavens, Mr Courtney! you will spoil all her femi-

nine graces; knowledge and learning, are insufferably masculine in a woman—born only for the soft solace of man! The mind of a young lady should be clear and unsullied, like a sheet of white paper, or her own fairer face: lines of thinking destroy the dimples of beauty; aping the reason of man, they lose the exquisite, *fascinating* charm, in which consists their true empire;*—Then strongest, when most weak—'

> 'Loveliest in their fears—
> And by this silent adulation, soft,
> To their protection more engaging man.'*

'Pshaw!' replied Mr Courtney, a little peevishly—'you will persuade Emma, that the age of chivalry is not yet over; and that giants and ravishers are as common now, as in the time of Charlemagne:* a young woman of sense and spirit needs no other protection; do not flatter the girl into affectation and imbecility. If blank paper be your passion, you can be at no loss; the town will supply quires and reams.'

'There I differ from you,' said the gentleman on the opposite side of the table; 'to preserve the mind a blank, we must be both deaf and blind, for, while any inlet to perception remains, your paper will infallibly contract characters of some kind, or be blotted and scrawled!'

'For God's sake! do not let us begin to philosophise,' retorted his antagonist, who was not to be easily silenced.

'I agree with you'—rejoined the other—'*thinking* is undoubtedly very laborious, and *principle* equally troublesome and impertinent.'

I looked at him as he finished speaking, and caught his eye for a moment; its expression methought was doubtful. The man of fashion continued to expatiate in rhetorical periods—He informed us, that he had fine feelings, but they never extended beyond selfish gratification. For his part, he had as much humanity as any man, for which reason he carefully avoided the scene or the tale of distress. He, likewise, had his opinions, but their pliability rendered them convenient to himself, and accommodat-

ing to his friends. He had courage to sustain fatigue and
hardship, when, not his country, but vanity demanded the
exertion. It was glorious to boast of having travelled two
hundred miles in eight and forty hours, and sat up three
nights, to be present, on two succeeding evenings, at a ball
in distant counties.

'This man,' said I to myself, while I regarded him with a
look of ineffable scorn—'takes a great deal of pains to
render himself ridiculous, he surely must have a vile heart,
or a contemptible opinion of mankind: if he be really the
character he describes, he is a compound of atrocity and
folly, and a pest to the world: if he slanders himself, what
must be that state of society, the applause of which he
persuades himself is to be thus acquired?' I sighed
deeply;—in either case the reflection was melancholy;—
my eyes enquired—'Am I to hate or to despise you?' I
know not whether he understood their language, but he
troubled me no more with his attentions.

I reflected a little too seriously:—I have since seen many
a prating, superficial coxcomb, who talks to display his
oratory—*mere words*—repeated by rote, to which few ideas
are affixed, and which are uttered and received with equal
apathy.

CHAPTER VIII

DURING three years, I continued my weekly visits to
Berkley square; I was not always allowed to join the parties
who assembled there, neither indeed would it have been
proper, for they were a motley groupe; when permitted so
to do, I collected materials for reflection. I had been educated by my good aunt, in strict principles of religion;
many of Mr Courtney's friends were men of wit and talents, who, occasionally, discussed important subjects with
freedom and ability: I never ventured to mingle in the
conversations, but I overcame my timidity sufficiently to
behave with propriety and composure; I listened attentively to all that was said, and my curiosity was awakened to
philosophic enquiries.

Mr Courtney now entrusted me with the keys of the bookcases, through which I ranged with ever new delight. I went through, by my father's direction, a course of historical reading, but I could never acquire a taste for this species of composition. Accounts of the early periods of states and empires, of the Grecian and Roman republics, I pursued with pleasure and enthusiasm: but when they became more complicated, grew corrupt, luxurious, licentious, perfidious, mercenary, I turned from them fatigued, and disgusted, and sought to recreate my spirits in the fairer regions of poetry and fiction.

My early associations rendered theology an interesting subject* to me; I read ecclesiastical history, a detail of errors and crimes, and entered deeply into polemic divinity: my mind began to be emancipated, doubts had been suggested to it, I reasoned freely, endeavoured to arrange and methodize my opinions, and to trace them fearlessly through all their consequences: while from exercising my thoughts with freedom, I seemed to acquire new strength and dignity of character. I met with some of the writings of Descartes,* and was seized with a passion for metaphysical enquiries. I began to think about the nature of the soul— whether it was a composition of the elements, the result of organized matter, or a subtle and etherial fire.

In the course of my researches, the Heloise of Rousseau* fell into my hands.—Ah! with what transport, with what enthusiasm, did I peruse this dangerous, enchanting, work!—How shall I paint the sensations that were excited in my mind!—the pleasure I experienced approached the limits of pain—it was tumult—all the ardour of my character was excited.—Mr Courtney, one day, surprised me weeping over the sorrows of the tender St Preux.* He hastily snatched the book from my hand, and, carefully collecting the remaining volumes, carried them in silence to his chamber: but the impression made on my mind was never to be effaced—it was even productive of a long chain of consequences, that will continue to operate till the day of my death.

My time at this period passed rapidly and pleasantly. My father never treated me with affection; but the austerity of his manner gradually subsided. He gave me, occasionally, useful hints and instructions. Without feeling for him any tenderness, he inspired me with a degree of respect. The library was a source of lively and inexhaustible pleasure to my mind; and, when admitted to the table of Mr Courtney, some new character or sentiment frequently sharpened my attention, and afforded me subjects for future enquiry and meditation. I delighted to expatiate, when returning to the kind and hospitable mansion of my beloved aunt, (which I still considered as my home), on the various topics which I had collected in my little emigrations. I was listened to by my cousins with a pleasure that flattered my vanity, and looked up to as a kind of superior being;—a homage particularly gratifying to a young mind.

CHAPTER IX

THE excellent woman, who had been my more than mother, took infinite pains to cure the foibles, which, like pernicious weeds, entangled themselves with, and sometimes threatened to choak, the embryo blossoms of my expanding mind. Ah! with what pleasure do I recall her beloved idea to my memory! Fostered by her maternal love, and guided by her mild reason, how placid, and how sweet, were my early days!—Why, my first, my tenderest friend, did I lose you at that critical period of life, when the harmless sports and occupations of childhood gave place to the pursuits, the passions, and the errors of youth?—With the eloquence of affection, with gentle, yet impressive persuasion, thou mightest have checked the wild career of energetic feeling, which thou hast so often remarked with hope and terror.

As I entered my eighteenth year, I lost, by a premature death, this tender monitor. Never shall I forget her last emphatic, affectionate caution.

'Beware, my dear Emma,' said this revered friend, 'beware of strengthening, by indulgence, those ardent and

impetuous sensations, which, while they promise vigour of
mind, fill me with apprehension for the virtue, for the
happiness of my child. I wish not that the canker-worm,
Distrust, should blast the fair fruit of your ripening virtues.
The world contains many benevolent, many disinterested,
spirits; but civilization is yet distempered and imperfect;
the inequalities of society, by fostering artificial wants, and
provoking jealous competitions, have generated selfish
and hostile passions. Nature has been vainly provident for
her offspring, while man, with mistaken avidity, grasping
more than he has powers to enjoy, preys on his fellow
man:—departing from simple virtues, and simple
pleasures, in their stead, by common consent, has a
wretched semblance been substituted. Endeavour to contract your wants, and aspire only to a rational independence; by exercising your faculties, still the importunate
suggestions of your sensibility; preserve your sincerity,
cherish the ingenuous warmth of unsophisticated feeling,
but let discernment precede confidence. I tremble even
for the excess of those virtues which I have laboured to
cultivate in your lively and docile mind. If I could form a
wish for longer life, it is only for my children, and that I
might be to my Emma instead of reason, till her own
stronger mind matures. I dread, lest the illusions of imagination should render those powers, which would give
force to truth and virtue, the auxiliaries of passion. Learn
to distinguish, with accuracy, the good and ill qualities of
those with whom you may mingle: while you abhor the
latter, separate the being from his errors; and while you
revere the former, the moment that your reverence becomes personal, that moment, suspect that your judgment
is in danger of becoming the dupe of your affections.'

Would to God that I had impressed upon my mind—
that I had recalled to my remembrance more frequently—
a lesson so important to a disposition like mine!—a
continual victim to the enthusiasm of my feelings; incapable of approving, or disapproving, with moderation—
the most poignant sufferings, even the study of mankind,
have been insufficient to dissolve the powerful enchant-

ment, to disentangle the close-twisted associations!—But I
check this train of overwhelming reflection, that is every
moment on the point of breaking the thread of my narration, and obtruding itself to my pen.

CHAPTER X

MR Courtney did not long survive the guardian of my
infancy:—his constitution had for some years been gradually impaired; and his death was hastened by a continuance of habitual dissipation, which he had not the
resolution to relinquish, and to which his strength was no
longer equal. It was an event I had long anticipated, and
which I contemplated with a sensation of solemnity, rather
than of grief. The ties of blood are weak, if not the mere
chimeras of prejudice, unless sanctioned by reason, or
cemented by habits of familiar and affectionate intercourse. Mr Courtney refusing the title of father, from a
conviction that his conduct gave him no claim to this
endearing appellation, had accustomed me to feel for him
only the respect due to some talents and good qualities,
which threw a veil over his faults. Courage and truth were
the principles with which he endeavoured to inspire me;—
precepts, which I gratefully acknowledge, and which forbid me to adopt the language of affection, when no
responsive sympathies exist in the heart.

My eyes were yet moist with the tears that I had shed for
the loss of my maternal friend, when I received a hasty
summons to Berkley-square. A servant informed me, that
his master was, at length, given over by his physicians, and
wished to speak to Miss Courtney, before his strength and
spirits were too much exhausted.

I neither felt, nor affected, surprize at this intelligence,
but threw myself, without reply, into the carriage which
had been dispatched for my conveyance.

On entering the house, a gloomy silence seemed to
reign throughout the late festive apartments; but, as I had
seldom been a partaker of the festivity, the contrast struck

me less forcibly than it might otherwise have done. My name was announced, and I was conducted, by the housekeeper, to the chamber of her dying master, who, supported on pillows, breathed with difficulty, but appeared to be free from pain, and tolerably composed. I met the physician in the antechamber; who, on my requesting earnestly to know the situation of his patient, informed me—That an internal mortification had taken place, and that he could not survive many hours.

Approaching the bed, considerably shocked at the intelligence I had received, Mr Courtney, in a low and faint voice, desired me to draw a chair near him. I obeyed in silence.

'Emma,' said he, 'I am about to quit a world, in which I have experienced little sincere enjoyment; yet, I leave it reluctantly. Had I been more temperate in my pleasures, perhaps, they might have been less destructive, and more protracted. I begin to suspect, that I have made some great mistakes; but it is now too late for retraction, and I will not, in my last moments, contradict, by my example, the lesson of fortitude, with which it has been a part of my plan to inspire you. You have now, unprotected, the world to encounter; for, I will frankly confess, that my affection for you has not been strong enough to induce me to forego my own more immediate gratification: but I have never deceived you. Your mother, when she married, reserved for her private expences a thousand pounds, which, on her deathbed, she desired might be invested in the funds on your account. This request I religiously complied with, and there it has remained untouched; and, being purchased in your name, you may claim it whenever you please. I have appointed you no guardians; for, already in your nineteenth year, and possessing an understanding superior to your sex and age, I chose to leave you unfettered, and at your own discretion. I spared from my pleasures what money was requisite to complete your education; for having no fortune to give you, and my health being precarious, I thought it just to afford you every advantage for the improvement of those talents which you evidently possess, and which must now enable you to make your way in the world; for the scanty pittance, that the interest of your fortune will produce, is, I doubt, insufficient for your support. Had I lived, it was my intention to have established you by marriage; but that is a scheme, to which, at present, I would not advise you to trust. Marriage, generally speaking, in the existing state of things, must of necessity be an affair of *finance*. My interest and introduction might have availed you something; but mere merit, wit, or beauty, stand in need of more powerful auxiliaries. My brother, Mr Morton,[1] called on me this morning:—he has agreed, for the present, to receive you into his family, where you must endeavour to make yourself useful and agreeable, till you can fix on a better and more independent plan. Finding me in so low a state, your uncle would have waited a few days in town, to have seen the result, and, in case of the worst, to have taken you down with him, but pressing business urged his departure. I would advise you, immediately after my decease, to set out for Morton Park. Proper persons are appointed to settle my affairs:—when every thing is turned into money, there will, I trust, be sufficient to discharge my just debts; but do not flatter yourself with the expectation of a surplus. Your presence here, when I am no more, will be equally unnecessary and improper.'

This was said at intervals, and with difficulty; when, seeming quite exhausted, he waved his hand for me to leave the room, and sunk into a sort of dose,* or rather stupor, which continued till within some minutes of his decease.

Mr Courtney had been, what is called, a man of pleasure:—he had passed thro' life without ever loving any one but himself—intent, merely, on gratifying the humour of the moment. A superior education, and an attentive observance, not of rational, but, of social man, in

---

[1] Mr Courtney's brother had taken the name of Morton, to qualify himself for the inheritance of an estate, bequeathed to him by a distant relation.

an extensive commerce with the world, had sharpened his sagacity; but he was inaccessible to those kindlings of the affections—those glowings of admiration—inspired by real, or fancied, excellence, which never fail to expand and advance the minds of such as are capable of sketching, with a daring hand, the dangerous picture:—or of those philosophic and comprehensive views, which teach us to seek a reflected happiness in benevolent exertions for the welfare of others. My mother, I suspected, had been the victim of her husband's unkindness and neglect: wonder not, then, that my heart revolted when I would have given him the tender appellation of father! If he coldly acknowledged any little merits which I possessed, he regarded them rather with jealousy than approbation; for he felt that they tacitly reproached him.

I will make no comment on the closing scene of his life. Among the various emotions which had rapidly succeeded each other in my mind, during his last address, surprize had no place; I had not then his character to learn.

CHAPTER XI

THE small pittance bequeathed to me was insufficient to preserve me from dependence.—*Dependence!*—I repeated to myself, and I felt my heart die within me. I revolved in my mind various plans for my future establishment.—I might, perhaps, be allowed to officiate, as an assistant, in the school where I had been placed in my childhood, with the mistress of which I still kept up an occasional correspondence; but this was a species of servitude, and my mind panted for freedom, for social intercourse, for scenes in motion, where the active curiosity of my temper might find a scope wherein to range and speculate. What could the interest of my little fortune afford? It would neither enable me to live alone, nor even to board in a family of any respectability. My beloved aunt was no more; her children were about to be dispersed, and to form various connections.

Cruel prejudices!—I exclaimed—hapless woman! Why
was I not educated for commerce, for a profession, for
labour? Why have I been rendered feeble and delicate by
bodily constraint, and fastidious by artificial refinement?
Why are we bound, by the habits of society, as with an
adamantine chain? Why do we suffer ourselves to be confined within a magic circle,* without daring, by a magnanimous effort, to dissolve the barbarous spell?

A child in the drama of the world, I knew not which way
to turn, nor on what to determine. I wrote to Mr Morton,
to enquire on what terms I was to be received by his family.
If merely as a visitor for a few weeks, till I had time to digest
my plans, I should meet, with pleasure, a gentleman whose
character I had been taught to respect; but I should not
consider myself as subject to controul. I ought, perhaps,
to have been satisfied with Mr Morton's answer to my
interrogatories.

He wished to embrace the daughter of his brother, his
family would be happy to render Morton park agreeable to
her, as long as she should think proper to favour them by
making it her residence. The young ladies expected both
pleasure and improvement from the society of their accomplished kinswoman, &c.

I believe I was unreasonable, the style of this letter was
civil, nay kind, and yet it appeared, to me, to want the
vivifying principle—what shall I say?—dictated merely by
the head, it reached not the heart.

The trials of my mind, I foreboded, were about to com-
mence, I shrunk from the world I had been so willing to
enter, for the rude storms of which I had been little fitted
by the fostering tenderness of my early guardians. Those
ardent feelings and lively expectations, with all the glowing
landscapes which my mind had sketched of the varied
pleasures of society, while in a measure secluded from
its enjoyments, gradually melted into one deep, undis-
tinguished shade. That sanguine ardour of temper, which
had hitherto appeared the predominant feature of my
character, now gave place to despondency. I wept, I suffered my tears to flow unrestrained: the solemnity of the

late events had seized my spirits, and the approaching change filled me with solicitude. I wandered over the scenes of my past pleasures, and recalled to my remembrance, with a sad and tender luxury, a thousand little incidents, that derived all their importance from the impossibility of their renewal. I gazed on every object, *for the last time*—What is there in these words that awakens our fanaticism? I could have done homage to these inanimate, and, till now, uninteresting objects; merely because I should *see them no more*.

How fantastic and how capricious are these sentiments! Ought I, or ought I not, to blush while I acknowledge them? My young friends, also, from whom I was about to separate myself!—how various might be our destinies, and how unconscious were we of the future! Happy ignorance, that by bringing the evils of life in succession, gradually inures us to their endurance.

> 'Had I beheld the sum of ills, which one
> By one, I have endured—my heart had broke.'*

CHAPTER XII

THE hour at length came, when, harrassed in body and in mind, I set out for Morton park. I travelled alone, and reached the end of my journey at the close of day. I entreated Mr Morton, who hastened to hand me from the carriage, and welcome my arrival, that I might be permitted to retire to my apartment, pleading fatigue, and wishing to wave* the ceremony of an introduction to the family till the next morning. My request was obligingly granted, and a servant ordered to attend me to my chamber.

Many years had elapsed fince I had seen this family, and my judgment was then so immature, that our meeting at the breakfast table had with each of us, I believe, the force of a first impression. You know my *fanaticism* on these occasions. I will attempt an imperfect sketch of the groupe, assembled in the saloon, to whom I was severally*

presented on my entrance, by the lord of the domain. Mr
Morton, himself, to whom precedence is due, seemed to
be about fifty years of age, was of the middle stature, his
features regular, and his countenance placid: he spoke but
little, but that little was always mild and often judicious. He
appeared not to be void of benevolent affections, and had
the character of a humane landlord, but his virtues were,
in a great measure, sunk in an habitual indolence of temper; he would sometimes sacrifice his principles to his
repose, though never to his interest. His lady—no, I will
not describe her; her character will, it may be, unfold
inself to you in future—Suffice it to say, that her person
was gross, her voice loud and discordant, and her features
rugged: she affected an air of openness and pleasantry; It
may be prejudiced, perhaps she did not *affect it*. Sarah
Morton, the eldest of the daughters, was about my own
age, she was under the middle height, fair, plump, lo-
quacious; there was a childish levity in her accent and
manners, which impressed strangers with an unfavourable
opinion of her understanding, but it was an acquired manner, for she was shrewd and sensible. Ann, the second
daughter, was a little lively brunette, with sharp features
and sparkling black eyes; volatile, giddy, vain and thoughtless, but good humoured and pretty. The other children
were much younger.

Two gentlemen joined us at our repast, visitors at
Morton park. Mr Francis, the elder, was in his fortieth
year,* his figure slender and delicate, his eye piercing,
and his manner impressive. It occurred to me, that I had
somewhere seen him before, and, after a few minutes
recollection, I recognized in him a gentleman who had
occasionally visited at my father's, and whom I have
already mentioned as the antagonist of the man of fashion,
whose sentiments and volubility excited my youthful astonishment and indignation. Mr Montague, the younger, the
son of a medical gentleman residing in a neighbouring
county, seemed about one and twenty, tall, elegantly
formed, full of fire and vivacity, with imperious manners,
an impetuous temper, and stubborn prejudices.

The introduction of a stranger generally throws some kind of restraint over a company; a break is made in their usual topics and associations, till the disposition and habits of the intruder have, in some degree, unfolded themselves. Mrs Morton took upon herself to entertain; she exhibited her talents on various subjects, with apparent self-approbation, till a few keen remarks from Mr Francis arrested the torrent of her eloquence. The young ladies scrutinized me with attention; even the lively Ann, while she minutely observed me, ceased to court play from Mr Montague, who attended to me with the air, and addressed me in the language of gallantry. I sometimes caught the penetrating eye of Mr Francis, and his glance seemed to search the soul.

After breakfast, Mr Morton having retired to his dressing-room, and the younger part of the company strolling into the pleasure grounds, whither I declined accompanying them, I took an opportunity, being ever desirous of active and useful employment, of offering my assistance to Mrs Morton, in the education of her younger children; proposing to instruct them in the rudiments either of music, drawing, French, or any other accomplishment, for which my own education had capacitated me. Mr Francis remained standing in a window, his back towards us, with a book in his hand, on which he seemed intent.

'If,' replied Mrs Morton, 'it is your wish, Miss Courtney, to procure the situation of governess in any gentleman's family, and it is certainly a very laudable desire in a young woman of your *small fortune*, Mr Morton will, I have no doubt, have it in his power to recommend you: but in the education of my family, I desire no interference; it is an important task, and I have my peculiar notions on the subject: their expectations are not great, and your *elegant* accomplishments might unfit them for their future, probable, stations.'

The manner in which this speech was uttered spoke yet more forcibly than the words.—I felt my cheeks glow.

'I was not asking favours, Madam, I was only desirous of being useful.'

'It is a pity, then, that your discernment had not corrected your vanity.'

The housekeeper entering, to consult her mistress on some domestic occasion, Mrs Morton quitted the room. Mr Francis closed his book, turned round, and gazed earnestly in my face: before sufficiently mortified, his observation, which I felt at this moment oppressive, did not relieve me. I attempted to escape, but, seizing my hand, he detained me by a kind of gentle violence.

'And why this confusion, my dear Miss Courtney; do you blush for having acted with propriety and spirit?' I burst into tears—I could not help it—'How weak is this, how unworthy of the good sense you have just manifested.'

'I confess it, but I feel myself, at this moment, a poor, a friendless, an unprotected being.'

'What prejudices! poverty is neither criminal, nor disgraceful; you will not want friends, while you continue to deserve them; and as for protection, (and he smiled) I had not expected from Emma Courtney's spirited letter to Mr Morton, and equally proper retort to his lady's impertinence, so plaintive, so feminine a complaint.—You have talents, cultivate them, and learn to rest on your own powers.'

'I thank you for your reproof, and solicit your future lessons.'

'Can you bear the truth?'

'Try me.'

'Have you not cherished a false pride?'

It is too true, thought I, and I sighed.

'How shall I cure this foible?'

'By self-examination, by resolution, and perseverance.'

'Be to me instead of a conscience.'

'What, then, is become of your own?'

'Prejudice, I doubt, has blinded and warped it.'

'I suspect so; but you have energy and candor, and are not, I hope, of a temper to despond.'

The return of the family terminated this singular conversation. The young ladies rallied me, on being found *tete-a-tete* with the philosopher; Mr Montague, I thought,

looked displeased. I stole out, while the party were dressing for dinner, and rambled into the gardens, which were
extensive, and laid out with taste.

CHAPTER XIII

I JUDGED my visit here would not be very long. I scarcely
knew whether I was most inclined to like or to fear Mr
Francis, but I determined, if possible, to cultivate his
friendship. I interrogated myself again and again—From
whence this restlessness, this languor, this disgust, with
all I hear and see?—Why do I feel wayward, querulous,
fastidious? Mr Morton's family had no hearts; they appeared to want a *sense*, that preyed incessantly on mine; I
could not love them, and my heart panted to expand its
sensations.

Sarah and Ann became jealous of me, and of each other;
the haughty, yet susceptible, Montague addressed each in
turn, with a homage equally fervent for the moment, and
equally transient. This young man was bold, ardent, romantic, and enterprizing, but blown about by every gust of
passion, he appeared each succeeding moment a different
character: with a glowing and rapid imagination, he had
never given himself time to reason, to compare, to acquire
principles: following the bent of a raised, yet capricious
fancy, he was ever in pursuit of meteors, that led him into
mischief, or phantoms, that dissolved at his approach.

Had my mind been more assured and at ease, I could
have amused myself with the whimsical flights of this eccentric being—One hour, attracted by the sportive graces
of Ann, he played with and caressed her, while the minutes
flew rapidly on the light wing of amusement, and, till
reminded by the grave countenance of Mr Morton,
seemed to forget that any other person was present. The
next minute, disgusted with her frivolity, all his attention
was absorbed by the less fascinating, but more artful and
ingenious, Sarah. Then, quitting them both, he would
pursue my steps, break in upon my meditations, and haunt

my retreats, from whence, when not disposed to be entertained by his caprice, I found it not difficult to drive him, by attacking some of his various prejudices:—accustomed to feel, and not to reason, his tastes and opinions were vehement and uncontroulable.

From this society, so uncongenial to my reflecting, reasoning, mind, I found some resource in the conversation of Mr Francis. The pride of Montague was evidently piqued by the decided preference which I gave to the company of his friend; but his homage, or his resentment, were alike indifferent to me: accustomed to speak and act from my convictions, I was but little solicitous respecting the opinion of others. My understanding was exercised by attending to the observations of Mr Francis, and by discussing the questions to which they led; yet it was exercised without being gratified: he opposed and bewildered me, convicted me of error, and harrassed me with doubt.

Mr Francis soon after prepared to return to town. I was affected at the idea of his departure; and felt, that in losing his society, I should be deprived of my only rational recreation, and should again be exposed to Mrs Morton's illiberal attacks, who appeared to have marked me out for her victim, though at present restrained by the presence of a man, who had found means to inspire, even her, with some degree of respect.

Mr Francis, on the evening preceding the day on which he purposed leaving Morton Park, passing under the open window of my chamber, in which I was sitting with a book to enjoy the refreshing breeze, invited me to come down, and accompany him in a ramble. I immediately complied with his request, and joined him in a few minutes, with a countenance clouded with regret at the idea of his quitting us.

'You are going,' said I, as I gave him my hand (which he passed under his arm), 'and I lose my friend and counsellor.'

'Your concern is obliging; but you are capable of standing alone, and your mind, by so doing, will acquire strength.'

'I feel as if this would not be the case: the world appears to me a thorny and a pathless wilderness;* I step with caution, and look around me with dread.—That I require protection and assistance, is, I confess, a proof of weakness, but it is nevertheless true.'

'Mr Montague,' replied he, with some degree of archness in his tone and manner, 'is a gallant knight, a pattern of chivalry, and appears to be particularly calculated for the defender of distressed damsels!'

'I have no inclination to trust myself to the guidance of one, who seems himself entangled in an inextricable maze of error, and whose versatile character affords little basis for confidence.'

'Tell me what it is you fear;—are your apprehensions founded in reason?'

'Recollect my youth, my sex, and my precarious situation.'

'I thought you contemned the plea of *sex*, as a sanction for weakness!'

'Though I disallow it as a natural, I admit it as an artificial, plea.'

'Explain yourself.'

'The character, you tell me, is modified by circumstances:* the customs of society, then, have enslaved, enervated, and degraded woman.'

'I understand you: there is truth in your remark, though you have given it undue force.'

I hesitated—my heart was full—I felt as if there were many things which I wished to say; but, however paradoxical, the manners of Mr Francis repressed, while they invited, confidence. I respected his reason, but I doubted whether I could inspire him with sympathy, or make him fully comprehend my feelings. I conceived I could express myself with more freedom on paper; but I had not courage to request a correspondence, when he was silent on the subject. That it would be a source of improvement to me, I could not doubt, but prejudice with-held me from making the proposal. He looked at me, and perceived my mind struggling with a suggestion, to which it dared not give utterance: he suspected the truth, but was unwilling to disturb the operations of my understanding. We walked for some time in silence:—my companion struck into a path that led towards the house—listened to the village clock as it struck nine—and observed, the hour grew late. He had distinguished me, and I was flattered by that distinction; he had supported me against the arrogance of Mrs Morton, retorted the sly sarcasms of Sarah, and even helped to keep the impetuous Montague in awe, and obliged him to rein in his offensive spirit, every moment on the brink of outrage. My heart, formed for grateful attachment, taking, in one instant, a hasty retrospect of the past, and a rapid glance into futurity, experienced at that moment so desolating a pang, that I endeavoured in vain to repress its sensations, and burst into a flood of tears. Mr Francis suddenly stopped, appeared moved, and, with a benevolent aspect and soothing accents, enquired into the cause of an emotion so sudden and unexpected. I wept a few minutes in silence, and my spirits seemed, in some measure, relieved.

'I weep, (said I,) because I am *friendless*; to be esteemed and cherished is necessary to my existence; I am an alien in the family where I at present reside, I cannot remain here much longer, and to whom, and whither, shall I go?'

He took my hand—'I will not, at present, say all that it might be proper to say, because I perceive your mind is in a feeble state;—My affairs call me to London:—yet, there is a method of conversing at a distance.'

I eagerly availed myself of this suggestion, which I had wished, without having the courage to propose.

'Will you, then, allow me, through the medium of pen and paper, to address, to consult you, as I may see occasion?'

'Will I? yes, most cheerfully! Propose your doubts and state your difficulties, and we shall see, (smiling) whether they admit of a solution.'

Thanking him, I engaged to avail myself of this permission, and we proceeded slowly to the house, and joined the party in the supper room. I never once thought of my red and swoln eyes, till Sarah, glancing a look half curious, half sarcastic, towards me, exclaimed from Shakespear, in an affected tone,

'Parting is such sweet sorrow'*

Mr Francis looked at her sternly, she blushed and was silent; Mr Montague was captious; Ann mortified, that she could not by her little tricks gain his attention. Mrs Morton sat wrapped in mock dignity; while Mr Morton, and his philosophic friend, canvassed the principles upon which an horizontal mill was about to be constructed on the estate of the former. After a short and scanty meal, I retired to my apartment, determined to rise early the next morning, and make breakfast for my friend before his departure.

CHAPTER XIV

M r Francis had ordered his horse to be ready at five o'clock. I left my chamber at four, to have the pleasure of preparing for him the last friendly repast, and of saying *farewel.* He was serene and chearful as usual, I somewhat more pensive; we parted with great cordiality, he gave me his address in town, and engaged me to write to him shortly. I accompanied him through the Park to the porter's lodge, where the servant and horses waited his coming. My eyes glistened as I bade him adieu, and reiterated my wishes for his safety and prosperity, while his features softened into a more than usual benignity, as he returned my salutation.

I wandered thoughtfully back towards the house, but the rich purple that began to illumine the east, the harbinger of the rising sun, the freshness of the morning air, the soft dews which already glittered on every fragrant plant and flower, the solemn stillness, so grateful to the reflecting mind, that pervaded the scene, induced me to prolong my walk. Every object appeared in unison with my feelings, my heart swelled with devotional affections, it aspired

to the Author of nature. After having bewildered ourselves
amid systems and theories, religion, in such situations,
returns to the susceptible mind as a *sentiment* rather
than as a principle. A passing cloud let fall a gentle,
drizzling shower; sheltered beneath the leafy umbrage of a
spreading oak, I rather heard than felt it; yet, the coolness
it diffused seemed to quench those ardent emotions,
which are but too congenial with my disposition, while
the tumult of the passions subsided into a delicious
tranquillity.

How mutable are human beings!—A very few hours
converted this sublime complacency into perturbation
and tumult. Having extended my walk beyond its accustomed limits, on my return, I retired, somewhat fatigued
to my apartment, and devoted the morning to my studies.
At the dinner hour I joined the family, each individual of
which seemed wrapped up in reserve, scarcely deigning to
practise the common ceremonies of the occasion. I was
not sufficiently interested in the cause of these appear-
ances to make any enquiries, and willingly resigned myself,
in the intervals of the entertainment, to meditation.

When the table was cleared, and the servants had withdrawn, perceiving the party not sociably inclined, I was
about to retire—when Mrs Morton observed, with features
full of a meaning which I did not comprehend, that—

'Their guest, Mr Francis, had, no doubt, left Morton
Park gratefully impressed by the *kindness* of Miss
Courtney.'

Montague reddened—bit his lips—got up—and sat
down again. The young ladies wore an air not perfectly
good-humoured, and a little triumphant. Mr Morton
looked very solemn.

'I hope so, Madam,' I replied, somewhat carelessly. 'I
felt myself indebted to Mr Francis for his civilities, and was
solicitous to make him all the return in my power—I wish
that power had been enlarged.'

She held up her hands and eyes with an affected, and
ridiculous, gesture.

'Mr Francis,' said Montague, abruptly, 'is very happy in having inspired you with sentiments *so partial.*'

'I am not partial—I am merely just. Mr Francis appeared to me a rational man, and my understanding was exercised and gratified by his conversation.'

I was about to proceed, but my uncle (who seemed to have been tutored for the occasion) interrupted me with much gravity.

'You are but little acquainted, Emma, with the customs of society; there is a great indecorum in a young lady's making these distinctions.'

'What distinctions, my dear Sir!—in prefering a reasonable man to fools and coxcombs?'

'Forgive me, my dear—you have a quick wit, but you want experience. I am informed, that you breakfasted with Mr Francis this morning, and attended him through the Park:—this, with your late walk yesterday evening, and evident emotion on your return, let me tell you, child, wears an indecorous appearance:—the world is justly attentive to the conduct of young women, and too apt to be censorious.'

I looked round me with unaffected surprize—'Good God!—did I suppose, in this family, it was necessary to be upon my guard against malicious constructions?'

'Pray,'—interrupted Sarah, pertly—'would you not have expressed some surprize, had I shewed Mr Montague similar attentions?'

I looked at her, I believe, a little too contemptuously.— 'Whatever sentiments might have been excited in my mind by the attentions of Miss Morton to Mr Montague, *surprize*, assuredly, would not have been among them.'

She coloured, and Montague's passions began to rise. I stopped him in the beginning of an impertinent harangue, by observing—

'That I did not think myself accountable to him for my conduct;—before I should be solicitous respecting his opinions, he must give me better reasons, than he had hitherto done, to respect his judgment.'

Ann wept, and prattled something, to which nobody thought it worth while to attend.

'Well, Sir,' continued I, turning to Mr Morton, 'be pleased to give me, in detail, what you have to alledge, that I may be enabled to justify myself.'

'Will you allow me to ask you a question?'

'Most certainly.'

'Has Mr Francis engaged you to correspond with him?'

I was silent a few moments.

'You hesitate!'

'Only, Sir, *how* to answer your question.——I certainly intend myself the pleasure of addressing Mr Francis on paper; but I cannot strictly say *he engaged* me so to do, as it was a proposal he was led to make, by conjecturing my wishes on the subject.'

Again, Mrs Morton, with uplifted hands and eyes— 'What effrontery!'

I seemed not to hear her.—'Have you any thing more to say, my dear uncle?'

'You are a strange girl. It would not, perhaps, be proper before this company to enquire'—and he stopped.

'Any thing is proper, Sir, to enquire of me, and in any company—I have no reserves, no secrets.'

'Well, then, I think it necessary to inform you, that, though a sensible, well-educated, liberal-minded, man, Mr Francis has neither estate nor fortune, nor does he practise any lucrative profession.'

'I am sorry for it, on his own account, and for those whom his generosity might benefit. But, what is it to me?'

'You affect to misunderstand me.'

'I *affect* nothing.'

'I will speak more plainly:—Has he made you any pro- posals?'

The purport of this solemn, but ludicrous, prep- aration, at once flashed upon my mind, the first time the thought had ever occurred. I laughed—I could not help it.

'I considered Mr Francis as a *philosopher*, and not as a *lover*. Does this satisfy you, Sir?'

My uncle's features, in spite of himself, relaxed into a half-smile.

'Very platonic—sweet simplicity!'—drauled out Mrs Morton, in ironical accents.

'I will not be insulted, Mr Morton!' quitting my seat, and rising in temper.—'I consider myself, merely, as your visitant, and not as responsible to any one for my actions. Conscious of purity of intention, and superior to all disguise or evasion, I was not aware of these feminine, indelicate, unfriendly suggestions. If this behaviour be a specimen of what I am to expect in the world—the world may do its will—but I will never be its slave: while I have strength of mind to form principles, and courage to act upon them, I am determined to preserve my freedom, and trust to the general candour and good sense of mankind to appreciate me justly. As the brother of my late father, and as entitled to respect from your own kind intentions, I am willing to enter into any explanations, which *you, Sir*, may think necessary:—neither my motives, nor my actions, have ever yet shrunk from investigation. Will you permit me to attend you in your library? It is not my intention to intrude longer on your hospitality, and I could wish to avail myself of your experience and counsels respecting my future destination.'

Mr Morton, at my request, withdrew with me into the library, where I quickly removed from his mind those injurious suspicions with which Mrs Morton had laboured to inspire him. He would not hear of my removal from the Park—apologized for what had passed—assured me of his friendship and protection—and entreated me to consider his house as my home. There was an honest warmth and sincerity in his manner, that sensibly affected me; I could have wept; and I engaged, at his repeated request, not to think, at present, of withdrawing myself from his protection. Thus we separated.

How were the virtues of this really good man tarnished by an unsuitable connection! In the giddy hours of youth, we thoughtlessly rush into engagements, that fetter our minds, and affect our future characters, without reflecting on the important consequences of our conduct. This is a subject on which I have had occasion to reflect deeply; yet, alas! my own boasted reason has been, but too often, the dupe of my imagination.

CHAPTER XV

NOTHING, here, occupied my heart—a heart to which it was necessary to love and admire. I had suffered myself to be irritated—the tumult of my spirits did not easily subside—I was mortified at the reflection—I had believed myself armed with patience and fortitude, but my philosophy was swept before the impetuous emotions of my passions like chaff before the whirlwind. I took up my pen to calm my spirits, and addressed myself to the man who had been, unconsciously, the occasion of these vexations.—My swelling heart needed the relief of communication.

TO MR FRANCIS

'I sought earnestly for the privilege of addressing you on paper. My mind seemed to overflow with a thousand sentiments, that I had not the courage to express in words; but now, when the period is arrived, that I can take up my pen, unawed by your penetrating glance, unchecked by your poignant reply, and pour out my spirit before you, I feel as if its emotions were too wayward, too visionary, too contradictory, to merit your attention.

'Every thing I see and hear is a disappointment to me:—brought up in retirement—conversing only with books—dwelling with ardour on the great characters, and heroic actions, of antiquity, all my ideas of honour and distinction were associated with those of virtue and talents. I conceived, that the pursuit of truth, and the advancement of reason, were the grand objects of universal attention, and I panted to do homage to those superior minds, who, teaching mankind to be wise, would at length lead them to happiness. Accustomed to think, to feel, to kindle into action, I am at a loss to understand the distinction between theory and practice, which every one seems eager to inculcate, as if the degrading and melancholy intelligence, which fills my soul with despondency, and pervades my understanding with gloom, was to them a subject of exultation.

'Is virtue, then, a chimera—does it exist only in the regions of romance?—Have we any interest in finding our fellow creatures weak and miserable?—Is the Being who formed them unjust, capricious, impotent, or tyrannical?

'Answer these questions, that press heavily on my mind, that dart across it, in its brightest moments, clouding its sunshine with a thick and impenetrable darkness. Must the benevolent emotions, which I have hitherto delighted to cherish, turn into misanthropy—must the fervent and social affections of my heart give place to inanity, to apathy—must the activity of a curious and vigorous mind sink into torpor and abhorred vacuity?

'While they teach me to distrust the existence of virtue, they endeavour to impose on me, in its stead, a fictitious semblance; and to substitute, for the pure gold of truth, a paltry tinsel. It is in vain I ask—what have those to do with "*seeming*," who still retain "that which *passeth shew*?"* However my actions may be corrupted by the contagious example of the world, may I still hold fast my integrity, and disdain to wear the *appearance* of virtue, when the substance shall no longer exist.

'To admire, to esteem, to love, are congenial to my nature—I am unhappy, because these affections are not called in to exercise. To venerate abstract perfection, requires too vigorous an exertion of the mental powers—I would see virtue exemplified, I would love it in my fellow creatures—I would catch the glorious enthusiasm, and rise from created to uncreated excellence.

'I am perplexed with doubts; relieve the wanderings of my mind, solve the difficulties by which it is agitated, prepare me for the world which is before me. The prospect, no longer beaming with light, no longer glowing with a thousand vivid hues, is overspread with mists, which the mind's eye vainly attempts to penetrate. I would feel, again, the value of existence, the worth of rectitude, the certainty of truth, the blessing of hope! Ah! tell me not— that the gay expectations of youth have been the meteors of fancy, the visions of a romantic and distempered imagination! If I must not live to realize them, I would not live at all.

'My harrassed mind turns to you! You will not ridicule its scruples—you will, at least, deign to reason with me, and, in the exercise of my understanding, I shall experience a temporary relief from the sensations which devour me, the suspicions that distress me, and which spread over futurity a fearful veil.

'EMMA.'

I walked to the next market town, and left my letter at the post-house.—I waited impatiently for a reply; my mind wanted *impression*, and sunk into languor. The answer, which arrived in a few days, was kind, because it was prompt, my sickly mind required a speedy remedy.

TO EMMA COURTNEY

'Why will you thus take things in masses, and continually dwell in extremes? You deceive yourself; instead of cultivating your reason, you are fostering an excessive sensibility, a fastidious delicacy. It is the business of reason to compare, to separate, to discriminate. Is there no medium —extraordinary exertions are only called forth by extraordinary contingences;—because every human being is not a hero, are we then to distrust the existence of virtue?

'The mind is modified by the circumstances in which it is placed, by the accidents of birth and education; the constitutions of society are all, as yet, imperfect; they have generated, and perpetuated, many mistakes—the consequences of those mistakes will, eventually, carry with them their antidote, the seeds of reproduction are, even, visible in their decay. The growth of reason is slow, but not the less sure; the increase of knowledge must necessarily prepare the way for the increase of virtue and happiness.*

'Look back upon the early periods of society, and, taking a retrospective view of what has been done, amidst the interruptions of barbarous inroads, falling empires, and palsying despotism, calculate what yet may be atchieved: while the causes, which have hitherto impeded the progress of civilization, must continue to decrease, in an accelerated ratio, with the wide, and still wider, diffusion of truth.

'We may trace most of the faults, and the miseries of mankind, to the vices and errors of political institutions,* their permanency having been their radical defect. Like children, we have dreamt, that what gratifies our desires, or contributes to our convenience, to-day, will prove equally useful and satisfactory to-morrow, without reflecting on the growth of the body, the change of humours, the new objects, and the new situations, which every succeeding hour brings in its train. That immutability, which constitutes the perfection of what we (from poverty of language) term the *divine mind*, would inevitably be the bane of creatures liable to error; it is of the constancy, rather than of the fickleness, of human beings, that we have reason to complain.

'Every improvement must be the result of successive experiments, this has been found true in natural science, and it must be universally applied to be universally beneficial. Bigotry, whether religious, political, moral, or commercial, is the canker-worm at the root of the tree of knowledge and of virtue. The wildest speculations are less mischievous than the torpid state of error: he, who tamely resigns his understanding to the guidance of another, sinks at once, from the dignity of a rational being, to a mechanical puppet, moved at pleasure on the wires of the artful operator.—*Imposition* is the principle and support of every varied description of tyranny, whether civil or ecclesiastical, moral or mental; its baneful consequence is to degrade both him who is imposed on, and him who imposes. *Obedience*, is a word, which ought never to have had existence: as we recede from conviction, and languidly resign ourselves to any foreign authority, we quench the principle of action, of virtue, of reason;*—we bear about the semblance of humanity, but the spirit is fled.

'These are truths, which will slowly, but ultimately, prevail; in the splendour of which, the whole fabric of superstition will gradually fade and melt away. The world, like every individual, has its progress from infancy to maturity—How many follies do we commit in childhood? how many errors are we precipitated into by the fervor and inexperience of youth! Is not every stable principle acquired through innumerable mistakes—can you wonder, that in society, amidst the aggregate of jarring interests and passions, reformation is so tardy? Though civilization has been impeded by innumerable obstacles, even these help to carry on the great work: empires may be overturned, and the arts scattered, but not lost. The hordes of barbarians, which overwhelmed ancient Rome,* adopted at length the religion, the laws, and the improvements of the vanquished, as Rome had before done those of Greece. As the stone, which, thrown into the water, spreads circles still more and more extended;—or (to adopt the gospel similitude) as the grain of mustard seed, growing up into a large tree, shelters the fowls of heaven in its branches*—so will knowledge, at length, diffuse itself, till it covers the whole earth.

'When the minds of men are changed, the system of things will also change; but these changes, though active and incessant, must be gradual. Reason will fall softly, and almost imperceptibly, like a gentle shower of dews, fructifying the soil, and preparing it for future harvests. Let us not resemble the ambitious shepherd, who, calling for the accumulated waters of the Nile upon his lands, was, with his flock, swept away in the impetuous torrent.

'You ask, whether—because human beings are still imperfect—you are to resign your benevolence, and to cherish misanthropy? What a question! Would you hate the inhabitants of an hospital for being infected with a pestilential disorder? Let us remember, that vice originates in mistakes of the understanding, and that, he who seeks happiness by means contradictory and destructive, *is em-*

phatically the sinner. Our duties, then, are obvious—If selfish and violent passions have been generated by the inequalities of society, we must labour to counteract them, by endeavouring to combat prejudice, to expand the mind, to give comprehensive views, to teach mankind their true interest, and to lead them to habits of goodness and greatness.* Every prejudice conquered, every mistake rectified, every individual improved, is an advance upon the great scale of virtue and happiness.

'Let it, then, be your noblest ambition to co-operate with, to join your efforts, to those of philosophers and sages, the benefactors of mankind. To waste our time in useless repinings is equally weak and vain; every one in his sphere may do something; each has a little circle where his influence will be availing. Correct your own errors, which are various—weeds in a luxuriant soil—and you will have done something towards the general reformation. But you are able to do more;—be vigilant, be active, beware of the illusions of fancy! I suspect, that you will have to suffer— may you, at length, reap the fruits of a wholesome, though it should be a bitter, experience.

'——FRANCIS.'

I perused the letter, I had received, again and again; it awakened a train of interesting reflections, and my spirits became tranquillized.

CHAPTER XVI

EARLY one fine morning, Ann tapped gently at the door of my chamber; I had already risen, and invited her to enter.

'Would I accompany her to breakfast, with a widow lady, who resided in a village about two miles from Morton Park, an occasional visitant in the family, a lady with whom, she was certain, I should be charmed.'

I smiled at her ardour, thanked her for her kindness, and readily agreed to her proposal. We strolled together through an adjacent wood, which, by a shady and winding path, conducted us towards the residence of this vaunted favourite of my little companion.

On our way, she entertained me with a slight sketch of the history of Mrs Harley and her family. She was the widow of a merchant, who was supposed to possess great property; but, practising occasionally as an underwriter, a considerable capture by the enemy (during war time) of some rich ships, reduced his fortune; and, by the consequent anxiety, completely destroyed a before debilitated constitution. He died in a few weeks after the confirmation of his loss, and, having neglected to make a will, a freehold estate of some value, which was all that remained of his effects, devolved of course to his eldest son;* his two younger sons and three daughters being left wholly unprovided for. Augustus Harley, the heir, immediately sold the estate, and divided the produce, in equal shares, between each individual of the family. His brothers had been educated for commerce, and were enabled, through the generous kindness of Augustus, to carry on, with advantage and reputation, their respective occupations; the sisters were, soon after, eligibly married. Augustus, who had been educated for the law, disgusted with its chicanery, relinquished the profession, content to restrain his expences within the limits of a narrow income. This income had since received an increase, by the bequest of a distant relation, a man of a whimsical character, who had married, early in life, a beautiful woman, for love; but his wife having eloped from him with an officer, and, in the course of the intrigue, practised a variety of deceptions, he had retired disgusted from society, cherishing a misanthropical spirit: and, on his decease, bequeathed an annual sum of four hundred pounds to Augustus Harley, (to whom in his childhood he had been particularly attached) on condition of his remaining unmarried. On his marriage, or death, this legacy passed into another branch of the family. On this acquisition Augustus determined on making the tour of Europe; and, after travelling on the continent for three years, on his return to his native country, alternately resided, either in the village of ——,

with his mother, or in the metropolis, where he divided his
time, between liberal studies, and rational recreation. His
visits to the country had, of late, been shorter and less
frequent: he was the idol of his mother, and universally
respected by his acquaintance, for his noble and generous
conduct.—'Ah! (added the lively narrator) 'could you
but see Augustus Harley, you would, infallibly, lose your
heart—so frank, so pleasant, so ingenuous are his manners, so intrepid, and yet so humane! Montague is a fine
gentleman, but Augustus Harley is more—*He is a man!*'

She began to grow eloquent on this, apparently, ex-
haustless theme, nor did she cease her panegyric till we
came in view of Mrs Harley's mansion.

'You will love the mother as well as the son,' continued
this agreeable prattler, 'when you come to know her; she is
very good and very sensible.'

Drawing near the house, she tripped from me, to enquire if its mistress had yet risen.

A small white tenement, half obscured in shrubbery, on
a verdant lawn, of dimensions equally modest, situated
on the side of a hill, and commanding an extensive and
variegated prospect, was too interesting and picturesque
an object, not to engage for some moments my attention.
The image of Augustus, also, which my lively companion
had pourtrayed with more than her usual vivacity, played
in my fancy—my heart paid involuntary homage to virtue,
and I entered the mansion of Mrs Harley with a swelling
emotion, made up of complicated feelings—half respectful, half tender—sentiments, too mingled to be distinctly
traced. I was introduced into a room that overlooked a
pleasant garden, and which the servant called a library. It
was hung with green paper, the carpet the same colour,
green venetian blinds to the windows, a sopha and chairs
covered with white dimity; some drawings and engravings
hung on the walls, arranged with exact symmetry; on one
side of the room stood a grand piano-forte, opposite
to which, was a handsome book-case, filled with books,
elegantly bound; in the middle of the apartment was
placed a table, covered with a green cloth, on which was a

reading desk, some books and pamphlets, with implements for writing and drawing. Nothing seemed costly, yet
neatness, order, and taste, appeared through the whole
apartment, bespeaking the elegant and cultivated mind of
the owner.

After amusing myself for a short time, in this charming
retirement, I was summoned by Ann to the breakfast
room, where Mrs Harley awaited me. I was interested, at
the first glance, in favour of this amiable woman—she
appeared to be near fifty, her person agreeable, her countenance animated, her address engaging, and her manners polished. Mutually pleased with each other, the hours
passed rapidly; and, till reminded by a significant look
from my little friend, I was unconscious, that I had made
my visit of an unreasonable length.

Mrs Harley spoke much of her son, he was the darling
and the pride of her heart; she lamented the distance that
separated them, and wished, that her health, and his tenderness, would allow of her residence with him in London.
When conversing on this favourite topic, a glow enlivened
her countenance, and her eyes sparkled with a humid
brightness. I was affected by her maternal love—tender
remembrances, and painful comparisons, crouded into
my mind—a tear fell, that would not be twinkled away—
she observed it, and seemed to feel its meaning; she held
out her hand to me, I took it and pressed it to my lips. At
parting, she entreated me speedily to renew my visit, to
come often without ceremony—I should cheer her solitude—my sympathy, for she perceived I had a feeling
heart, would help to console her in the absence of her
Augustus.

CHAPTER XVII

ON our way home, Ann was in high spirits, congratulating
herself upon her sagacity.

'Mrs Harley, (said she, archly leering in my face) 'will
console you for the departure of Mr Francis.'

I smiled without replying. At dinner our visit of the morning was canvassed (Ann had wished me to conceal it, but this I positively refused). Mr Morton spoke of Mrs Harley and her son with great respect, Mrs Morton with a sarcastic sneer, accompanied with a reprimand to her daughter, for the improper liberty she had taken.

I quitted the table, immediately after the desert,* to stifle my disgust, and, taking a book, wandered into the pleasure grounds, but incapable of fixing my attention, I presently shut my book, and, sauntering slowly on, indulged in a reverie. My melancholy reflections again returned—How could I remain in a house, where I was every day marked out for insult by its mistress—and where was I to dispose of myself? My fortune was insufficient to allow of my boarding in a respectable family. Mrs Harley came across my mind—Amiable woman!—Would she, indeed, accept of my society, and allow me to soften her solitude!—But her income was little less limited than my own—it must not be thought of. I reflected on the inequalities of society, the source of every misery and of every vice, and on the peculiar disadvantages of my sex. I sighed bitterly; and, clasping my hands together, exclaimed, unconsciously—

'Whither can I go—and where shall I find an asylum?'

'Allow me to propose one,' said a voice, in a soft accent, suddenly, behind me.

I started, turned, and beheld Mr Montague. After some expressions of sympathy for the distress which he had witnessed, apologies for his intrusion, and incoherent expressions of respect and regard, he somewhat abruptly offered his hand and heart to my acceptance, with the impetuosity which accompanied all his sentiments and actions; yet, he expressed himself with the air of a man who believes he is conferring an obligation. I thanked him for his generous proposal—

But, as my heart spake not in his favour—'I must be allowed to decline it.'

'That heart,' said he, rudely, 'is already bestowed upon another.'

'Certainly not, Mr Montague; if it were, I would frankly tell you.'

He pronounced the name of Mr Francis—

'Mr Francis is a man for whom I feel a sincere respect and veneration—a man whom I should be proud to call my friend; but a thought beyond that, I dare venture to say, has never occurred to either of us.'

He knew not how to conceive—that a woman in my situation, unprepossessed, could reject so advantageous an establishment!

This, I told him, was indelicate, both to me and to himself. Were my situation yet more desolate, I would not marry any man, merely for an *establishment*, for whom I did not feel an affection.

Would I please to describe to him the model of perfection which I should require in a husband?

It was unnecessary; as I saw no probability of the portrait bearing any resemblance to himself.

He reddened, and turned pale, alternately; bit his lips, and muttered to himself.—'Damned romantic affectation!'

I assumed a firmer tone—methought he insulted me.— ' I beg you will leave me, Sir—I chuse to be alone—By what right do you intrude upon my retirements?'

My determined accent abashed him:—he tried, but with an ill grace, to be humble; and entreated me to take time for consideration.

'There is no need of it. It is a principle with me, not to inflict a moment's suspence on any human being, when my own mind is decided.'

'Then you absolutely refuse me, and prefer the being exposed to the mean and envious insults of the vulgar mistress of this mansion!'

'Of the two evils, I consider it as the least, because it involves no permanent obligation.'

His countenance was convulsed with passion. His love, he told me, was converted into vengeance by my scorn: he was not to be contemned with impunity; and he warned me to beware.

I smiled, I believe, a little too contemptuously. 'You love me not, Sir: I am glad, for your own sake, that you never loved me.'

'My hatred may be more terrible!'

'You cannot intimidate me——I am little accustomed to fear.'

I turned from him somewhat disdainfully: but, instantly recollecting myself, I stepped back, and apologized for the harsh manner into which I had been betrayed by his abrupt address, vehement expostulation, and the previous irritated state of my mind.

'I acknowledge,' said I, 'the disinterestedness of your proposal, and the *distinction* which it implies. Will you allow my own wounded feelings to be an excuse for the too little consideration with which I have treated *your's*? Can you forgive me?' added I, in a conciliating tone, holding out my hand.

The strong emotions, which rapidly succeeded each other in his mind, were painted in his countenance. After a moment's hesitation, he snatched the hand I offered him, pressed it to his lips, and, murmuring a few incoherent words, burst into tears. My spirits were already depressed—affected by these marks of his sensibility, and still more distressed by the recollection of the pain I had occasioned him by my inconsiderate behaviour, I wept with him for some minutes in silence.

'Let us no more,' resumed I, making an effort to recover myself, 'renew these impressions. I thank you sincerely for the sympathy you have manifested for my situation. I am sensible that I have yielded to weak and wayward feelings.—I have youth, health, and activity—I ought not—neither do I despair.— The mortifications I have experienced, since my residence here, will afford me a useful lesson for the future—they have already taught me, what I before merely conjectured, *the value of independence!*'

'Why, then,' interrupted he with quickness, 'do you reject an opportunity of placing yourself out of the reach of insult?'

'Stop, my good friend,' replied I, smilingly looking in his face; 'there is a possibility of exchanging evils. You are yet too young, and too unstable, maturely to have weighed the importance of the scheme you propose. Remember, like-wise, that you are, yourself, in a great measure, dependent on the will of your father; and that much reflection is requisite before we fetter ourselves with engagements, that, once entered into, are not easily dissolved.'

'You allow me, then, to hope!'

'Indeed I meant not to imply any such thing. I wish to soften what I have already expressed—but, there are a variety of reasons which oblige me to assure you, that I see no probability of changing my sentiments on the subject.'

'Why, then, this cruel ostentation? I would either love or hate, bless or curse you.'

'You shall do neither, if I can prevent it. If my esteem is of any value to you, you must learn to respect both me and yourself.'

'Esteem!—Is that to be my frigid reward!'

'If *mine* be worthless, propose to yourself *your own* as a recompense.'

'I have already forfeited it, by seeking to move a heart, that triumphs in its cold inflexibility.'

'Is this just—is it kind? Is it, indeed, *my welfare* you seek, while you can thus add to the vexations and embar-rassment, which were before sufficiently oppressive? I would preserve you from an act of precipitation and im-prudence;—in return, you load me with unmerited reproaches. But it is time to put an end to a con-versation, that can answer little other purpose than vain recrimination.'

He was about to speak—'Say no more—I feel myself, again, in danger of losing my temper—my spirits are agi-tated—I would not give you pain—Allow me to retire, and be assured of my best wishes.'

Some of the family appearing in sight, as if advancing towards us, favoured my retreat. I quitted the place with precipitation, and retired to my chamber, where I sought, by employing myself, to calm the perturbation of my heart.

CHAPTER XVIII

IN a few days I renewed my visit to Mrs Harley:—a strong sympathy united us, and we became almost inseparable. Every day I discovered in this admirable woman a new and indissoluble tie, that bound me to her. Her cultivated understanding afforded an inexhaustible fund of instruction and entertainment; and her affectionate heart spread a charm over her most indifferent actions. We read, we walked, we conversed together; but, with whatever subjects these conversation commenced, some associated idea always led them to terminate in an eulogium on the virtues and talents, or an expression of regret, for the absence of Augustus. There was a portrait of him (drawn by a celebrated artist, which he had lately sent from town as a present to his mother) hung up in the library. I accustomed myself to gaze on this resemblance of a man, in whose character I felt so lively an interest, till, I fancied, I read in the features all the qualities imputed to the original by a tender and partial parent.

Cut off from the society of mankind, and unable to expound my sensations, all the strong affections of my soul seemed concentrated to a single point. Without being conscious of it myself, my grateful love for Mrs Harley had, already, by a transition easy to be traced by a philosophic mind, transferred itself to her son. He was the St Preux, the Emilius,* of my sleeping and waking reveries. I now spent almost my whole time in the cottage of my friend, returning to Morton Park late in the evening, and quitting it early in the morning, and sometimes being wholly absent for weeks together.

Six months thus passed away in tranquillity, with but little variation. Mr Montague, during this period, had several times left Mr Morton's, and returned again abruptly: his manners became sullen, and even, at times, ferocious. I carefully avoided encountering him, fearful of exasperating a spirit, that appeared every moment on the verge of excess.

Hastening one evening to my friend, after a longer separation than common, (having been prevailed on by Mr
Morton and his daughters to accompany them on a distant
visit, where business of Mr Morton's detained us for some
days) I ran into the library, as usual, and threw myself into
the arms of Mrs Harley, that opened spontaneously to
receive me.

'Ah! you little truant,' said she, in a voice of kindness,
'where have you been so long? My son has visited me in
your absence; he passed through this part of the country,
in his way to the seat of a friend. He staid with me two days,
during which I sent half a dozen messages to Morton Park,
but you were flown away, it seems, nor could I learn any
tidings of you. Augustus,' continued she, without observing the emotions she excited, 'had scarcely quitted the
house an hour when you arrived.'

I made no reply; an unaccountable sensation seized, and
oppressed, my heart—sinking on the sopha, I burst into a
convulsive flood of tears.

My friend was struck: all the indiscretion of her conduct
(as she has since told me) flashed suddenly into her mind;
she felt that, in indulging her own maternal sensations,
she had, perhaps, done me an irreparable injury, and she
shuddered at the probable consequences. It was some
moments before either of us recovered;—our conversation was that evening, for the first time, constrained, reserved, and painful; and we retired at an early hour to our
respective apartments.

I spent the night in self-examination. I was compelled to
acknowledge, to myself, that solitude, the absence of other
impressions, the previous circumstances that had operated
on my character, my friendship for Mrs Harley, and her
eloquent, affectionate, reiterated, praises of her son, had
combined to awaken all the exquisite, though dormant,
sensibilities of my nature; and, however romantic it might
appear to others, and did appear even to myself, I felt, that
I loved an ideal object (for such was Augustus Harley to
me) with a tender and fervent excess; an excess, perhaps,
involving all my future usefulness and welfare. 'People, in
general,' says Rousseau, 'do not sufficiently consider the

influence which the first attachments, between man and woman, have over the remainder of their lives; they do not perceive, that an impression, so strong, and so lively, as that of love, is productive of a long chain of effects, which pass unobserved in a course of years, yet, nevertheless, continue to operate till the day of their deaths.'* It was in vain I attempted to combat this illusion; my reason was but an auxiliary to my passion, it persuaded me, that I was only doing justice to high and uncommon worth; imagination lent her aid, and an importunate sensibility, panting after good unalloyed, completed the seduction.

From this period Mrs Harley was more guarded in her conduct; she carefully avoided the mention of her son.— Under pretence of having an alteration made in the frame, she removed his picture from the library; but the constraint she put upon herself was too evident and painful; we no longer sought, with equal ardour, an interchange of sentiment, reserve took place of the tender confidence of friendship; a thousand times, while I gazed upon her dear averted countenance, I yearned to throw myself upon her bosom, to weep, to unfold to her the inmost recesses of my mind—that ingenuous mind, which languished for communication, and preyed upon itself! Dear and cruel friend, why did you transfix my heart with the barbed and envenomed arrow, and then refuse to administer the only healing balsam?

My visits to Mrs Harley became less frequent; I shut myself up whole days in my apartment, at Morton Park, or wandered through its now leafless groves, absorbed in meditation—fostering the sickly sensibility of my soul, and nursing wild, improbable, chimerical, visions of felicity, that, touched by the sober wand of truth, would have 'melted into thin air.'* 'The more desires I have (observes an acute, and profound French Philosopher[1]) the less ardent they are. The torrents that divide themselves into many branches, are the least dangerous in their course. A strong passion is a solitary passion, that concentrates all our desires within one point.'*

---

[1] Helvetius.

CHAPTER XIX

I HAD not seen my friend for many days, when, on a dark and stormy night, in the month of January, between nine and ten o'clock, the family at Morton Park were alarmed, by a loud and violent knocking at the hall door.

On opening it, a servant appeared—and a chaise,* the porter having unbolted the great gates, drew up to the door. The man delivered a note addressed to Miss Courtney. I was unacquainted with the hand writing, and unfolded it with trepidation. It contained but a few lines, written in a female character, and signed with the name of a lady, who resided about twelve miles from Morton Park, at whose house Mrs Harley sometimes made a visit of a few days. It stated—

'That my friend was seized at the mansion of this lady with an apoplectic fit, from which she had been restored, after some hours of insensibility: that the physicians were apprehensive of a relapse, and that Mrs Harley had expressed a desire of seeing Miss Courtney—A carriage and servants were sent for her conveyance.'

Mr Morton was from home, his lady made no offer of any of her own domestics to accompany me. Montague, who had been at the Park for some days past, solicited permission to be my escort. I hesitated a moment, and would willingly have declined this proposal, but he repeated and enforced it with a vehemence, that, in the present hurried state of my mind, I had not spirits to oppose. Shocked, alarmed, distressed, I wrapped a shawl round me, and sprang into the chaise. Montague stepped in after me, and seated himself by my side; the horses galloped, or rather flew down the avenue, that led to the high road.

We travelled with great swiftness, and in uninterrupted silence, for some miles: the darkness was so thick and profound, that I could not discover the road we took, and I began to feel very impatient to arrive at the place of our destination. I questioned my companion respecting his knowledge of our situation, and expressed an apprehension, that we might possibly have missed the way. He made no reply to my interrogation, but, starting as if from a reverie, seized my hand, while his own trembled with a visible agitation, and began once more to urge a suit, which I had hoped the steadiness and consistency of my conduct had induced him entirely to relinquish.

'Is this a time, Mr Montague, for an address of this nature—do you believe, that my favour is to be gained by these proofs of inconsideration? Have some respect for the claims of humanity and friendship, and, in seeking my affection, do not forfeit my esteem.'

He was about to reply, and I could perceive by the few words which he uttered, and by the tone of his voice, that he struggled, in vain, to rein in his quick and irascible spirit; when, in turning a sharp angle of the road, the horses took fright at some object, indistinctly seen, and ran precipitately down a steep hill, with a velocity that threatened immediate destruction.

My companion, forcing open the door, seemed inclined to leap from the carriage, but hesitated, as if unwilling to desert me in so imminent a danger; I exhorted him to think only of providing for his own safety, and, letting down the glasses on the side on which I sat, I resigned myself to my fate. In springing from the chaise, by some means, Montague entangled his coat in the step—he fell, without clearing it, and I felt, with a horror that congealed my blood, the wheel go over him. In a few minutes, I perceived a traveller, at the risque of his own life, endeavouring to stop that horses—the pole of the chaise striking him with great force, he was obliged to relinquish his humane efforts—but this impediment occasioning the restive animals to turn out of the road, they ran furiously up a bank, and overset the carriage. I felt it going, and sitting, with my arms folded, close in the lower corner, fell with it, without attempting to struggle, by which means I escaped unhurt.

The stranger, once more, came to our assistance, and, the mettle of the horses being now pretty well exhausted,

my deliverer was enabled to cut the traces, and then hastened to extricate me from my perilous situation. It was
some time before I recovered myself sufficiently to thank
him for his humanity, and to assure him, that I had received no other injury than from my fears. I then mentioned to him, my apprehensions for the fate of my fellow
traveller, entreating that he would return with me in
search of him. With this request he immediately complied,
leaving the horses in the care of the servants, neither of
which had received any material hurt.

We soon discovered the unfortunate Montague, lying in
the road, in a melancholy situation: the wheel had gone
over one of his legs, the bone of which was broken and
splintered in a terrible manner, and, having fainted from
the pain, we were at first apprehensive that he was already
dead. Turning from this shocking spectacle, a faint sickness overspread my heart, the stranger supported me in
his arms, while a violent burst of tears preserved me from
swooning. My companion examining the body, perceived
signs of life, and, by our united efforts, sense and recollection were soon restored.

I remained with Montague while the stranger returned
to the carriage, to enquire what damages it had received,
and whether it was in a condition to proceed to the
next village, which, the postilion informed him, was near
two miles from the spot where the accident had
happened, and we were, yet, five miles from the place
whither we were going. The axle-tree and one of the hind
wheels, upon examination, were found broken, the traces
had been cut in pieces, and the horses, had the chaise
been in a better condition, were so unmanageable, in
consequence of their late flight, that it would have been
dangerous to have attempted putting them again into
harness.

With this intelligence our kind friend came back to us—
We held a short consultation, on the means most proper to
be adopted, and, at length it was determined, that, after
placing Montague in the carriage, where he would be
sheltered from the inclemency of the elements, and leav-

ing him in the charge of the servants, the traveller and
myself should walk onward to the village, and send a
chaise, or litter,* for the conveyance of our unfortunate
companion.

To this proposal Montague assented, at the same time,
declaring it to be his intention, to proceed directly across
the country, to the house of his father, which could not, he
conjectured, be at any great distance, and where he should
be assured of meeting with greater attention, and more
skilful assistance, than at a petty inn, in a paltry village.
Having thus adjusted our plan, and, with the help of the
servants, carefully placed Montague in the chaise, we proceeded towards the village.

CHAPTER XX

THE night was tempestuous, and, though the moon was
now rising, her light was every moment obscured by dark
clouds, discharging frequent and heavy showers of rain,
accompanied by furious gusts of wind. After walking near
a mile we entered upon a wide heath, which afforded no
shelter from the weather. I perceived my companion's
steps began to grow feeble, and his voice faint. The moon
suddenly emerging from a thick cloud, I observed his
countenance, and methought his features seemed familiar
to me; but they were overspread by a palid and death-like
hue. He stopped suddenly——

'I am very ill,' said he, in a tone of voice that penetrated
into my soul, 'and can proceed no further.'

He sunk upon the turf. Seating myself beside him, while
his head fell on my shoulder, I threw around him my
supporting arms. His temples were bedewed with a cold
sweat, and he appeared to be in expiring agonies. A violent
sickness succeeded, followed by an hemorrhage.

'Gracious God!' I exclaimed, 'you have broken a blood
vessel!'

'I fear so,' he replied. 'I have felt strangely disordered
since the blow I received from the pole of the carriage;

but, till this moment, I have not been at leisure to attend
to my sensations.'

'Do not talk,' cried I, wildly; 'do not exhaust yourself.'

Again the clouds gathered; an impetuous gust of wind
swept over the heath, and the rain fell in torrents. Unconscious what I did, I clasped the stranger to my throbbing
bosom,—the coldness of death seemed upon him—I
wrapped my shawl around him, vainly attempting to
screen him from the piercing blast. He spake not; my
terrified imagination already represented him as a lifeless
corpse; I sat motionless for some minutes, in the torpor of
despair.

From this horrible situation, I was, at length, roused, by
the sound of a distant team: breathless, I listened for a few
moments; I again distinctly heard it wafted upon the wind;
when, gently reclining my charge on the grass, I started
from the ground, and ran swiftly towards the highway. The
sound approached, and the clouds once more breaking,
and discovering a watery moonlight gleam, I perceived,
with joy, a waggon loaded with hay. I bounded over a part
of the turf that still separated me from the road, and
accosting the driver, explained to him, in a few words, as
much of my situation as was necessary; and, entreating his
assistance, allured him by the hope of a reward.

We returned together to my patient: he raised his head
on my approach, and attempted to speak; but, enjoining
him silence, he took my hand, and, by a gentle pressure,
expressed his sense of my cares more eloquently than
by words. I assisted the countryman in supporting him
to the road. We prepared for him, in the waggon, a soft
bed of hay, upon which we placed him; and, resting his
head on my lap, we proceeded gently to the nearest village.
On our arrival at an indifferent inn, I ordered a bed to
be immediately prepared for him, and sent a man and
horse express, to the next town, for medical assistance:
at the same time, relating in brief the accidents of the
night, I dispatched a carriage for the relief of Montague,
who was conveyed, according to his wishes, to the house of
his father.

Notwithstanding all my precautions, the moving brought on a relapse of the alarming symptoms; the discharge of blood returned with aggravated violence, and, when the physician arrived, there appeared in the unfortunate sufferer but little signs of life; but by the application of styptics and cordials he once more began to revive; and, about five in the morning, I was prevailed on, by the joint efforts of the landlady and the humane Dr——, to resign my seat at the bed's head to a careful servant, and to recruit my exhausted strength by a few hours' repose.

The vivid impressions, which had so rapidly succeeded each other in my mind, for some time kept me waking, in a state of feverish agitation; but my harrassed spirits were at length relieved by wearied nature's kind restorer, and I slept for four hours profoundly.

On waking, my first enquiry was after my companion, in whose fate I felt an unusual degree of interest; and I heard, with pleasure, that the hemorrhage had not returned; that he had rested with apparent tranquillity, and appeared revived. I dressed myself hastily, and passed into his apartment: he faintly smiled on perceiving my approach, and gave me his hand.—The physician had ordered him to be kept quiet, and I would not suffer him to speak; but, contemplating more attentively his countenance, which had the night before struck me with a confused recollection—what were my emotions, on tracing the beloved features of Augustus Harley! His resemblance, not only to the portrait, but to his mother, could not, as I thought, be mistaken. A universal trembling seized me—I hastened out of the apartment with tottering steps, and shutting myself into my chamber, a tide of melancholy emotions gushed upon my heart. I wept, without knowing wherefore, tears half delicious, half agonizing! Quickly coming to myself, I returned to the chamber of my patient, (now more tenderly endeared) which, officiating as a nurse for five days, I never quitted, except to take necessary rest and refreshment.

I had written to Mr Morton a minute account of all that happened, merely suppressing the name of my deliverer:

to this letter I received no reply; but had the pleasure of hearing, on the return of my messenger (who was commissioned to make enquiries), that Mrs Harley had suffered no return of her disorder, and was daily acquiring health and strength.—I feared, yet, to acquaint her with the situation of her son; not only on the account of her own late critical situation, but, also, lest any sudden agitation of spirits from the arrival of his mother, might, in his present weak state, be fatal to Augustus.

I now redoubled for him my cares and attentions: he grew hourly better; and, when permitted to converse, expressed in lively terms his grateful sense of my kindness. Ah! why did I misconstrue these emotions, so natural in such circumstances—why did I flatter my heart with the belief of a sympathy which did not, could not, exist!

CHAPTER XXI

As my patient began to acquire strength, I demanded of him his name and family, that I might inform his friends of his situation. On his answering 'Harley,' I enquired, smiling—

If he remembered hearing his mother speak of a little *Protegé*, Emma Courtney, whom she favoured with her partial friendship?

'Oh, yes!'—and his curiosity had been strongly awakened to procure a sight of this lady.

'Behold her, then, in your nurse!'

'Is it possible!' he exclaimed, taking my hand, and pressing it with his lips—'My sister!—my friend!—how shall I ever pay the debt I owe you?'

'We will settle that matter another time; but it is now become proper that I should inform your excellent mother of what has happened, which I have hitherto delayed, lest surprise should be prejudicial to you, and retard your recovery.'

I then recounted to him the particulars of the late occurrences, of which he had before but a confused notion;

adding my surprise, that I had neither seen, nor heard, any thing from Mr Morton.

He informed me, in his turn, that, having received an express,* informing him of his mother's alarming situation, he immediately quitted the seat of his friend, where he was on a visit, to hasten to her; that, for this purpose, riding late, he by some means bewildered himself through the darkness of the evening, by which mistake he encountered our chaise, and he hoped was, in some measure, notwithstanding the accidents which ensued, accessary to my preservation.

I quitted him to write to my friend, whom I, at length, judged it necessary to acquaint with his situation. On the receipt of my letter, she flew to us on the wings of maternal tenderness—folded her beloved Augustus, and myself, alternately to her affectionate bosom, calling us 'her children—her darling children!——I was her guardian angel—*the preserver of her son!*—and *he* only could repay my goodness!' I ventured to raise my eyes to him—they met his—mine were humid with tears of tenderness: a cloud passed over his brow—he entreated his mother to restrain her transports—he was yet too enfeebled to bear these emotions. She recollected herself in an instant; and, after again embracing him, leaning on my arm, walked out into the air, to relieve the tumultuous sensations that pressed upon her heart.

Once more she made me recite, minutely, the late events—strained me in her arms, repeatedly calling me—

'Her beloved daughter—the meritorious child of her affections—the preserver of her Augustus!'

Every word she uttered sunk deep into my soul, that greedily absorbed the delicious poison,* prepared for me by the cruel hand of more than maternal fondness.

I mentioned to her my having written to Mr Morton, and my astonishment at his silence.

He had not yet returned, she informed me, to Morton Park; and intimated, that some malicious stories, respecting my sudden disappearance, had been circulated by Mrs Morton through the neighbourhood. She had herself been under extreme solicitude on my account. It was generally believed, from the turn Mrs Morton's malice had given to the affair, that I had eloped with Mr Montague:— the accident which had befallen him had been rumoured; but the circumstances, and the occasion of it, had been variously related. Confiding in my principles, she had waited with anxiety for the elucidation of these mysterious accounts; lamenting herself as the innocent occasion of them, yet assured they would, eventually, prove to my honour. She commended the magnanimity, which her partial friendship imputed to my behaviour, with all the enthusiasm of affection, and execrated the baseness of Mrs Morton, who, having received my letter, must have been acquainted with the real truth.

Her narration gave me many complicated, and painful, sensations; but the good opinion of the world, however desirable it may be, as connected with our utility, has ever been with me but a secondary consideration. Confiding in the rectitude of my own conduct, I composed my spirits; depending on that rectitude, and time, for removing the malignant aspersions which at present clouded my fame. The tale of slander, the basis of which is falsehood, will quietly wear away; and should it not—how unfounded, frequently, are the censures of the world—how confused its judgments! I entreated my friend to say nothing, at present, to her son on this subject; it was yet of importance that his mind should be kept still and tranquil.

We rejoined Augustus at the dinner hour, and spent the day together in harmony and friendship. The physician calling in the evening, Mrs Harley consulted him, whether it would be safe to remove her son, as she was impatient to have him under her own roof. To this the doctor made no objection, provided he was conveyed in an easy carriage, and by short stages. On Mrs Harley's thanking him for this polite and humane attention to his patient, smilingly pointing to me, he replied—'Her thanks were misplaced.' His look was arch and significant; it called a glow into my cheeks. I ventured, once more, to steal a glance at Augustus: his features were again overspread with a more than usual seriousness, while his eyes seemed designedly averted. Mrs Harley sighed, and, abruptly changing the subject, asked the physician an indifferent question, who soon after took his leave.

CHAPTER XXII

In a few days we returned to the peaceful mansion of my maternal friend. Augustus seemed revived by the little journey, while every hour brought with it an increase of health and spirits. Mrs Harley would not suffer me to speak of going to Morton Park in the absence of its master; neither could Augustus spare his kind nurse:—'I must stay,' he added, and methought his accents were softened, 'and complete my charitable purpose.' My appearance again in the village, the respectability, and the testimony, of my friends, cleared my fame; and it was only at Morton Park, that any injurious suspicions were affected to be entertained.

The hours flew on downy pinions:—my new *brother*, for so he would call himself, endeavoured to testify his gratitude, by encouraging and assisting me in the pursuit of learning and science: he gave us lectures on astronomy and philosophy—

'While truths divine came mended from his tongue.'*

I applied myself to the languages, and, aided by my preceptor, attained a general knowledge of the principles, and philosophy, of criticism and grammar, and of the rules of composition. Every day brought with it the acquisition of some new truth; and our intervals from study were employed in music, in drawing, in conversation, in reading the *belles lettres*—in—

'The feast of reason, and the flow of souls.'*

The spring was advancing:—we now made little excursions, either on horseback, in a chaise, or in a boat on the river, through the adjacent country. The fraternal relation, which Augustus had assumed, banished restraint, and assisted me in deceiving myself. I drank in large and intoxicating draughts of a delicious poison, that had circulated through every vein to my heart, before I was aware of its progress. At length, part of a conversation, which I accidentally overheard between Mrs Harley and her son, recalled me to a temporary recollection.

I was seeking them in the garden, towards the dusk of the evening, and a filbert hedge separated us. I heard the voice of my friend, as speaking earnestly, and I unconsciously stopped.

'It would be a comfort to my declining years to see you the husband of a woman of virtue and sensibility: domestic affections meliorate the heart; no one ought to live wholly to himself.'

'Certainly not, neither does any one; but, in the present state of society, there are many difficulties and anxieties attending these connections: they are a lottery, and the prizes are few. I think, perhaps, nearly with you, but my situation is, *in many respects, a peculiar one,*'—and he sighed deeply:—'Need I enumerate these peculiarities to you? Neither do I pretend to have lived so long in the world without imbibing many of its prejudices, and catching the contagion of its habits.'

'They are unworthy of you.'

'Perhaps so—but we will, if you please, change the subject; this to me is not a pleasant one. What is become of my pupil? It is likely to be a clear night; let us go in, and prepare for some astronomical observations.'

My heart reproved me for listening, I crept back to my chamber—shed one tear—heaved a convulsive, struggling, sigh—breathed on my handkerchief, applied it to my eyes, and joined my friends in the library.

Four months had passed rapidly—'the spot of azure in the cloudy sky'*—of my destiny. Mr Morton, I was informed, had returned to the Park, and Augustus, whose health was now thoroughly restored, talked of quitting the country. I advised with my friends, who agreed with me, that it was now become proper for me to visit my uncle, and, explaining to him the late events, justify my conduct. Mrs Harley and her son offered to accompany me; but this, for many reasons, I declined; taking my leave of them with a heavy heart, and promising, if I were not kindly received, an immediate return.

CHAPTER XXIII

ON my arrival at Mr Morton's, the porter informed me, he was ordered, by his lady, to deny my entrance. My swelling heart!—a sentiment of indignation distended it almost to suffocation.—At this moment, Ann tripped lightly through the court-yard, and, seeing me, ran to embrace me. I returned her caresses with warmth.

'Ah!' said she, 'you are not, you cannot be, guilty. I have been longing to see you, and to hear all that has happened, but it was not permitted me.' She added, in a whisper, 'I cannot love my mother, for she torments and restrains me—my desire of liberty is stronger than my duty—but I shall one day be able to outwit her.'

'Will not your father, my love, allow me to speak to him? I have a right to be heard, and I demand his attention.'

'He is in his dressing-room,' said Ann, 'I will slide softly, to him, and tell him you are here.'

Away she flew, and one of the footmen presently returned, to conduct me to his master. I found him alone, he received me with a grave and severe aspect. I related to him, circumstantially, the occurrences which had taken place during his absence. My words, my voice, my manner, were emphatic—animated with the energy of truth—they extorted, they commanded, they, irresistibly, compelled assent. His features softened, his eyes glistened, he held out his hand, he was about the speak—he hesitated a moment, and sighed. At this instant, Mrs Morton burst into the room, with the aspect of a fury—her bloated countenance yet more swelled and hideous—I shrunk back involuntarily—she poured forth a torrent of abuse and invective. A momentary recollection reassured me—

waiting till she had exhausted her breath, I turned from her, and to her husband, with calm dignity—

'I thank you, Sir, for all the kindness I have received from you—I am convinced you do me justice—*for this I do not thank you*, it was a duty to which I had a claim, and which you owed, not only to me, but, to yourself. My longer continuance in this house, I feel, would be improper. For the present, I return to Mrs Harley's, where I shall respectfully receive, and maturely weigh, any counsels with which you may in future think proper to favour me.'

Mr Morton bowed his head; poor man! his mild spirit was overborne, he dared not assert the dictates of his own reason. I hurried out of the apartment, and hastily embracing Ann, who awaited me in the hall, charging myself with a hundred kisses for Mrs Harley, I took the way to the hospitable mansion of my friend.

I had proceeded about half a mile, when I beheld Augustus, advancing towards me; he observed my tremulous emotions, and pallid countenance; he took my hand, holding it with a gentle pressure, and, throwing his other arm round me, supported my faultering steps. His voice was the voice of kindness—his words spake assurance, and breathed hope—*fallacious hope!*—My heart melted within me—my tremor encreased—I dissolved into tears.

'A deserted outcast from society—a desolate orphan—what was to become of me—to whom could I fly?'

'Unjust girl! have I then forfeited all your confidence—have you not a mother and a friend, who love you—' he stopped—paused—and added 'with maternal, with *fraternal*, tenderness? to whom would you go?—remain with us, your society will cheer my mother's declining years'—again he hesitated—'I am about to return to town, assure me, that you will continue with Mrs Harley—it will soften the pain of separation.'

I struggled for more fortitude—hinted at the narrowness of my fortune—at my wish to exert my talents in some way, that should procure me a less dependent situation—

spoke of my active spirit—of my abhorrence of a life of indolence and vacuity.

He insisted on my waving these subjects for the present. 'There would be time enough, in future, for their consideration. In the mean while, I might go on improving myself, and whether present; or absent, might depend upon him, for every assistance in his power.'

His soothing kindness, aided by the affectionate attentions of my friend, gradually, lulled my mind into tranquillity. My bosom was agitated, only, by a slight and sweet emotion—like the gentle undulations of the ocean, when the winds, that swept over its ruffled surface, are hushed into repose.

CHAPTER XXIV

ANOTHER month passed away—every hour, I imbibed, in large draughts, the deceitful poison of hope. A few days before that appointed for the departure of Augustus, I received a visit from Mr Montague, of whose situation, during his confinement, I had made many enquiries, and it was with unaffected pleasure that I beheld him perfectly restored to health. I introduced him to my friends, who congratulated him upon his recovery, and treated him with that polite and cordial hospitality which characterized them. He was on his way to Morton Park, and was particular in his enquiries respecting the late conduct of the lady of the mansion, of which he had heard some confused reports. I could not conceal from him our final separation, but, aware of his inflammable temper, I endeavoured to soften my recital as far as was consistent with truth and justice. It was with difficulty, that our united persuasions induced him to restrain his fiery spirit, which broke out into menaces and execrations. I represented to him—

'That every thing had been already explained; that the affair had now subsided; that a reconciliation was neither probable nor desirable; that any interference, on his part, would only tend to mutual exasperation, from which I must eventually be the sufferer.'

I extorted from him a promise—that, as he was necessitated to meet Mr Morton on business, he would make no allusion to the past—I should be mortified, (I added) by having it supposed, that I stood in need of a *champion*.—Mr Morton had no doubts of the rectitude of my conduct, and it would be barbarous to involve him in a perpetual domestic warfare.

Mr Montague, at the request of Augustus, spent that day, and the next, with us. I thought, I perceived, that he regarded Mr Harley with a scrutinizing eye, and observed my respect for, and attention to, him, with jealous apprehension. Before his departure, he requested half an hour's conversation with me alone, with which request I immediately complied, and withdrew with him into an adjoining apartment. He informed me—

'That he was going to London to pursue his medical studies—that, on his return, his father had proposed to establish him in his profession—that his prospects were very favourable, and that he should esteem himself completely happy if he might, yet, hope to soften my heart in his favour, and to place me in a more assured and tranquil situation.'

I breathed a heavy sigh, and sunk into a melancholy reverie.

'Speak to me, Emma,' said he, with impatience, 'and relieve the anxiety I suffer.'

'Alas! What can I say?'

'Say, that you will try to love me, that you will reward my faith and perseverance.'

'Would to God, I could'—I hesitated—my eyes filled with tears—'Go to London,' resumed I; 'a thousand new objects will there quickly obliterate from your remembrance a romantic and ill-fated attachment, to which retirement, and the want of other impression, has given birth, and which owes its strength merely to opposition.'

'As that opposition,' retorted he, 'is the offspring of pride and insensibility—'

I looked at him with a mournful air—'Do not reproach me, Montague, my situation is far more pitiable than yours. *I am, indeed, unhappy,*'—added I, after a pause; 'I, like you, am the victim of a raised, of, I fear, a distempered imagination.'

He eagerly entreated me to explain myself.

'I will not attempt to deceive you—I should accuse myself, were I to preserve any sentiment, however delicate its nature, that might tend to remove your present illusion. It is, I confess, with extreme reluctance—with real pain'—I trembled—my voice faultered, and I felt my colour vary— 'that I constrain myself to acknowledge a hopeless, an extravagant'—I stopped, unable to proceed.

Fire flashed from his eyes, he started from his seat, and took two or three hasty strides across the room.

'I understand you, but too well—Augustus Harley shall dispute with me a prize'—

'Stop, Sir, be not unjust—make not an ungenerous return to the confidence I have reposed in you. Respect the violence which, on your account, I have done to my own feelings. I own, that I have not been able to defend my heart against the accomplishments and high qualities of Mr Harley—I respected his virtues and attainments, and, by a too easy transition—at length—*loved his person.* But my tenderness is a secret to all the world but yourself—It has not met with'—a burning blush suffused my cheek—'It has little hope of meeting, a return. To your *honor* I have confided this cherished *secret*—dare you betray my confidence? I know, you dare not!'

He seemed affected—his mind appeared torn by a variety of conflicting emotions, that struggled for victory—he walked towards me, and again to the door, several times. I approached him—I gave him my hand—

'Adieu, Montague,' said I, in a softened accent—'Be assured of my sympathy—of my esteem—of my best wishes! When you can meet me with calmness, I shall rejoice to see you—*as a friend.* Amidst some excesses, I perceive the seeds of real worth in your character, cultivate them, they may yield a noble harvest. I shall not be forgetful of the distinction you have shewn me, *when almost a deserted orphan*—Once again—farewel, my friend, and—may God bless you!'

I precipitately withdrew my hand from his, and rushed out of the room. I retired to my chamber, and it was some hours before my spirits became sufficiently composed to allow me to rejoin my friends. On meeting them, Mrs Harley mentioned, with some surprize, the abrupt departure of Montague, who had quitted the house, without taking leave of its owners, by whom he had been so politely received.

'He is a fine young man,' added she, 'but appears to be very eccentric.'

Augustus was silent, but fixed his penetrating eyes on my face, with an expression that covered me with confusion.

CHAPTER XXV

THE day fixed for the departure of Mr Harley, for London, now drew near—I had anticipated this period with the most cruel inquietude. I was going to lose, perhaps for ever, my preceptor, my friend! He, from whom my mind had acquired knowledge, and in whose presence my heart had rested satisfied. I had hitherto scarcely formed a wish beyond that of daily beholding, and listening to him—I was now to gaze on that beloved countenance, to listen to those soothing accents, no longer. He was about to mix in the gay world—to lose in the hurry of business, or of pleasure, the remembrance of those tender, rational, tranquil, moments, sacred to virtue and friendship, that had left an indelible impression on my heart. Could I, indeed, flatter myself, that the idea of the timid, affectionate, Emma, would ever recur to his mind in the tumultuous scenes of the crouded metropolis, it would doubtless quickly be effaced, and lost in the multiplicity of engagements and avocations. How should I, buried in solitude and silence, recall it to his recollection, how contrive to mingle it with his thoughts, and entangle it with his associations? Ah! did he but know my tenderness—*the desire of being beloved*, of inspiring sympathy, is congenial to the human heart—why should I hesitate to inform him of my affection—why do I blush and tremble at the mere idea? It is a false shame! It is a pernicious system of morals, which teaches us that hypocrisy can be virtue! He is well acquainted with the purity, and with the sincerity, of my heart—he will at least regard me with esteem and tender pity—and how often has 'pity melted the soul to love!'* The experiment is, surely, innocent, and little hazardous. What have I to apprehend? Can I distrust, for a moment, those principles of rectitude, of honour, of goodness, which gave birth to my affection? Have I not witnessed his humanity, have I not experienced his delicacy, in a thousand instances? Though he should be obliged to wound, he is incapable of insulting, the heart that loves him; and that, loving him, believed, alas! for a long time, *that it loved only virtue!*

The morning of our separation, at last, arrived. My friend, too much indisposed to attend the breakfast table, took leave of her son in her own apartment. I awaited him, in the library, with a beating heart, and, on his departure, put into his hands a paper.—

'Read it not,' said I, in a low and almost inarticulate tone of voice, 'till arrived at the end of your journey; or, at least, till you are ten miles from hence.'

He received it in silence; but it was a silence more expressive than words.

'Suffer me,' it said, 'for a few moments, to solicit your candour and attention. You are the only man in the world, to whom I could venture to confide sentiments, that to many would be inconceivable; and by those, who are unacquainted with the human mind, and the variety of circumstances by which characters are variously impressed and formed—who are accustomed to consider mankind in masses—who have been used to bend implicitly, to custom and prescription—the deviation of a solitary individual from *rules* sanctioned by usage, by prejudice, by expediency, would be regarded as romantic. I frankly avow, while my cheeks glow with the blushes of *modesty*, not of shame, that your virtues and accomplishments have excited in my bosom an affection, as pure as the motives which gave it birth, and as animated as it is pure.—This ingenuous avowal may perhaps affect, but will scarcely (I suspect) surprise, you; for, incapable of dissimulation, the emotions of my mind are ever but too apparent in my expressions, and in my conduct, to deceive a less penetrating eye than yours—neither have I been solicitous to disguise them.

'It has been observed, that, "the strength of an affection is generally in the same proportion, as the character of the species, in the object beloved, is lost in that of the individual,"[1]* and, that individuality of character is the only fastener of the affections. It is certain, however singular it may appear, that many months before we became personally acquainted, the report of your worth and high qualities had generated in my mind, an esteem and reverence, which has gradually ripened into a tenderness, that has, at length, mixed itself with all my associations, and is become interwoven with every fibre of my heart.

'I have reflected, again and again, on the imprudence of cherishing an attachment, which a variety of circumstances combine to render so unpromising, and——What shall I say?—So peculiar is the constitution of my mind, that those very circumstances have had a tendency directly opposite to what might reasonably have been expected; and have only served to render the sentiment, I have delighted to foster, more affecting and interesting.—Yes! I am aware of the tenure upon which you retain your fortunes—of the cruel and unnatural conditions imposed on you by the capricious testator: neither can I require a sacrifice which I am unable to recompence. But while these melancholy convictions deprive me of hope, they encourage me, by proving the disinterestedness of my attachment, to relieve my heart by communication.—Mine is a whimsical pride, which dreads nothing so much as the

[1] Woolstonecraft's Rights of Woman.

imputation of sordid, or sinister motives. Remember, then—should we never meet again—if in future periods you should find, that the friendship of the world is—"a shade that follows wealth and fame;"*—if, where you have conferred obligation, you are repaid with ingratitude— where you have placed confidence, with treachery—and where you have a claim to zeal, with coldness! Remember, *that you have once been beloved, for yourself alone,* by one, who, in contributing to the comfort of your life, would have found the happiness of her own.

'Is it possible that a mind like yours, neither hardened by prosperity, nor debased by fashionable levity—which vice has not corrupted, nor ignorance brutalized—can be wholly insensible to the balmy sweetness, which natural, unsophisticated, affections, shed through the human heart?

> "Shall those by heaven's own influence join'd,
> By feeling, sympathy, and mind,
> The sacred voice of truth deny,
> And mock the mandate of sky?"*

'But I check my pen:—I am no longer—

> "The hope-flush'd enterer on the stage of life."*

The dreams of youth, chaced by premature reflection, have given place to soberer, to sadder, conclusions; and while I acknowledge, that it would be inexpressibly sooth-ing to me to believe, that, in happier circumstances, my artless affection might have awakened in your mind a sympathetic tenderness:—this is the extent of my hopes! ——I recollect you once told me "It was our duty to make our reason conquer the sensibility of our heart." Yet, why? Is, then, apathy the perfection of our nature—and is not that nature refined and harmonized by the gentle and social affections? The Being who gave to the mind its reason, gave also to the heart its sensibility.

'I make no apologies for, because I feel no conscious-ness of, weakness. An attachment sanctioned by nature, reason, and virtue, ennobles the mind capable of conceiving and cherishing it: of such an attachment a corrupt heart is utterly incapable.

'You may tell me, perhaps, "that the portrait on which my fancy has dwelt enamoured, owes all its graces, its glowing colouring—like the ideal beauty of the ancient artists—to the imagination capable of sketching the dangerous picture."—Allowing this, for a moment, *the sentiments it inspires are not the less genuine*; and without some degree of illusion, and enthusiasm, all that refines, exalts, softens, embellishes, life—genius, virtue, love itself, languishes. But, on this subject, my opinions have not been lightly formed:—it is not to the personal graces, though "the body charms, because the mind is seen,"* but to the virtues and talents of the individual (for without intellect, virtue is an empty name), that my heart does homage; and, were I never again to behold you—were you even the husband of another—my tenderness (a tenderness as innocent as it is lively) would never cease!

'But, methinks, I hear you say,—"Whither does all this tend, and what end does it propose?" Alas! this is a question I scarcely dare to ask myself!—Yet, allow me to request, that you will make me one promise, and resolve me one question:—ah! do not evade this enquiry; for much it imports me to have an explicit reply, lest, in indulging my own feelings, I should, unconsciously, plant a thorn in the bosom of another:—*Is your heart, at present, free?* Or should you, in future, form a tender engagement, tell me, that I shall receive the first intimation of it from yourself; and, in the assurance of your happiness, I will learn to forget my own.

'I aspire to no higher title than that of the most faithful of your friends, and the wish of becoming worthy of your esteem and confidence shall afford me a motive for improvement. I will learn of you moderation, equanimity, and self-command; and you will, perhaps, continue to afford me direction, and assistance, in the pursuit of knowledge and truth.

'I have laid down my pen, again and again, and still taken it up to add something more, from an anxiety, lest even you, of whose delicacy I have experienced repeated proofs, should misconstrue me.—"Oh! what a world is this!—into what false habits has it fallen! Can hypocrisy be virtue? Can a desire to call forth all the best affections of the heart, be misconstrued into something too degrading for expression?"[1]* But I will banish these apprehensions; I am convinced they are injurious.

'Yes!—I repeat it—I relinquish my pen with reluctance. A melancholy satisfaction, from what source I can scarcely define, diffuses itself through my heart while I unfold to you its emotions.—Write to me; *be ingenuous*; I desire, I call for, truth!

'EMMA.'

CHAPTER XXVI

I HAD not courage to make my friend a confident* of the step I had taken; so wild, and so romantic, did it appear, even to myself—a false pride, a false shame, with-held me. I brooded in silence over the sentiment, that preyed on the bosom which cherished it. Every morning dawned with expectation, and every evening closed in disappointment. I walked daily to the post-office, with precipitate steps and a throbbing heart, to enquire for letters, but in vain; and returned slow, dejected, spiritless. *Hope*, one hour, animated my bosom and flushed my cheek; the next, pale *despair* shed its torpid influence through my languid frame. Inquietude, at length, gradually gave place to despondency, and I sunk into lassitude.

My studies no longer afforded me any pleasure. I turned over my books, incapable of fixing my attention; took out my drawings, threw them aside; moved, restless and dissatisfied, from seat to seat; sought, with unconscious steps, the library, and throwing myself on the sopha, with folded arms, fixed my eyes on the picture of Augustus, which had

[1] Holcroft's Anna St Ives.

lately been replaced, and sunk into waking dreams of ideal prefection and visionary bliss. I gazed on the lifeless features, engraven on my heart in colours yet more true and vivid—but where was the benignant smile, the intelligent glance, the varying expression? Where the pleasant voice, whose accents had been melody in my ear; that had cheered me in sadness, dispelled the vapours of distrust and melancholy, and awakened my emulation for science and improvement? Starting from a train of poignant and distressing emotions, I fled from an apartment once so dear, presenting now but the ghosts of departed pleasures—fled into the woods, and buried myself in their deepest recesses; or shutting myself in my chamber, avoided the sight of my friend, whose dejected countenance but the more forcibly reminded me—

'That such things were, and were most dear.'*

In this state of mind, looking one day over my papers, without any known end in view, I accidentally opened a letter from Mr Francis (with whom I still continued, occasionally, to correspond), which I had recently received. I eagerly seized, and re-perused, it. My spirits were weakened; the kindness which it expressed affected me—it touched my heart—it excited my tears. I determined instantly to reply to it, and to acknowledge my sense of his goodness.

My mind was overwhelmed with the pressure of its own thoughts; a gleam of joy darted through the thick mists that pervaded it; communication would relieve the burthen. I took up my pen, and, though I dared not betray the fatal secret concealed, as a sacred treasure, in the bottom of my heart, I yet gave a loose to, I endeavoured to paint, its sensations.

After briefly sketching the events that had driven me from Morton Park (of which I had not hitherto judged it necessary to inform him), without hinting the name of my deliverer, or suffering myself to dwell on the services he had rendered me, I mentioned my present temporary residence at the house of a friend, and expressed an impatience at my solitary, inactive, situation.

I went on——'To what purpose should I trouble you with a thousand wayward, contradictory, ideas and emotions, that I am, myself, unable to disentangle—which have, perhaps, floated in every mind, that has had leisure for reflection—which are distinguished by no originality, and which I may express (though not feel) without force? I sought to cultivate my understanding, and exercise my reason, that, by adding variety to my resources, I might increase the number of my enjoyments: for *happiness* is, surely, the only desirable *end* of existence! But when I ask myself, Whether I am yet nearer to the end proposed?—I dare not deceive myself—sincerity obliges me to answer in the negative. I daily perceive the gay and the frivolous, among my sex, amused with every passing trifle; gratified by the insipid *routine* of heartless, mindless, intercourse; fully occupied, alternately, by domestic employment, or the childish vanity of varying external ornaments, and "hanging drapery on a smooth block."* I do not affect to despise, and I regularly practise, the necessary avocations of my sex; neither am I superior to their vanities. The habits acquired by early precept and example adhere tenaciously, and are never, perhaps, entirely eradicated. But all these are insufficient to engross, to satisfy, the active, aspiring, mind. Hemmed in on every side by the constitutions of society, and not less so, it may be, by my own prejudices—I perceive, indignantly perceive, the magic circle, without knowing how to dissolve the powerful spell. While men pursue interest, honor, pleasure, as accords with their several dispositions, women, who have too much delicacy, sense, and spirit, to degrade themselves by the vilest of all interchanges, remain insulated beings, and must be content tamely to look on, without taking any part in the great, though often absurd and tragical, drama of life. Hence the eccentricities of conduct, with which women of superior minds have been accused—the struggles, the despairing though generous struggles, of an ar-

dent spirit, denied a scope for its exertions! The strong
feelings, and strong energies, which properly directed, in a
field sufficiently wide, might—ah! what might they not
have aided? forced back, and pent up, ravage and destroy
the mind which gave them birth!

'Yes, I confess, *I am unhappy*, unhappy in proportion as
I believe myself (it may be, erringly) improved. Philosophy, it is said, should regulate the feelings, but it has
added fervor to mine! What are passions, but another
name for powers?* The mind capable of receiving the
most forcible impressions is the sublimely improveable
mind! Yet, into whatever trains such minds are accidentally
directed, they are prone to enthusiasm, while the vulgar
stupidly wonder at the effects of powers, to them wholly
inconceivable: the weak and the timid, easily discouraged,
are induced, by the first failure, to relinquish their pursuits. "They make the impossibility they fear!" But the bold
and the persevering, from repeated disappointment, derive only new ardor and activity. "They conquer difficulties, by daring to attempt them."*

'I feel, that I am writing in a desultory manner, that I am
unable to crowd my ideas into the compass of a letter, and,
that could I do so, I should perhaps only weary you. There
are but few persons to whom I venture to complain, few
would understand, and still fewer sympathise with me. You
are in health, they would say, in the spring of life, have
every thing supplied you without labour (so much the
worse) nature, reason, open to you their treasures! All this
is, partly, true—but, with inexpressible yearnings, my soul
pants for something more, something higher! The
morning rises upon me with sadness, and the evening
closes with disgust—Imperfection, uncertainty, is impressed on every object, on every pursuit! I am either
restless or torpid, I seek to-day what to-morrow, wearies
and offends me.

'I entered life, flushed with hope—I have proceeded but
a few steps, and the parterre of roses, viewed in distant
prospect, nearer seen, proves a brake of thorns. The few
worthy persons I have known appear, to me, to be strug-

gling with the same half suppressed emotions.—Whence is all this? Why is intellect and virtue so far from conferring happiness? Why is the active mind a prey to the incessant conflict between truth and error? Shall I look beyond the disorders which, *here*, appear to me so inexplicable?—shall I expect, shall I demand, from the inscrutable Being to whom I owe my existence, in future unconceived periods, the *end* of which I believe myself capable, and which capacity, like a tormenting *ignis fatuus*,* has hitherto served only to torture and betray? The animal rises up to satisfy the cravings of nature, and lies down to repose, undisturbed by care—has man superior powers, only to make him preeminently wretched?—wretched, it seems to me, in proportion as he rises? Assist me, in disentangling my bewildered ideas—write to me—reprove me—spare me not!

'EMMA.'

To this letter I quickly received a kind and consolatory reply, though not unmingled with the reproof I called for. It afforded me but a temporary relief, and I once more sunk into inanity; my faculties rusted for want of exercise, my reason grew feeble, and my imagination morbid.

CHAPTER XXVII

A PACQUET of letters, at length, arrived from London—Mrs Harley, with a look that seemed to search the soul, put one into my hands—The superscription bore the well known characters—yes, it was from Augustus, and addressed to Emma—I ran, with it, into my chamber, locked myself in, tore it almost asunder with a tremulous hand, perused its contents with avidity—scarce daring to respire—I reperused it again and again.

'I had trusted my confessions (it said) to one who had made the human heart his study, who could not be affected by them improperly. It spoke of the illusions of the passions—of the false and flattering medium through which they presented objects to our view. He had an-

swered my letter earlier, had it not involved him in too
many thoughts to do it with ease. There was a great part of
it to which he knew not how to reply—perhaps, on some
subjects, it was not necessary to be explicit. And now, it
may be, he had better be silent—he was dissatisfied with
what he had written, but, were he to write again, he
doubted if he should please himself any better.—He was
highly flattered by the favourable opinion I entertained of
him, it was a grateful proof, not of his merit, but of the
warmth of my friendship, &c. &c.'

This letter appeared to me vague, obscure, enigmatical.
Unsatisfied, disappointed, I felt, I had little to hope—and,
yet, had no *distinct* ground of fear. I brooded over it, I
tortured its meaning into a hundred forms—I spake of it
to my friend, but in general terms, in which she seemed to
acquiesce: she appeared to have made a determination,
not to enquire after what I was unwilling to disclose; she
wholly confided both in my principles, and in those of her
son: I was wounded by what, entangled in prejudice, I
conceived to be a necessity for this reserve.

Again I addressed the man, whose image, in the absence
of all other impressions, I had suffered to gain in my mind
this dangerous ascendency.

TO AUGUSTUS HARLEY

'I, once more, take up my pen with a mind so full of
thought, that I foresee I am about to trespass on your time
and patience—yet, perhaps, to one who makes "the human heart his study," it may not be wholly uninteresting
to trace a faithful delineation of the emotions and sentiments of an ingenuous, uncorrupted, mind—a mind
formed by solitude, and habits of reflection, to some
strength of character.

'If to have been more guarded and reserved would have
been more discreet, I have already forfeited all claim to
this discretion—to affect it now, would be vain, and, by
pursuing a middle course, I should resign the only advantage I may ever derive from my sincerity, the advantage of
expressing my thoughts and feelings with freedom.

'The conduct, which I have been led to adopt, has been the result of a combination of peculiar circumstances, *and is not what I would recommend to general imitation*—To say nothing of the hazards it might involve, I am aware, generally speaking, arguments might be adduced, to prove, that certain customs, of which I, yet, think there is reason to complain, may not have been unfounded in nature—I am led to speak thus, because I am not willing to spare myself, but would alledge all which you might have felt inclined to hint, had you not been with-held by motives of delicate consideration.

'Of what then, you may ask, do I complain?—Not of the laws of nature! But when mind has given dignity to natural affections; when reason, culture, taste, and delicacy, have combined to chasten, to refine, to exalt (shall I say) to sanctify them—Is there, then, no cause to complain of rigor and severity, that such minds must either passively submit to a vile traffic, or be content to relinquish all the endearing sympathies of life? Nature has formed woman peculiarly susceptible of the tender affections. "The voice of nature is too strong to be silenced by artificial precepts."* To feel these affections in a supreme degree, a mind enriched by literature and expanded by fancy and reflection, is necessary—for it is intellect and imagination only, that can give energy and interest to—

> "The thousand soft sensations—
> Which vulgar souls want faculties to taste,
> Who take their good and evil in the gross."*

'I wish we were in the vehicular state, and that you understood the sentient language;[1]* you might then comprehend the whole of what I mean to express, but find too delicate for *words*. But I do you injustice.

'If the affections are, indeed, generated by sympathy, where the principles, pursuits, and habits, are congenial—where the *end*, sought to be attained, is—

> "Something, than beauty dearer,"*

[1] See Light of Nature pursued. An entertaining philosophical work.

'You may, perhaps, agree with me, that it is *almost* indifferent on which side the sentiment originates. Yet, I confess, my frankness has involved me in many after thoughts and inquietudes; inquietudes, which all my reasoning is, at times, insufficient to allay. The shame of being singular, it has been justly observed,[1] requires strong principles, and much native firmness of temper, to surmount.*—Those who deviate from the beaten track must expect to be entangled in the thicket, and wounded by many a thorn—my wandering feet have already been deeply pierced.

'I should vainly attempt to describe the struggles, the solicitudes, the doubts, the apprehensions, that alternately rend my heart! I feel, that I have "put to sea upon a shattered plank, and placed my trust in miracles for safety."* I dread, one moment, lest, in attempting to awaken your tenderness, I may have forfeited your respect; the next, that I have mistaken a delusive meteor for the sober light of reason. In retirement, numberless contradictory emotions revolve in my disturbed mind:—in company, I start and shudder from accidental allusions, in which no one but myself could trace any application. The end of doubt is the beginning of repose. Say, then, to me, that it is a principle in human nature, however ungenerous, to esteem lightly what may be attained without difficulty.—Tell me to make distinctions between love and friendship, of which I have, hitherto, been able to form no idea.—Say, that the former is the caprice of fancy, founded on external graces, to which I have little pretension, and that it is vain to pretend, that—

> "Truth and good are one,
> And beauty dwells with them."*

'Tell me, that I have indulged too long the wild and extravagant chimeras of a romantic imagination. Let us walk together into the palace of Truth,* where (it is fancifully related by an ingenious writer,[2] that) every one was compelled by an irresistible, controuling, power, to reveal his

[1] Aikin's Letters.
[2] Madame de Genlis's Tales of the Castle.

inmost sentiments! All this I will bear, and will still respect
your integrity, and confide in your principles; but I can no
longer sustain a suspense that preys upon my spirits. It is
not the Book of Fate*—it is your mind, only, I desire to
read. A sickly apprehension overspreads my heart——I
pause here, unable to proceed.

'EMMA.'

CHAPTER XXVIII

WEEK after week, month after month, passed away in the
anguish of vain expectation: my letter was not answered,
and I again sunk into despondency.—Winter drew near. I
shuddered at the approach of this dreary and desolate
season, when I was roused by the receipt of a letter from
one of the daughters of the maternal aunt, under whose
care I had spent the happy, thoughtless, days of childhood.
My cousin informed me—
    'That she had married an officer in the East India Ser-
vice;* that soon after their union he was ordered abroad,
and stationed in Bengal for three years, during which
period she was to remain in a commodious and pleasant
house, situated in the vicinity of the metropolis. She had
been informed of my removal from Morton Park, and had
no doubt but I should be able to give a satisfactory account
of the occasion of that removal. She purposed, during the
absence of her husband, to let out a part of her house; and
should I not be fixed in my present residence, would be
happy to accommodate me with an apartment, on terms
that should be rather dictated by friendship than interest.
She also hinted, that a neighbouring lady, of respectable
character, would be glad to avail herself of the occasional
assistance of an accomplished woman in the education of
her daughters; that she had mentioned me to her in advantageous terms, conceiving that I should have no objection, by such a means, to exercise my talents, to render
myself useful, and to augment my small income.'
    This intelligence filled me with delight: the idea of

change, of exertion, of new scenes—shall I add, *of breathing the same air with Augustus,* rushed tumultuously through my imagination. Flying eagerly to my friend, to impart these tidings, I was not aware of the ungrateful and inconsiderate appearance which these exultations must give me in her eyes, till I perceived the starting tear.—It touched, it electrified, my heart; and, throwing myself into her arms, I caught the soft contagion, and wept aloud.

'Go, Emma—my daughter,' said this excellent woman; 'I banish the selfish regret that would prompt me to detain thee. I perceive this solitude is destructive to thy ardent mind. Go, vary your impressions, and expand your sensations; gladden me only from time to time with an account of your progress and welfare.'

I had but little preparation to make. I canvassed over, with my friend, a thousand plans, and formed as many expectations and conjectures; but they all secretly tended to one point, and concentrated in one object. I gave my cousin notice that I should be with her in a few days—settled a future correspondence with my friend—embraced her, at parting, with unfeigned, and tender, sorrow—and, placing myself in a stage-coach, that passed daily through the village, took the road, once more, with a fluttering heart, to London. We travelled all night—it was cold and dreary—but my fancy was busied with various images, and my bosom throbbing with lively, though indistinct sensations.

The next day, at noon, I arrived, without accident, at the residence of my relation, Mrs Denbeigh. She received me with unaffected cordiality: our former amity was renewed; we spent the evening together, recalling past scenes; and, on retiring, I was shewn into a neat chamber, which had been prepared for me, with a light closet adjoining. The next day, I was introduced to the lady, mentioned to me by my kind hostess, and agreed to devote three mornings in the week to the instruction of the young ladies (her daughters), in various branches of education.

END OF THE FIRST VOLUME

VOLUME II

TO AUGUSTUS HARLEY

'MY friend, my son, it is for your benefit, that I have
determined on reviewing the sentiments, and the incidents, of my past life. Cold declamation can avail but little
towards the reformation of our errors. It is by tracing, by
developing, the passions in the minds of others; tracing
them, from the seeds by which they have been generated,
through all their extended consequences, that we learn,
the more effectually, to regulate and to subdue our own.

'I repeat, it will cost me some pain to be ingenuous in
the recital which I have pledged myself to give you; even in
the moment when I resume my pen, prejudice continues
to struggle with principle, and I feel an inclination to
retract. While unfolding a series of error and mortification, I tremble, lest, in warning you to shun the rocks
and quicksands amidst which my little bark has foundered,
I should forfeit your respect and esteem, the pride, and
the comfort, of my declining years. But you are deeply
interested in my narrative, you tell me, and you entreat me
to proceed.'

CHAPTER I

CHANGE of scene, regular employment, attention to my
pupils, and the conscious pride of independence, afforded
a temporary relief to my spirits. My first care, on my arrival
in town, was to gladden the mind of my dear benefactress, by a minute detail of my present comforts and
occupations.

She had charged me with affectionate remembrance
and letters to her son. I enclosed these letters; and, after
informing him (in the cover) of the change in my situ-

ation, and the incident which had occasioned it, complained of the silence he had observed towards my last
letter.

—'If,' said I, 'from having observed the social and sympathetic nature of our feelings and affections, I suffered
myself to yield, involuntarily, to the soothing idea, that the
ingenuous avowal of an attachment so tender, so sincere,
so artless, as mine, could not have been unaffecting to a
mind with which my own proudly claimed kindred:—if I
fondly believed, that simplicity, modesty, truth—the eye
beaming with sensibility, the cheek mantling with the glow
of affection, the features softened, the accents modulated,
by ineffable tenderness, might, in the eyes of a virtuous
man, have supplied the place of more dazzling accomplishments, and more seductive charms: if I over-rated my
own merit, and my own powers—surely my mistakes were
sufficiently humiliating! You should not, indeed you
should not, have obliged me to arrive at the conviction
through a series of deductions so full of mortification and
anguish. You are too well acquainted with the human
heart not to be sensible, that no certainty can equal the
misery of conjecture, in a mind of ardour—the agonizing
images which *suspense* forces upon the tender and sensible
heart! You should have written, in pity to the situation of
my mind. I would have thanked you for being ingenuous,
even though, like Hamlet, you had *spoke daggers*.* I expected it, from your character, and I had a claim to your
sincerity.

'But it is past!—the vision is dissolved! The barbed arrow
is not extracted with more pain, than the enchantments of
hope from the ardent and sanguine spirit! But why am I to
lose your friendship? My heart tells me, I have not deserved this! Do not suspect, that I have so little justice, or
so little magnanimity, as to refuse you the privilege, the
enviable privilege, of being master of your own affections.
I am unhappy, I confess; the principal charm of my life is
fled, and the hopes that should enliven future prospects
are faint: melancholy too often obscures reason, and a
heart, perhaps too tender, preys on itself.

'I suspect I had formed some vain and extravagant expectations. I could have loved you, had you permitted it, with no mean, nor common attachment.—My words, my looks, my actions, betrayed me, ere I suffered my feelings to dictate to my pen. Would to God I had buried this fatal secret in the bottom of my soul! But repentance is, now, too late. Yet the sensible heart yearns to disclose itself— and to whom can it confide its sentiments, with equal propriety, as to him who will know how to pity the errors, of which he feels himself, however involuntarily, the cause? The world might think my choice in a confident* singular; it has been my misfortune seldom to think with the world, and I ought, perhaps, patiently to submit to the inconveniences to which this singularity has exposed me.

'I know not how, without doing myself a painful violence, to relinquish your society; and why, let me again ask, should I? I now desire only that repose which is the end of doubt, and this, I think, I should regain by one hour's frank conversation with you; I would compose myself, listen to you, and yield to the sovereignty of reason. After such an interview, my mind—no longer harrassed by vague suspicion, by a thousand nameless apprehensions and inquietudes—should struggle to subdue itself—at least, I would not permit it to dictate to my pen, not to bewilder my conduct. I am exhausted by perturbation. I ask only certainty and rest.

'EMMA.'

A few days after I had written the preceding letter, Mr Harley called on me, Mrs Denbeigh was with me on his entrance; I would have given worlds to have received him alone, but had not courage to hint this to my relation. Overwhelmed by a variety of emotions, I was unable for some time to make any reply to his friendly enquiries after my health, and congratulations on my amended prospects. My confusion and embarrassment were but too apparent; perceiving my distress, he kindly contrived to engage my hostess in discourse, that I might have time to rally my spirits. By degrees, I commanded myself sufficiently to join in the conversation—I spoke to him of his mother, expressed the lively sense I felt of her goodness, and my unaffected regret at parting with her. Animated by my subject, and encouraged by the delicacy of Augustus, I became more assured: we retraced the amusements and studies of H——shire, and two hours passed delightfully and insensibly away, when Mrs Denbeigh was called out of the room to speak to a person who brought her letters and intelligence from the India House.* Mr Harley, rising at the same time from his seat, seemed about to depart, but hesitating, stood a few moments as if irresolute.

'You leave me,' said I, in a low and tremulous tone, 'and you leave me still in suspense?'

'Could you,' replied he, visibly affected, 'but have seen me on the receipt of your last letter, you would have perceived that my feelings were not enviable—Your affecting expostulation, added to other circumstances of a vexatious nature, oppressed my spirits with a burthen more than they were able to sustain.'

He resumed his seat, spoke of his situation, of the tenure on which he held his fortune,—'I am neither a stoic nor a philosopher,' added he,—'I knew not how— *I could not answer your letter.* What shall I say?—I am withheld from explaining myself further, by reasons—*by obligations*—Who can look back on every action of his past life with approbation? Mine has not been free from error! I am distressed, perplexed—*Insuperable obstacles* forbid what otherwise'——

'I feel,' said I, interrupting him, 'that I am the victim of my own weakness and vanity—I feel, that I have been rushing headlong into the misery which you kindly sought to spare me—I am sensible of your delicacy—of your humanity!—And is it with the full impression of your virtues on my heart that I must teach that heart to renounce you—renounce, for ever, the man with whose pure and elevated mind my own panted to mingle? My reason has been blinded by the illusions of my self-love—and, while I severely suffer, I own my sufferings just—yet, the sentiments you inspired were worthy of you! I understand little of—I have violated common forms—seeking your tenderness, I have perhaps forfeited your esteem!'

'Far, *very far,* from it—I would, but cannot, say more.'

'Must we, then, separate for ever—will you no longer assist me in the pursuit of knowledge and truth—will you no more point out to me the books I should read, and aid me in forming a just judgment of the principles they contain—Must all your lessons be at an end—all my studies be resigned? How, without your counsel and example, shall I regain my strength of mind—to what *end* shall I seek to improve myself, when I dare no longer hope to be worthy of him—'

A flood of tears choked my utterance; hiding my face with my hands, I gave way to the kindly relief, but for which my heart had broken. I heard footsteps in the passage, and the voice of Mrs Denbeigh as speaking to her servant—covered with shame and grief, I dared not in this situation appear before her, but, rushing out at an opposite door, hid myself in my chamber. A train of confused recollections tortured my mind, I concluded, that Augustus had another, a prior attachment; I felt, with this conviction, that I had not the fortitude, and that perhaps I ought not, to see him again. I wrote to him under this impression; I poured out my soul in anguish, in sympathy, in fervent aspirations for his happiness. These painful and protracted conflicts affected my health, a deep and habitual depression preyed upon my spirits, and, surveying every object through the medium of a distempered imagination, I grew disgusted with life.

CHAPTER II

I BEGAN, at length, to think, that I had been too precipitate, and too severe to myself.—Why was I to sacrifice a friend, from whose conversation I had derived improvement and pleasure? I repeated this question to myself, again and again; and I blushed and repented. But I deceived myself. I had too frequently acted with precipitation, I determined, now, to be more prudent—I waited three months, fortified my mind with many reflections, and resumed my pen—

TO AUGUSTUS HARLEY

'Near three months have elapsed, since I last addressed you. I remind you of this, not merely to suppress, as it arises, any apprehension which you may entertain of further embarrassment or importunity: for I can no longer afflict myself with the idea, that my peace, or welfare, are indifferent to you, but will rather adopt the sentiment of Plato—who on being informed, that one of his disciples, whom he had more particularly distinguished, had spoken ill of him, replied, to the slanderer—"I do not believe you, for it is impossible that I should not be esteemed by one whom I so sincerely regard."*

'My motive, for calling to your remembrance the date of my last, is, that you should consider what I am now about to say, as the result of calmer reflection, the decision of judgment after having allowed the passions leisure to subside. It is, perhaps, unnecessary to premise, that I am not urged on by pride, from an obscure consciousness of having been betrayed into indiscretion, to endeavour to explain away, or to extenuate, any part of my former expressions or conduct. To a mind like yours, such an attempt would be impertinent; from one like mine, I hope, superfluous. I am not ashamed of being a human being, nor blush to own myself liable to "the shakes and agues of his fragile nature."* I have ever spoken, and acted, from the genuine dictates of a mind swayed, at the time, by its own views and propensities, nor have I hesitated, as those views and propensities have changed, to avow my further convictions—"Let not the coldly wise exult, that their heads were never led astray by their hearts."* I have all along used, and shall continue to use, the unequivocal language of sincerity.

'However *romantic* (a vague term applied to every thing we do not understand, or are unwilling to imitate) my views and sentiments might appear to many, I dread not, from you, this frigid censure. "The ideas, the associations, the circumstances of each man are properly his own, and it is a pernicious system, that would lead us to require all men, however different their circumstances, to act in many of the common affairs of life, by a precise, general rule."[1]* The genuine effusions of the heart and mind are easily distinguished, by the penetrating eye, from the vain ostentation of sentiment, lip deep, which, causing no emotion, communicates none—Oh! how unlike the energetic sympathies of truth and feeling—darting from mind to mind, enlightening, warming, with electrical rapidity!

'My ideas have undergone, in the last three months, many fluctuations. My *affection* for you (why should I seek for vague, inexpressive phrases?) has not ceased, has not diminished, but it has, in some measure, changed its nature. It was originally generated by the report, and cemented by the knowledge, of your virtues and talents; and to virtue and talents my mind had ever paid unfeigned, enthusiastic, homage! It is somewhere said by Rousseau— "That there may exist such a suitability of moral, mental, and personal, qualifications, as should point out the propriety of an union between a prince and the daughter of an executioner."* Vain girl that I was! I flattered myself that between us this sympathy really existed. I dwelt on the union between mind and mind—sentiments of nature gently insinuated themselves—my sensibility grew more tender, more affecting—and my imagination, ever lively, traced the glowing picture, and dipped the pencil in rainbow tints! Possessing one of those determined spirits, that is not easily induced to relinquish its purposes—while I conceived that I had only your pride, or your insensibility, to combat, I wildly determined to persevere.—A further recapitulation would, perhaps, be unnecessary:—my situation, alas! is now changed.

[1] Godwin's Political Justice.

'Having then examined my heart, attentively and delib-
erately, I suspect that I have been unjust to myself, in
supposing it incapable of a disinterested attachment.—
Why am I to deprive you of a faithful friend, and myself of
all the benefits I may yet derive from your conversation
and kind offices? I ask, why? And I should, indeed, have
cause to blush, if, after having had time for reflection, I
could really think this necessary. Shall I, then, sign the
unjust decree, that women are incapable of energy or
fortitude? Have I exercised my understanding, without
ever intending to apply my principles to practice? Do I
mean always to deplore the prejudices which have, system-
atically, weakened the female character, without making
any effort to rise above them? Is the example you have
given me, of a steady adherence to honour and principle,
to be merely respected, without exciting in my bosom any
emulation? Dare I to answer these questions in the affirm-
ative, and still ask your esteem—the esteem of the wise and
good?—I dare not! No longer weakened by alternate
hopes and fears, like the reed yielding to every breeze, I
believe myself capable of acting upon firmer principles;
and I request, with confidence, the restoration of your
friendship! Should I afterwards find, that I have over-rated
my own strength, I will frankly tell you so, and expect from
your humanity those allowances, which are but a poor
substitute for respect.

'Believe, then, my views and motives to be simply such as
I state them; at least, such, after severely scrutinizing my
heart, they appear to myself; and reply to me with similar
ingenuousness. My expectations are very moderate:
answer me with simplicity—my very soul sickens at evasion!
You have, undoubtedly, a right to judge and to determine
for yourself; but it will be but just to state to me the reasons
for, and the result of, that judgment; in which case, if I
cannot obviate those reasons, I shall be bound, however
reluctantly, to acquiesce in them. Be assured, I will never
complain of any consequences which may ensue, even,
from the utterance of all truth.

                                                          'EMMA.'

CHAPTER III

THIS letter was succeeded by a renewal of our intercourse
and studies. Mrs Denbeigh, my kind hostess, was usually of
our parties. We read together, or conversed only on general topics, or upon subjects of literature. I was introduced
by Mr Harley to several respectable families, friends of his
own and of his mother's. I made many indirect enquiries
of our common acquaintance, with a view to discover the
supposed object of my friend's attachment, but without
success. All that he had, himself, said, respecting such an
engagement, had been so vague, that I began to doubt of
the reality of its existence.—When, in any subsequent
letters (for we continued occasionally to correspond) I
ventured to allude to the subject, I was warned 'not to
confound my own conceptions with real existences.' When
he spoke of a susceptibility to the tender affections, it was
always in the past time, 'I *have* felt,'—'I *have* been—' Once
he wrote—'His situation had been rendered difficult, by a
combination of *peculiar circumstances*; circumstances, with
which but few persons were acquainted.' Sometimes he
would affect to reflect upon his past conduct, and warn me
against appreciating him too highly. In fine,* he was a
perfect enigma, and every thing which he said or wrote
tended to increase the mystery.

A restless, an insatiable, curiosity,* devoured me, height-
ened by feelings that every hour became more imperious,
more uncontroulable. I proposed to myself, in the gratification of this curiosity, a satisfaction that should compensate for all the injuries I might suffer in the career.
This inquietude prevented my mind from resting;
and, by leaving room for conjecture, left room for the
illusions of fancy, and of hope. Had I never expressed
this, he might have affected ignorance of my sensations;
he might have pleaded guiltless, when, in the agony
of my soul, I accused him of having sacrificed my
peace to his disingenuousness—but vain were all my
expostulations!

'If,' said I, 'I have sought, too earnestly, to learn the state
of your affections, it has been with a view to the more
effectually disciplining of my own—of stifling every *ignis
fatuus* of false hope,* that making, even, impossibilities
possible, will still, at times, continue to mislead me. Objects seen through obscurity, imperfectly discerned, allow
to the fancy but too free a scope; the mind grows debilitated, by brooding over its apprehensions; and those apprehensions, whether real or imaginary, are carried with
accumulated pain to the heart. I have said, on this subject,
you have a right to be free; but I am, now, doubtful of this
right: the health of my mind being involved in the question, has rendered it a question of *utility**—and on what
other basis can morals rest?'

I frequently reiterated these reasonings, always with
encreased fervor and earnestness: represented—'that
every step I took in advance would be miles in return—
every minute that the blow was suspended, prepared it to
descend with accumulated force.' I required no particulars, but merely requested to be assured of *a present, existing, engagement.* I continued, from time to time, to urge this
subject.

'Much,' said I, 'as I esteem you, and deeply as a thousand associations have fixed your idea in my heart—in true
candour of soul, I, yet, feel myself your superior.—I recollect a sentiment of Richardson's Clarissa that always
pleased me, and that may afford a test, by which each of us
may judge of the integrity of our own minds—"I should be
glad that you, and all the world, knew my heart; let my
enemies sit in judgment upon my actions; fairly scanned, I
fear not the result. Let them ask me my most secret
thoughts; and, whether they make for me, or against me, I
will reveal them."*

'This is the principle, my friend, upon which I have
acted towards you. I have said many things, I doubt not,
which make against me; but I trusted them to one, who
told me, that he had made the human heart his study: and
it is only in compliance with the prejudices of others, if I
have taken any pains to conceal all I have thought and felt

on this, or on any other, subject, from the rest of the world. Had I not, in the wild career of fervent feeling, had sufficient strength of mind to stop short, and to reason calmly, how often, in the bitterness of my spirit, should I have accused you of sporting with my feelings, by involving me in a hopeless maze of conjecture—by leaving me a prey to the constant, oppressive, apprehension of hearing something, which I should not have the fortitude to support with dignity; which, in proportion as it is delayed, still contributes to harrass, to weaken, to incapacitate, my mind from bearing its disclosure.

'I know you might reply—and more than nine-tenths of the world would justify you in this reply—"That you had already said, what ought to have been sufficient, and would have been so to any other human being;—that you had not sought the confidence I boast of having reposed in you;—and that, so far from affording you any satisfaction, it has occasioned you only perplexity. If my own destiny was not equivocal, of what importance could it be to me, and what right had I to enquire after circumstances, in which, however affecting, I could have no real concern."

'You may think all this, perhaps—I will not spare myself—and it may be reasonable. *But could you say it*—and have you, indeed, studied the human heart—*have you, indeed, ever felt the affections?*—Whatever may be the event—and it is in the mind of powers only that passions are likely to become fatal—and however irreproachable every other part of your conduct may have been, I shall, *here*, always say, you were culpable!'

I changed my style. 'I know not,' said I, 'the nature of those stern duties, which oblige you to with-hold from me your tenderness; neither do I any longer enquire. I dread, only, lest I should acquire this knowledge when I am the least able to support it. Ignorant, then, of any reasons which should prevent me from giving up my heart to an attachment, now become interwoven with my existence, I yield myself up to these sweet and affecting emotions, so necessary to my disposition—to which apathy is abhorrent.

"The affections (truly says Sterne) must be exercised on something; for, not to love, is to be miserable. Were I in a desart,* I would find out wherewith in it to call forth my affections. If I could do no better, I would fasten them upon some sweet myrtle, or seek some melancholy cypress to connect myself to—I would court their shade, and greet them kindly for their protection. I would cut my name upon them, and swear they were the loveliest trees throughout the desart. If their leaves withered, I would teach myself to mourn; and, when they rejoiced, I would rejoice with them."*

'An attachment, founded upon a full conviction of worth, must be both safe and salutary. My mind has not sufficient strength to form an abstract idea of perfection. I have ever found it stimulated, improved, advanced, by its affections. I will, then, continue to love you with fervor and purity; I will see you with joy, part from you with regret, grieve in your griefs, enter with zeal into your concerns, interest myself in your honour and welfare, and endeavour, with all my little power, to contribute to your comfort and satisfaction.—Is your heart so differently constituted from every other human heart, that an affection, thus ardent and sincere, excites in it no grateful, and soothing, emotions? Why, *then*, withdraw yourself from me, and by that means afflict, and sink into despondency, a mind that entrusts its peace to your keeping.

'EMMA.'

We met the next day at the house of a common friend. My accents, involuntarily, were softened, my attentions pointed.—Manifestly agitated, embarrassed, even distressed, Augustus quitted the company at an early hour.

It would be endless to enumerate all the little incidents that occurred; which, however trifling they might appear in the recital, continued to operate in one direction. Many letters passed to the same purport. My curiosity was a consuming passion; but this inflexible, impenetrable, man, was still silent, or alternately evaded, and resented, my enquiries. We continued, occasionally, to meet, but generally in company.

CHAPTER IV

DURING the ensuing summer, Mr Harley proposed making a visit to his mother, and, calling to take his leave of me, on the evening preceding his journey, accidentally found me alone.—We entered into conversation on various subjects: twilight stole upon us unperceived. The obscure light inspired me with courage: I ventured to resume a subject, so often discussed; I complained, gently, of his reserve.

'Could I suppose,' he asked, 'that he had been without *his share* of suffering?'

I replied something, I scarce know what, adverting to his stronger mind.

'Strength!' said he, turning from me with emotion, 'rather say, weakness!'

I reiterated the important, the so often proposed, enquiry—'Had he, or had he not, a *present, existing, engagement*?'

He endeavoured to evade my question—I repeated it— He answered, with a degree of impatience, '*I cannot tell you*; if I could, do you think I would have been silent so long?'—as once, before, he spoke of the circumstances of his past life, as being of '*a singular, a peculiar, nature.*'

At our separation, I asked, if he would write to me during his absence. 'Certainly, he would.' The next morning, having some little commissions to execute for Mrs Harley, I sent them, accompanied by a few lines, to her son.

'Why is it,' said I, 'that our sagacity, and penetration, frequently desert us on the most interesting occasions? I can read any mind with greater facility than I can read your's; and, yet, what other have I so attentively studied? This is a problem I know not how to solve. One conclusion will force itself upon me—if a mistaken one, whom have you to blame?—That an *honourable*, suitable, engagement, could have given no occasion for mystery.' I added, 'I should depend on hearing from him, according to his promise.'

Week after week, month after month, wore away, and no letter arrived. Perturbation was succeeded by anxiety and apprehension; but hearing, through my maternal friend, Mrs Harley, of the welfare of this object of our too tender cares, my solicitude subsided into despondency. The pressure of one corroding train of ideas preyed, like a canker-worm, upon my heart, and destroyed all its tranquility.

In the beginning of the winter, this mysterious, inexplicable, being, again returned to town. I had undertaken a little business, to serve him, during his absence.—I transmitted to him an account of my proceedings; subjoining a gentle reproach for his unkind silence.

'You promised you would write to me,' said I, 'during your residence in ——shire. I therefore depended upon hearing from you; and, yet, I was disappointed. You should not, indeed you should not, make these experiments upon my mind. My sensibility, originally acute, from having been too much exercised, has become nearly morbid, and has almost unfitted me for an inhabitant of the world. I am willing to believe, that your conduct towards me has originated in good motives, nevertheless, you have made some sad mistakes—you have *deeply*, though undesignedly, wounded me: I have been harrassed, distressed, mortified. You know not, neither will I attempt to describe, all I have suffered! language would be inadequate to paint the struggles of a delicate, susceptible, mind, in some peculiar and interesting situations.

'You may suspect me of wanting resolution, but strong, persevering affections, are no mark of a weak mind. To have been the wife of a man of virtue and talents was my dearest ambition, and would have been my glory: I judged myself worthy of the confidence and affection of such a man—I felt, that I could have united in his pursuits, and shared his principles—aided the virtuous energies of his mind, and assured his domestic comfort. I earnestly sought to inspire you with tenderness, from the conviction, that I could contribute to your happiness, and to the worth of your character. And if, from innumerable associations, I at length loved your person, it was the magnanimity of your conduct, it was your virtues, that first excited my admiration and esteem. But you have rejected an attachment originating in the highest, the purest, principles—you have thrown from you a heart of exquisite sensibility, and you leave me in doubt, whether you have not sacrificed that heart to prejudice. Yet, contemned affection has excited in my mind no resentment; true tenderness is made up of gentle and amiable emotions; nothing hostile, nothing severe, can mix with it: it may gradually subside, but it will continue to soften the mind it has once subdued.

'I see much to respect in your conduct, and though, it is probable, some parts of it may have originated in mistaken principles, I trust, that their source was pure! I, also, have made many mistakes—have been guilty of many extravagances. Yet, distrust the morality, that sternly commands you to pierce the bosom that most reveres you, and then to call it virtue—*Yes! distrust and suspect its origin!*' I concluded with expressing a wish to see him—'*merely as a friend*'—requesting a line in reply.

He wrote not, but came, unexpectedly came, the next evening. I expressed, in lively terms, the pleasure I felt in seeing him. We conversed on various subjects, he spoke affectionately of his mother, and of the tender interest she had expressed for my welfare. He enquired after my pursuits and acquirements during his absence, commending the progress I had made. Just before he quitted me, he adverted to the reproach I had made him, for not having written to me, according to his engagement.

'Recollect,' said he, 'in the last letter I received from you, before I left London, you hinted some suspicions—' I looked at him, 'and what,' added he, 'could I reply?'

I was disconcerted, I changed colour, and had no power to pursue the subject.

CHAPTER V

FROM this period, he continued to visit me (I confess at my solicitation) more frequently. We occasionally resumed our scientific pursuits, read together, or entered into discussion on various topics. At length he grew captious, disputatious, gloomy, and imperious—the more I studied to please him, the less I succeeded. He disapproved my conduct, my opinions, my sentiments; my frankness offended him. This change considerably affected me. In company, his manners were studiously cold and distant; in private capricious, yet reserved and guarded. He seemed to overlook all my efforts to please, and, with a severe and penetrating eye, to search only for my errors—errors, into which I was but too easily betrayed, by the painful, and delicate, situation, in which I had placed myself.

We, one day, accompanied Mrs Denbeigh on a visit of congratulation to her brother (eldest son of my deceased uncle Mr Melmoth), who had, when a youth, been placed by his father in a commercial house in the West Indies, and who had just returned to his native country with an ample fortune. His sister and myself anticipated the pleasure of renewing our early, fraternal, affection and intimacy, while I felt a secret pride in introducing to his acquaintance a man so accomplished and respectable as Mr Harley. We were little aware of the changes which time and different situations produce on the character, and, with hearts and minds full of the frank, lively, affectionate, youth, from whom we had parted, seven years since, with mutual tears and embraces, shrunk spontaneously, on our arrival at Mr Melmoth's elegant house in Bedford square,* from the cold salutation, of the haughty, opulent, purse-proud, Planter, surrounded by ostentatious luxuries, and evidently valuing himself upon the consequence which he imagined they must give him in our eyes.

Mr Harley received the formal compliments of this favourite of fortune with the easy politeness which distinguishes the gentleman and the man of letters, and the dignified composure which the consciousness of worth and talents seldom fails to inspire. Mr Melmoth, by his awkward and embarrassed manner, tacitly acknowledged the impotence of wealth, and the real superiority of his guest. We were introduced by our stately relation to his wife, the lady of the mansion, a young woman whom he had accidentally met with in a party of pleasure at Jamaica, whither she had attended a family in the humble office of companion or chief attendant to the lady. Fascinated by her beauty and lively manner, our trader had overlooked an empty mind, a low education, and a doubtful character, and, after a very few interviews, tendered to her acceptance his hand and fortune; which, though not without some affectation of doubt and delay, were in a short time joyfully accepted.

A gentleman joined our party in the dining-room, whom the servant announced by the name of Pemberton, in whom I presently recognized, notwithstanding some years had elapsed since our former meeting, the man of fashion and gallantry who had been the antagonist of Mr Francis, at the table of my father. He had lately (we were informed by our host) been to Jamaica, to take possession of an estate bequeathed to him, and had returned to England in the same vessel with Mr and Mrs Melmoth. After an elegant dinner of several courses had been served up and removed for the desert, a desultory conversation took place.

Mr Pemberton, it appeared, held a commission in the militia, and earnestly solicited Mrs Melmoth, on whom he lavished a profusion of compliments, to grace their encampment, which was to be stationed in the ensuing season near one of the fashionable watering places, with her presence.

This request the lady readily promised to comply with, expressing, in tones of affected softness, her admiration of military men, and of the

'Pride, pomp, and circumstance of glorious war!'*

'Do you not think, Miss Courtney,' said she, turning to me,

'that soldiers are the most agreeable and charming men in the world?'

'Indeed I do not, Madam; their trade is *murder*, and their trappings, in my eyes, appear but as the gaudy pomp of sacrifice.'

'*Murder*, indeed! What a harsh word—I declare you are a shocking creature—There always have been wars in the world, and there always must be: but surely you would not confound the brave fellows, who fight to protect their King and Country, and *the ladies*, with common ruffians and housebreakers!'

'All the difference between them is, that the one, rendered desperate by passion, poverty, or injustice, endeavours by *wrong* means to do himself *right*, and through this terrible and pitiable mistake destroys the life or the property of a fellow being—The others, wantonly and in cold blood, cut down millions of their species, ravage whole towns and cities, and carry devastation through a country.'

'What *odd notions!* Dear, Mr Pemberton, did you ever hear a lady talk so strangely?'

Thus called upon, Mr Pemberton thought it incumbent upon him to interfere—'*Courtney*, I think, Madam, your name is! The daughter of an old friend of mine, if I am not mistaken, and who, I remember, was, when a very young lady, a great admirer of *Roman virtues*.'

'Not of *Roman virtues*, I believe, Sir; they had in them too much of the destructive spirit which Mrs Melmoth thinks so admirable.'

'Indeed, I said nothing about *Roman virtues*, nor do I trouble myself with such subjects—I merely admired the soldiers because they are so brave and so polite; besides, the military dress is so very elegant and becoming—Dear, Mr Pemberton, how charmingly you must look in your regimentals!'

Mr Pemberton, bowing in return to the compliment, made an animated eulogium of the taste and beauty of the speaker.

'Pray, Sir,' resumed she, addressing herself to Mr Harley, whose inattention seemed to pique her, and whose notice she was determined to attract, 'are you of Miss Courtney's opinion—do you think it right to call soldiers *murderers*?'

'Upon my word, Madam,' with an air of irony, 'you must excuse me from entering into such *nice** *distinctions*—when *ladies* differ, who shall presume to decide?'

Mr Melmoth interposed, by wishing, 'that they had some thousands more of these *murderers* in the West Indies, to keep the slaves in subordination, who, since absurd notions of liberty had been put into their heads, were grown very troublesome and refractory, and, in a short time, he supposed, would become as insolent as the English servants.'

'Would you believe it, Mrs Denbeigh,' said the Planter's lady, addressing the sister of her husband, 'Mr Melmoth and I have been in England but a month, and have been obliged three times to change our whole suit of servants?'

'This is a land of freedom, my dear sister; servants, here, will not submit to be treated like the slaves in Jamaica.'

'Well, I am sure it is very provoking to have one's will disputed by such low, ignorant, creatures. How should they know what is right? It is enough for them to obey the orders of their superiors.'

'But suppose,' replied Mrs Denbeigh, 'they should happen to think their superiors unreasonable!'

'*Think!* sister,' said the lordly Mr Melmoth, with an exulting laugh, 'what have *servants*, or *women*, to do with *thinking*?'

'Nay, now,' interrupted Mr Pemberton, 'you are too severe upon the ladies—how would the elegant and tasteful arrangement of Mrs Melmoth's ornaments have been produced without thinking?'

'Oh, you flatterer!' said the lady.

'Let them think only about their dress, and I have no objection, but don't let them plague us with *sermonizing*.'

'Mrs Melmoth,' said I, coolly, 'does not often, I dare say, offend *in this way*. That some of the gentlemen, present, should object to a woman's exercising her discriminating powers, is not wonderful, since it might operate greatly to their disadvantage.'

'A blow on the right cheek, from so fair a hand,' replied Mr Pemberton, affectedly bending his body, 'would almost induce one to adopt the christian maxim, and turn the left, also.* What say you, Mr Harley?'

'Mr Harley, I believe, Sir, does not feel himself included in the reflection.'

'He is a happy man then.'

'No, Sir, merely a *rational one*!'

'You are pleased to be severe; of all things I dread a female wit.'

'It is an instinctive feeling of self-preservation—nature provides weak animals with timidity as a guard.'

Mr Pemberton reddened, and, affecting a careless air, hummed a tune. Mr Melmoth again reverted to the subject of English servants, which gave rise to a discussion on the Slave Trade.* Mr Harley pleaded the cause of freedom and humanity with a bold and manly eloquence, expatiating warmly on the iniquity as well as impolicy of so accursed a traffic. Melmoth was awed into silence. Mr Pemberton advanced some trite arguments in opposition, respecting the temporary mischiefs which might ensue, in case of an abolition, to the planters, landholders, traders, &c. Augustus explained, by contending only for the gradual emancipation, after their minds had been previously prepared, of the oppressed Africans. The conversation grew interesting. Pemberton was not devoid of talents when he laid aside his affectation; the subject was examined both in a moral and a political point of view. I listened with delight, while Augustus exposed and confuted the specious reasoning and sophistry of his antagonist: exulting in the triumph of truth and justice, I secretly gloried—'with more than selfish vanity'*—in the virtue and abilities of my friend. Though driven from all his resources, Mr Pemberton was too much the courtier to be easily discon-

certed, but, complimenting his adversary on his eloquence, declared he should be happy to hear of his having
a seat in Parliament.

Mrs Melmoth, who had yawned and betrayed various
symptoms of weariness during the discussion, now proposed the adjournment of the ladies into the drawing-
room, whither I was compelled, by a barbarous and odious
custom, reluctantly to follow, and to submit to be entertained with a torrent of folly and impertinence.

'I was ill-natured,' she told me.—'How could I be so
severe upon the *charming* and *elegant* Mr Pemberton?'

It was in vain I laboured to convince her, that to be
treated like *ideots* was no real compliment; and that the
men who condescend to flatter our foibles, despised the
weak beings they helped to form.*

My remonstrances were as fatiguing, and as little to be
comprehended by this *fine lady*, as the arguments respecting the Slave Trade:—she sought refuge from them in
interrogating Mrs Denbeigh respecting the last new
fashions, and in consulting her taste on the important
question—whether blue or violet colour was the most
becoming to a brunette complexion? The gentlemen
joined us, to our great relief, at the tea-table:—other company dropped in, and the evening was beguiled with cards
and the chess-board;—at the latter Mr Melmoth and Mr
Harley were antagonists;—the former was no match for
Augustus. I amused myself by observing their moves, and
overlooking the game.

During our return from this visit, some conversation
occurred between Mr Harley, my cousin, and myself,
respecting the company we had quitted. I expressed my
disappointment, disgust, and contempt, in terms, it may
be, a little too strong.

'I was *fastidious*,' Augustus told me, 'I wanted a world
made on purpose for me, and beings formed after one
model. It was both amusing, and instructive, to contem-
plate varieties of character. I was a romantic enthusiast—
and should endeavour to become more like an inhabitant
of the world.'

Piqued at these remarks, and at the tone and manner in which they were uttered, I felt my temper rising, and replied with warmth; but it was the glow of a moment; for, to say truth, vexation and disappointment, rather than reason, had broken and subdued my spirit. Mrs Denbeigh, perceiving I was pained, kindly endeavoured to give a turn to the conversation; yet she could not help expressing her regret, on observing the folly, levity, and extravagance, of the woman whom her brother had chosen for a wife.

'No doubt,' said Augustus, a little peevishly, 'he is fond of her—she is a fine woman—there is no accounting for the *caprices* of the affections.'

I sighed, and my eyes filled with tears—'Is, then, affection so *capricious* a sentiment—is it possible to love what we despise?'

'I cannot tell,' retorted Mr Harley, with quickness. 'Triflers can give no *serious* occasion for uneasiness:— the humours of superior women are sometimes still less tolerable.'

'Ah! how unjust. If gentleness be not *the perfection of reason*, it is a quality which I have never, yet, properly understood.'

He made no reply, but sunk into silence, reserve, and reverie. On our arrival at my apartments, I ventured (my cousin having left us) to expostulate with him on his un-kind behaviour; but was answered with severity. Some retrospection ensued, which gradually led to the subject ever present to my thoughts.—Again I expressed a solici-tude to be informed of the real state of his heart, of the nature of those mysterious obstacles, to which, when clearly ascertained, I was ready to submit.—'Had he, or had he not, an attachment, that looked to, as its *end*, a serious and legal engagement?' He appeared ruffled and discomposed.—'I ought not to be so urgent—he had al-ready sufficiently explained himself.' He then repeated to me some particulars, apparently adverse to such a supposi-tion—asking me, in his turn, 'If these circumstances be-spoke his having any such event in view?'

CHAPTER VI

FOR some time after this he absented himself from me; and, when he returned, his manners were still more unequal; even his sentiments, and principles, at times, appeared to me equivocal, and his character seemed wholly changed. I tried, in vain, to accommodate myself to a disposition so various. My affection, my sensibility, my fear of offending—a thousand conflicting, torturing, emotions, threw a constraint over my behaviour.—My situation became absolutely intolerable—time was murdered, activity vain, virtue inefficient: yet, a secret hope inspired me, that *indifference* could not have produced the irritations, the inequalities, that thus harrassed me. I thought, I observed a conflict in his mind; his fits of absence, and reflection, were unusual, deep, and frequent: I watched them with anxiety, with terror, with breathless expectation. My health became affected, and my mind disordered. I perceived that it was impossible to proceed, in the manner we had hitherto done, much longer—I felt that it would, inevitably, destroy me.

I reflected, meditated, reasoned, with myself—'That one channel, into which my thoughts were incessantly impelled, was destructive of all order, of all connection.'* New projects occurred to me, which I had never before ventured to encourage—I revolved them in my mind, examined them in every point of view, weighed their advantages and disadvantages, in a moral, in a prudential, scale.—Threatening evils appeared on all sides—I endeavoured, at once, to free my mind from prejudice, and from passion; and, in the critical and *singular* circumstances in which I had placed myself, coolly to survey the several arguments of the case, and nicely to calculate their force and importance.

'If, as we are taught to believe, the benevolent Author of nature be, indeed, benevolent,' said I, to myself, 'he surely must have intended the *happiness* of his creatures. Our morality cannot extend to him, but must consist in the knowledge, and practice, of those duties which we owe to ourselves and to each other.—Individual happiness constitutes the general good:——*happiness* is the only true *end* of existence;*—all notions of morals, founded on any other principle, involve in themselves a contradiction, and must be erroneous. Man does right, when pursuing interest and pleasure—it argues no depravity—this is the fable of superstition: he ought only to be careful, that, in seeking his own good, he does not render it incompatible with the good of others—that he does not consider himself as standing alone in the universe. The infraction of established *rules* may, it is possible, in some cases, be productive of mischief; yet, it is difficult to state any *rule* so precise and determinate, as to be alike applicable to every situation: what, in one instance, might be a *vice*, in another may possibly become a *virtue*.—a thousand imperceptible, evanescent, shadings, modify every thought, every motive, every action, of our lives—no one can estimate the sensations of, can form an exact judgment for, another.

'I have sometimes suspected, that all mankind are pursuing phantoms, however dignified by different appellations.—The healing operations of time, had I patience to wait the experiment, might, perhaps, recover my mind from its present distempered state; but, in the meanwhile, the bloom of youth is fading, and the vigour of life running to waste.—Should I, at length, awake from a delusive vision, it would be only to find myself a comfortless, solitary, shivering, wanderer, in the dreary wilderness of human society. I feel in myself the capacities for increasing the happiness, and the improvement, of a few individuals—and this circle, spreading wider and wider, would operate towards the grand end of life—*general utility*.'*

Again I repeated to myself—'Ascetic virtues are equally barbarous as vain:—the only just morals, are those which have a tendency to increase the bulk of enjoyment. My plan tends to this. The good which I seek does not appear to me to involve injury to any one—it is of a nature, adapted to the disposition of my mind, for which every event of my life, the education both of design and accident, have fitted me. If I am now put out, I may, perhaps, do mischief:—the placid stream, forced from its channel, lays waste the meadow. I seem to stand as upon a wide plain, bounded on all sides by the horizon:—among the objects which I perceive within these limits, some are so lofty, my eyes ache to look up to them; others so low, I disdain to stoop for them. *One*, only, seems fitted to my powers, and to my wishes—*one, alone*, engages my attention! Is not its possession worthy an arduous effort? *Perseverance* can turn the course of rivers, and level mountains! Shall I, then, relinquish my efforts, when, perhaps, on the very verge of success?

'The mind must have an object:—should I desist from my present pursuit, after all it has cost me, for what can I change it? I feel, that I am neither a philosopher, nor a heroine—but a *woman, to whom education has given a sexual character*. It is true, I have risen superior to the generality of my *oppressed sex*; yet, I have neither the talents for a legislator, nor for a reformer, of the world. I have still many female foibles, and shrinking delicacies, that unfit me for rising to arduous heights. Ambition cannot stimulate me, and to accumulate wealth, I am still less fitted. Should I, then, do violence to my heart, and compel it to resign its hopes and expectations, what can preserve me from sinking into, the most abhorred of all states, *languor and inanity*?—Alas! that tender and faithful heart refuses to change its object—it can never love another. Like Rousseau's Julia,* my strong individual attachment has annihilated every man in the creation:—him I love appears, in my eyes, something more—every other, something less.

'I have laboured to improve myself, that I might be worthy of the situation I have chosen. I would unite myself to a man of worth—I would have our mingled virtues and talents perpetuated in our offspring—I would experience those sweet sensations, of which nature has formed my heart so exquisitely susceptible. My ardent sensibilities incite me to love—to seek to inspire sympathy—to be beloved! My heart obstinately refuses to renounce the man, to whose mind my own seems akin! From the centre of private affections, it will at length embrace—like spreading circles on the peaceful bosom of the smooth and expanded lake—the whole sensitive and rational creation. Is it virtue, then, to combat, or to yield to, my passions?'

I considered, and reconsidered, these reasonings, so specious, so flattering, to which passion lent its force. One moment, my mind seemed firmly made up on the part I had to act;—I persuaded myself, that I had gone too far to recede, and that there remained for me no alternative:—the next instant, I shrunk, gasping, from my own resolves, and shuddered at the important consequences which they involved. Amidst a variety of perturbations, of conflicting emotions, I, at length, once more, took up my pen.

CHAPTER VII

TO AUGUSTUS HARLEY

'I BLUSH, when I reflect what a weak, wavering, inconsistent, being, I must lately have appeared to you. I write to you on important subjects—I forbid you to answer me on paper; and, when you seem inclined to put that period to the present, painful, high-wrought, and trying, state of my feelings, which is now become so necessary, I appear neither to hear, now to comprehend you. I fly from the subject, and thicken the cloud of mystery, of which I have so often, and, I still think, so justly complained.—These are some of the effects of the contradictory systems, that have so long bewildered our principles and conduct. A combination of causes, added to the conflict between a thousand delicate and nameless emotions, have lately conspired to confuse, to weaken, my spirits. You can conceive, that these acute, mental, sensations, must have had a temporary effect on the state of my health. To say truth (and, had I not said it, my countenance would have betrayed me), I have not, for some time past, been so thoroughly disordered.

'Once more, I have determined to rally my strength; for I feel, that a much longer continuance in the situation, in which my mind has been lately involved, would be insupportable:—and I call upon you, *now*, with a resolution to summon all my fortitude to bear the result, for the *written* state of your mind, on the topic become so important to my future welfare and usefulness.

'You may suppose, that a mind like mine must have, repeatedly, set itself to examine, on every side, all that could possibly have a relation to a subject affecting it so materially. You have hinted at *mysterious* obstacles to the wish, in which every faculty of my soul has been so long absorbed—the wish of forming with you, a connection, nearer, *and more tender*, than that of friendship. This mystery, by leaving room for conjecture (and how frequently have I warned you of this!), left room for the illusions of imagination, and of hope—left room for the suspicion, that you might, possibly, be sacrificing *your own feelings*, as well as mine, to a mistaken principle. Is it possible that you were not aware of this—you, who are not unacquainted with the nature of mind! Still less were you ignorant of the nature of my mind—which I had so explicitly, so unreservedly, laid open? I had a double claim upon your confidence—a confidence, that I was utterly incapable of abusing, or betraying—a confidence, which must have stopped my mind in its career—which would have saved me the bitter, agonizing, pangs I have sustained. Mine were not common feelings—It is *obscurity* and *mystery* which has wrought them up to frenzy—*truth* and *certainty* would, long ere this, have caused them temperately to subside into their accustomed channels. You understand little of the human heart, if you cannot conceive this—"Where the imagination is vivid, the feelings strong, the views and desires not bounded by common rules;—in such minds, passions, if not subdued, become ungovernable and fatal: where there is much warmth, much enthusiasm, there is much danger.—My mind is no less ardent than yours, though education and habit may have given it a different turn—it glows with equal zeal to attain its end."[1]* Yes, I must continue to repeat, there has been in your conduct *one grand mistake*; and the train of consequences which may, yet, ensue, are uncertain, and threatening.—But, I mean no reproach——we are all liable to errors; and my own, I feel, are many, and various. But to return——

'You may suppose I have revolved, in my thoughts, every possible difficulty on the subject alluded to; balancing their degrees of probability and force:—and, I will frankly confess, such is the sanguine ardour of my temper, that I can conceive but one obstacle, that would be *absolutely invincible*; which is, supposing that you have already contracted a *legal, irrevocable*, engagement. Yet, this I do not suppose. I will arrange, under five heads, (on all occasions, I love to class and methodize) every other possible species of objection, and subjoin all the reasonings which have occurred to me on the subjects.

'And, first, I will imagine, as the most serious and threatening difficulty, that you love another. I would, then, ask—Is she capable of estimating your worth—does she love you—has she the magnanimity to tell you so—would she sacrifice to that affection every meaner consideration—has she merit to secure, as well as accomplishments to attract, your regard?——You are too well acquainted with the human heart, not to be aware, that what is commonly called love is of a fleeting nature, kept alive only by hopes and fears, if the qualities upon which it is founded afford no basis for its subsiding into tender confidence, and rational esteem. Beauty may inspire a transient desire, vivacity amuse, for a time, by its sportive graces; but the first will quickly fade and grow familiar—the last degenerate into impertinence and insipidity. Interrogate your own heart—Would you not, when the ardour of the passions, and the fervor of the imagination, subsided, wish to find the sensible, intelligent, friend, take place of the engaging

[1] Holcroft's *Anna St Ives*.

mistress?—Would you not expect the economical manager of your affairs, the rational and judicious mother to your offspring, the faithful sharer of your cares, the firm friend to your interest, the tender consoler of your sorrows, the companion in whom you could wholly confide, the discerning participator of your nobler pursuits, the friend of your virtues, your talents, your reputation—who could understand you, who was formed to pass the ordeal of honour, virtue, friendship?—Ask yourself these questions—ask them closely, without sophistry, and without evasion. You are not, now, an infatuated boy! Supposing, then, that you are, at present, entangled in an engagement which answers not this description—Is it virtue to fulfil, or to renounce, it? Contrast with it my affection, with its probable consequences, and weigh our different claims! *Would you have been the selected choice, of this woman, from all mankind*—would no other be capable of making her equally happy—would nothing compensate to her for your loss—are you the only object that she beholds in creation—might not another engagement suit her equally well, or better—is her whole soul absorbed but by one sentiment, that of fervent love for you—is her future usefulness, as well as peace, at stake—does she understand your high qualities better than myself—will she emulate them more?—Does the engagement promise a favourable issue, or does it threaten to wear away the best period of life in protracted and uncertain feeling—*the most pernicious, and destructive, of all states of mind*? Remember, also, that the summer of life will quickly fade; and that he who has reached the summit of the hill, has no time to lose— if he seize not the present moment, age is approaching, and life melting fast away.—I quit this, to state my second hypothesis—

'That you esteem and respect me, but that your heart has hitherto refused the sympathies I have sought to awaken in it. If this be the case, it remains to search for the reason; and, I own, I am at a loss to find it, either in moral, or physical, causes. Our principles are in unison, our tastes and habits not dissimilar, our knowledge of, and confidence in, each other's virtues is reciprocal, tried, and established—our ages, personal accomplishments, and mental acquirements do not materially differ. From such an union, I conceive, mutual advantages would result. I have found myself distinguished, esteemed, beloved, by others, where I have not sought for this distinction. How, then, can I believe it compatible with the nature of mind, that so many strong efforts, and reiterated impressions, can have produced no effect upon yours? Is your heart constituted differently from every other human heart?—I have lately observed an inequality in your behaviour, that has whispered something flattering to my heart. Examine yourself—Have you felt no peculiar interest in what concerns me—would the idea of our separation affect you with no more than a slight and common emotion?——One more question propose to yourself, as a test—Could you see me form a new, and a more fortunate, attachment, with indifference? If you cannot, without hesitation, answer these questions, I have still a powerful pleader in your bosom, though unconscious of it yourself, that will, ultimately, prevail. If I have, yet, failed of producing an unequivocal effect, it must arise from having mistaken the *means* proper to produce the desired *end*. My own sensibility, and my imperfect knowledge of your character may, here, have combined to mislead me. The first, by its suffocating and depressing powers, clouding my vivacity, incapacitating me from appearing to you with my natural advantages—these effects would diminish as assurance took place of doubt. The last, every day would contribute to correct. Permit me, then, *to hope for*, as well as to seek your affections, and if I do not, at length, gain and secure them, it will be a phenomenon in the history of mind!

'But to proceed to my third supposition—The peculiar, pecuniary, embarrassments of your situation—Good God! did this barbarous, insidious, relation, allow himself to consider the pernicious consequences of his absurd bequest?—threatening to undermine every manly principle, to blast every social virtue! Oh! that I had the eloquence to rouse you from this tame and unworthy acquiescence—to stimulate you to exercise your talents, to trust to the independent energies of your mind, to exert yourself to procure the honest rewards of virtuous industry. In proportion as we lean for support on foreign aid, we lose the dignity of our nature, and palsey* those powers which constitute that nature's worth. Yet, I will allow, from my knowledge of your habits and associations, this obstacle its full force. But there remains one method of obviating, even this! I will frankly confess, that could I hope to gain the interest in your heart, which I have so long and so earnestly sought—my confidence in your honour and integrity, my tenderness for you, added to the wish of contributing to your happiness, would effect, what no lesser considerations could have effected—would triumph, not over my principles, (*for the individuality of an affection constitutes its chastity*) but over my prudence. I repeat, I am willing to sacrifice every inferior consideration—retain your legacy, so capriciously bequeathed—retain your present situation, and I will retain mine. This proposition, though not a violation of modesty, certainly involves in it very serious hazards—*It is, wholly, the triumph of affection!* You cannot suppose, that a transient engagement would satisfy a mind like mine; I should require a reciprocal faith plighted and returned—an after separation, otherwise than by mutual consent, would be my destruction—I should not survive your desertion. My existence, then, would be in your hands. Yet, having once confided, your affection should be my recompence—my sacrifice should be a cheerful and a voluntary one; I would determine not to harrass you with doubts nor jealousies, I would neither reflect upon the past, nor distrust the future: I would rest upon you, I would confide in you fearlessly and entirely! but, though I would not enquire after the past, my delicacy would require the assurance of your present, undivided, affection.

'The fourth idea that has occurred to me, is the probability of your having formed a plan of seeking some agreeable woman of fortune, who should be willing to reward a man of merit for the injustice of society. Whether you may already have experienced some disappointments of this nature, I will not pretend to determine. I can conceive, that, by many women, a coxcomb might be preferred to you——however this may be, the plan is not unattended with risque, nor with some possible degrading circumstances—and you may succeed, and yet be miserable: happiness depends not upon the abundance of our possessions.

'The last case which I shall state, and on which I shall lay little comparative stress, is the possibility of an engagement of a very inferior nature—a mere affair of the senses. The arguments which might here be adduced are too obvious to be repeated. Besides, I think highly of your refinement and delicacy—Having therefore just hinted, I leave it with you.

'And now to conclude—After considering all I have urged, you may, perhaps, reply—That the subject is too nice* and too subtle for reasoning, and that the heart is not to be compelled. These, I think, are mistakes. There is no subject, in fact, that may not be subjected to the laws of investigation and reasoning. What is it that we desire— *pleasure—happiness*? I allow, pleasure is the supreme good: but it may be analyzed—it must have a stable foundation— to this analysis I now call you! This is the critical moment, upon which hangs a long chain of events*—This moment may decide your future destiny and mine—it may, even, affect that of unborn myriads! My spirit is pervaded with these important ideas—my heart flutters—I breathe with difficulty—*My friend—I would give myself to you*—the gift is not worthless. Pause a moment, ere you rudely throw from you an affection so tried, so respectable, so worthy of you! The heart may be compelled—compelled by the touching sympathies which bind, with sacred, indissoluble ties, mind to mind! Do not prepare for yourself future remorse—when lost, you may recollect my worth, and my affection, and remember them with regret—Yet mistake me not, I have no intention to intimidate—I think it my duty to live, while I may possibly be useful to others, however bitter and oppressive may be that existence. I will live *for duty*, though peace and enjoyment should be for ever fled. You may rob me of my happiness, you may rob me of my strength, but, even, you cannot destroy my principles. And, if no other motive with-held me from rash determinations, my tenderness for you (it is not a selfish tenderness), would prevent me from adding, to the anxieties I have already given you, the cruel pang, of feeling yourself the occasion, however unintentionally, of the destruction of a fellow creature.

'While I await your answer, I summon to my heart all its remaining strength and spirits. Say to me, in clear and decisive terms, that the obstacles which oppose my affection *are absolutely, and altogether, insuperable*—Or that there is a possibility of their removal, but that time and patience are, yet, necessary to determine their force. In this case, I will not disturb the future operations of your mind, assuring myself, that you will continue my suspence no longer than is proper and requisite—or frankly accept, and return, the faith of her to whom you are infinitely dearer than life itself!

'Early to-morrow morning, a messenger shall call for the paper, which is to decide the colour of my future destiny. Every moment, that the blow has been suspended, it has acquired additional force—since it must, at length, descend, it would be weakness still to desire its protraction—We have, already, refined too much—*I promise to live*—more, alas! *I cannot promise.*

'*Farewel!* dearest and most beloved of men—whatever may be my fate—*be happiness yours!* Once more, my lingering, foreboding heart, repeats *farewel!*

'EMMA.'

It would be unnecessary to paint my feelings during the interval in which I waited a reply to this letter—I struggled to repress hope, and to prepare my mind for the dissolution of a thousand air-built fabrics. The day wore tediously away in strong emotion, and strong exertion. On the

subsequent morning, I sat, waiting the return of my messenger, in a state of mind, difficult even to be conceived—
I heard him enter—breathless, I flew to meet him—I held
out my hand—I could not speak.

'Mr Harley desired me to tell you, *he had not had time to
write.*'

Gracious God! I shudder, even now, to recall the convulsive sensation! I sunk into a chair—I sat for some time
motionless, every faculty seemed suspended. At length,
returning to recollection, I wrote a short incoherent note,
entreating—

'To be spared another day, another night, like the
preceding—I asked only *one single line*! In the morning I
had made up my mind to fortitude—it was now sinking—
another day, I could not answer for the consequences.'

Again an interval of suspense—again my messenger returned with a verbal reply—'*He would write to-morrow.*' Unconsciously, I exclaimed—'*Barbarous, unfeeling, unpitying,
man*!' A burst of tears relieved—no—*it did not relieve
me*. The day passed—I know not how—I dare not
recollect.

The next morning, I arose, somewhat refreshed; my
exhausted strength and spirits had procured me a few
hours of profound slumber. A degree of resentment gave
a temporary firmness to my nerves. 'What happiness (I
repeated to myself) could I have expected with a man,
thus regardless of my feelings?' I composed my spirits—
hope was at an end—into a sort of sullen resignation to my
fate—a half stupor!

At noon the letter arrived, coldly, confusedly written;
methought there appeared even a degree of irritation
in it.

'*Another, a prior attachment*—His behaviour had been
such, as necessarily resulted from such an engagement—
unavoidable circumstances had prevented an earlier reply.' My swollen heart—but it is enough—'He blamed my
impatience—he would in future, perhaps, when my mind
had attained more composure, make some remarks on my
letter.'

CHAPTER VIII

To write had always afforded a temporary relief to my spirits—The next day I resumed my pen.

'If, after reflecting upon, and comparing, many parts of your past conduct, you can acquit yourself, at the sacred bar of humanity—it is well! How often have I called for— urged, with all the energy of truth and feeling—but in vain—such a letter as you have at length written—and, *even, now,* though somewhat late, I thank you for it. Yet, what could have been easier, than to repeat so plain and so simple a tale? The vague hints, you had before given, I had repeatedly declared to be insufficient. Remember, all my earnestness, and all my simplicity, and *learn the value of sincerity*! "Oh! with what difficulty is an active mind, once forced into any particular train, persuaded to desert it as hopeless!"[1]*

'This recital, then, was not to be confirmed, till the whole moral conformation of my mind was affected—till the barbed arrow had fixed, and rankled in, and poisoned, with its envenomed point, every vein, every fibre, of my heart. This, I confess, is now the case—Reason and self-respect sustain me—but the wound you have inflicted *is indelible*—it will continue to be the corroding canker at the root of my peace. My youth has been worn in anguish— and the summer of life will probably be overshadowed by a still thicker and darker cloud. But I mean not to reproach you—it is not given me to contribute to your happiness—the dearest and most ardent wish of my soul— I would not then inflict unnecessary pain—yet, I would fix upon your mind, the value of *unequivocal sincerity*.

'Had the happiness of any human being, the meanest, the vilest, depended as much upon me, as mine has done upon you, I would have sacrificed, for their relief, the

---

[1] Godwin's *Caleb Williams.*

dearest secret of my heart—the secret, even upon which my very existence had depended. It is true, you did not directly deceive me—but is that enough for the delicacy of humanity? May the past be an affecting lesson to us both—it is written upon my mind in characters of blood. I feel, and acknowledge, my own errors, in yielding to the illusion of vague, visionary, expectation; but my faults have originated in a generous source—they have been the wild, ardent, fervent, excesses, of a vigorous and an exalted mind!

'I checked my tears, as they flowed, and they are already dried—uncalled, unwished, for—why do they, thus, struggle to force their way? my mind has, I hope, too much energy, utterly to sink—I know what it is to suffer, and to combat with, if not to subdue, my feelings—and *certainty*, itself, is some relief. I am, also, supported by the retrospect of my conduct; with all its mistakes, and all its extravagances, it has been that of a virtuous, ingenuous, uncorrupted, mind. You have contemned a heart of no common value, you have sported with its exquisite sensibilities—but it will, still, know how to separate your virtues from your errors.

'You reprove, perhaps justly, my impatience—I can only say, that circumstanced as you were, I should have stolen an hour from rest, from company, from business, however important, to have relieved and soothed a fellow-creature in a situation, so full of pain and peril. Every thought, during a day scarcely to be recollected without agony, *was a two-edged sword*—but some hours of profound and refreshing slumber recruited my exhausted spirits, and enabled me, yesterday, to receive my fate, with a fortitude but little hoped for.

'You would oblige me exceedingly by the remarks you allow me to hope for, on my letter of the ——th. You know, I will not shrink from reproof—that letter afforded you the last proof of my affection, and I repent not of it. I loved you, first, for what, I conceived, high qualities of mind—from nature and association, my tenderness became personal—till at length, I loved you, not only rationally and tenderly—*but passionately*—it became a pervading and a devouring fire! And, yet, I do not blush—my affection was modest, if intemperate, *for it was individual*—it annihilated in my eyes every other man in the creation. I regret these natural sensations and affections, their forcible suppression injures the mind—it converts the mild current of gentle, and genial sympathies, into a destructive torrent. This, I have the courage to avow it, has been one of the miserable mistakes in morals, and, like all other partial remedies, has increased the evil, it was intended to correct. From monastic institutions and principles have flowed, as from a polluted source, streams, that have at once spread through society a mingled contagion of dissoluteness and hypocrisy.

'You have suddenly arrested my affections in their full career—in all their glowing effervescence—you have taken

> "The rose
> From the fair forehead of an innocent love,
> And placed a blister there."*

'And, yet, I survive the shock, and determine to live, not for future enjoyment—that is now, for ever, past—*but for future usefulness*—Is not this virtue?

'I am sorry your attachment has been, and I fear is likely to be, protracted—I know, too well, the misery of these situations, and I should, now, feel a melancholy satisfaction in hearing of its completion—In that completion, may you experience no disappointment! I do not wish you to be beloved, as I have loved you; this, perhaps, is unnecessary; such an affection, infallibly, enslaves the heart that cherishes it; and slavery is the tomb of virtue and of peace.

'I believe it would not be proper for us to meet again—at least at present—should I hear of sickness, or calamity, befalling you, I shall, I suspect, be impelled, by an irresistible impulse to seek you—but I will no more interrupt your repose—Though you have contemned my affection, my friendship will still follow you.

'If you really *love*, I think you ought to make some sacri-
fices, and not render yourself, and the happy object of
your tenderness, the victims of factitious notions.—Remember—youth and life will quickly fade. Relinquish, call
upon her to relinquish, her prejudices—should she refuse,
she is unworthy of you, and you will regret, too late, the
tender, faithful, ingenuous, heart, that you have pierced
through and through—*that you have almost broken*! Should
she make you happy, I will esteem, though I may never
have an opportunity of thanking, her—Were she informed
of my conduct, she might rejoice in the trial of your affection—though I should not.

'The spirits, that had crouded round my heart, are
already subsiding—a flood of softness, a tide of overwhelming reflection, gushes upon it—and I feel sinking
into helpless, infantine, distress! Hasten to me your promised remarks—they will rouse, they will strengthen, me.—
Truth I will never call either indelicate or inhuman—it is
only the virtuous mind can dare to practise, to challenge,
it:—simplicity is true refinement.

'Let us reap from the past all the good we can—a close,
and searching, knowledge of the secret springs and
foldings of our hearts. Methinks, I could wish you justified, *even at my own expence.*—I ask, unshrinking, a frank
return.

'A heart-rending sigh accompanies my farewel—the last
struggles of expiring nature will be far less painful—but
my philosophy, now, *sternly* calls upon me to put its precepts in practice——trembling—shuddering—I obey!
              '*Farewel!*

                                        'EMMA.'

Perhaps it cost me some efforts to make the preceding
letter so moderate—yet, every victory gained over ourselves is attended with advantages. But this apparent calm
was the lethargy of despair——it was succeeded by severer
conflicts, by keener anguish. A week passed, and near a
second—I received no answer.

CHAPTER IX

A LETTER from the country made it necessary for me, again, to address Mr Harley, to make some enquiries which respected business of his mother's. It may be, that I felt a mixture of other motives;——it is certain, that when I wrote, I spoke of more than business.

'I had hoped,' I told him, 'ere this, to have received the promised letter—Yet, I do not take up my pen,' said I, 'either to complain of, or to importune, you. If I have already expressed myself with bitterness, let the harrassed state of my mind be my excuse. My own conduct has been too erroneous, too eccentric, to enable me to judge impartially of your's. Forgive me, if, by placing you in an embarrassed situation, I have exposed you to consequent mistake or uneasiness. I feel, that whatever errors we may either of us have committed, *originated only with myself*, and I am content to suffer all the consequences. It is true, had you reposed in me an early, generous, confidence, much misery would have been avoided—I had not been wounded

"There, where the human heart most exquisitely feels!"*

'You had been still my friend, and I had been comparatively happy. Every passion is, in a great measure, the growth of indulgence: all our desires are, in their commencement, easily suppressed, when there appears no probability of attaining their object; but when strengthened, by time and reflection, into habit, in endeavouring to eradicate them, we tear away part of the mind. In my attachments there is a kind of savage tenacity—they are of an elastic nature, and, being forced back, return with additional violence.

'My affection for you has not been, altogether, irrational or selfish. While I felt that I loved you, as no other woman, I was convinced, would love you—I conceived, could I once engage your heart, I could satisfy, and, even, purify it.

While I loved your virtues, I thought I saw, and I lamented, the foibles which sullied them. I suspected you, perhaps erroneously, of pride, ambition, the love of distinction; yet your ambition could not, I thought, be of an ignoble nature—I feared that the gratifications you sought, if, indeed, attainable, were factitious—I even fancied I perceived you, against your better judgment, labouring to seduce yourself! "He is under a delusion," said I, to myself;—"reason may be stunned, or blinded, for awhile; but it will revive in the heart, and do its office, when sophistry will be of no avail." I saw you struggling with vexations, that I was assured might be meliorated by tender confidence— I longed to pour its balms into your bosom. My sensibility disquieted you, and myself, only *because it was constrained.* I thought I perceived a conflict in your mind—I watched its progress with attention and solicitude. A thousand times has my fluttering heart yearned to break the cruel chains that fettered it, and to chace the cloud, which stole over your brow, by the tender, yet chaste, caresses and endearments of ineffable affection! My feelings became too high wrought, and altogether insupportable. Sympathy for your situation, zeal for your virtues, love for your mind, tenderness for your person—a complication of generous, affecting, exquisite, emotions, impelled me to make one great effort—"The world might call my plans absurd, my views romantic, my pretensions extravagant—Was I, or was I not, guilty of any crime, when, in the very acme of the passions, I so totally disregarded the customs of the world?"[1]* Ah! what were my sensations—what did I not suffer, in the interval?—and you prolonged that cruel interval—and still you suffer me to doubt, whether, at the moment in my life when I was actuated by the highest, the most fervent, the most magnanimous, principles—whether, at that moment when I most deserved your respect, I did not for ever forfeit it.

'I seek not to extenuate any part of my conduct—I confess that it has been wild, extravagant, romantic—I

---

[1] Holcroft's *Anna St. Ives.*

confess, that, even for your errors, I am justly blameable—
and yet I am unable to bear, because I feel they would be
unjust, your hatred and contempt. I cherish no resentment—my spirit is subdued and broken—your unkindness
sinks into my soul.

'EMMA.'

Another fortnight wore away in fruitless expectation—the
morning rose, the evening closed, upon me, in sadness.
I could not, yet, think the mystery developed: on a concentrated view of the circumstances, they appeared to me
contradictory, and irreconcileable. A solitary enthusiast, a
child in the drama of the world, I had yet to learn, that
those who have courage to act upon advanced principles,
must be content to suffer moral martyrdom.[1] In subduing
our own prejudices, we have done little, while assailed
on every side by the prejudices of others. My own heart
acquitted me; but I dreaded that distortion of mind,
that should wrest guilt out of the most sublime of its
emanations.

I ruminated, in gloomy silence, on my forlorn, and
hopeless, situation. 'If there be not a future state of being,'
said I to myself, 'what is this!—Tortured in every stage of it,
"Man cometh forth like a flower, and is cut down—he
fleeth, as a shadow, and continueth not!"*——I looked
backward on my past life, and my heart sickened—its confidence in humanity was shaken—I looked forward, and all
was cheerless. I had certainly committed many errors!——
Who has not—who, with a fancy as lively, feelings as acute,
and a character as sanguine, as mine? "What, in fact," says
a philosophic writer,[2] "is character?—the production of a
lively and constant affection, and, consequently, of a
strong passion;"*—eradicate that passion, that ferment,
that leaven, that exuberance, which raises and makes the
mind what it is, and what remains? Yet, let us beware how

[1] This sentiment may be just in some particular cases, but it is by
no means of general application, and must be understood with great
limitations.
[2] Helvetius.

we wantonly expend this divine, this invigorating, power. Every grand error, in a mind of energy, in its operation and consequences, carries us years forward—*precious years, never to be recalled!*' I could find no substitute for the sentiment I regretted—for that sentiment formed my character; and, but for the obstacles which gave it force, though I might have suffered less misery, I should, I suspect, have gained less improvement; still adversity *is a real evil*; and I foreboded that this improvement had been purchased too dear.

CHAPTER X

Weeks elapsed ere the promised letter arrived—a letter still colder, and more severe, than the former. I wept over it, bitter tears! It accused me 'of adding to the vexations of a situation, before sufficiently oppressive.'——Alas! had I known the nature of those vexations, could I have merited such a reproof? The Augustus, I had so long and so tenderly loved, no longer seemed to exist. Some one had, surely, usurped his signature, and imitated those characters, I had been accustomed to trace with delight. He tore himself from me, *nor would he deign to soften the pang of separation.* Anguish overwhelmed me—my heart was pierced. Reclining my head on my folded arms, I yielded myself up to silent grief. Alone, sad, desolate, no one heeded my sorrows—no eye pitied me—no friendly voice cheered my wounded spirit! The social propensities of a mind forbidden to expand itself, forced back, preyed incessantly upon that mind, secretly consuming its powers.

I was one day roused from these melancholy reflections by the entrance of my cousin, Mrs Denbeigh. She held in her hand a letter, from my only remaining friend, Mrs Harley. I snatched it hastily; my heart, lacerated by the seeming unkindness of him in whom it had confided, yearned to imbibe the consolation, which the gentle tenderness of this dear, maternal, friend, had never failed to administer. The first paragraph informed me—

'That she had, a few days since, received a letter from the person to whom the legacy of her son devolved, should he fail in observing the prescribed conditions of the testator: that this letter gave her notice, that those conditions had already been infringed, Mr Harley having contracted a marriage, three years before, with a foreigner, with whom he had become acquainted during his travels; that this marriage had been kept a secret, and, but very lately, by an accidental concurrence of circumstances, revealed to the person most concerned in the detection. Undoubted proofs of the truth of this information could be produced; it would therefore be most prudent in her son to resign his claims, without putting himself, and the legal heir, to unnecessary expence and litigation. Ignorant of the residence of Mr Harley, the writer troubled his mother to convey to him these particulars.'

The paper dropped from my hand, the colour forsook my lips and cheeks;—yet I neither wept, nor fainted. Mrs Denbeigh took my hands—they were frozen—the blood seemed congealed in my veins—and I sat motionless—my faculties suspended, stunned, locked up! My friend spake to me—embraced, shed tears over, me—but she could not excite mine;—my mind was pervaded by a sense of confused misery. I remained many days in this situation— it was a state, of which I have but a feeble remembrance; and I, at length, awoke from it, as from a troublesome dream.

With returning reason, the tide of recollection also returned. Oh! how complicated appeared to me the guilt of Augustus! Ignorant of his situation, I had been unconsciously, and perseveringly, exerting myself to seduce the affections of a *husband* from his *wife*. He had made me almost criminal in my own eyes—he had risqued, at once, by a disingenuous and cruel reserve, the virtue and the happiness of three beings. What is virtue, but a calculation of *the consequences of our actions?* Did we allow ourselves to reason on this principle, to reflect on its truth and importance, we should be compelled to shudder at many parts of our conduct, which, *taken unconnectedly*, we have habituated ourselves to consider as almost indifferent. Virtue can exist only in a mind capable of taking comprehensive views. How criminal, then, is ignorance!

During this sickness of the soul, Mr Francis, who had occasionally visited me since my residence in town, called, repeatedly, to enquire after my welfare; expressing a friendly concern for my indisposition. I saw him not—I was incapable of seeing any one—but, informed by my kind hostess of his humane attentions, soothed by the idea of having yet a friend who seemed to interest himself in my concerns, I once more had recourse to my pen (Mrs Denbeigh having officiously placed the implements of writing in my way), and addressed him in the wild and incoherent language of despair.

TO MR FRANCIS

'You once told me, that I was incapable of heroism; and you were right—yet, I am called to great exertions! a blow that has been suspended over my head, days, weeks, months, years, has at length fallen—still I live! My tears flow—I struggle, in vain, to suppress them, but they are not tears of blood!—My heart, though pierced through and through, is not broken!

'My friend, come and teach me how to acquire forti-tude—I am wearied with misery—All nature is to me a blank—an envenomed shaft rankles in my bosom—philos-ophy will not heal the festering wound—*I am exquisitely wretched!*

'Do not chide me till I get more strength—I speak to you of my sorrows, for your kindness, while I was yet a stranger to you, inspired me with confidence, and my desolate heart looks round for support.

'I am indebted to you—how shall I repay your goodness? Do you, indeed, interest yourself in my fate? Call upon me, then, for the few incidents of my life—I will relate them simply, and without disguise. There is nothing uncommon in them, but the effect which they have produced upon my mind—yet, that mind they formed.

'After all, my friend, what a wretched farce is life! Why cannot I sleep, and, close my eyes upon it for ever? But something whispers, *"this would be wrong."*—How shall I tear from my heart all its darling, close-twisted, associ-ations?—And must I live—*live for what?* God only knows! Yet, how am I sure that there is a God—is he wise—is he powerful—is he benevolent? If he be, can he sport himself in the miseries of poor, feeble, impotent, beings, forced into existence, without their choice—impelled, by the iron hand of necessity, through mistake, into calamity?—Ah! my friend, who will condemn the poor solitary wanderer,* whose feet are pierced with many a thorn, should he turn suddenly out of the rugged path, seek an obscure shade to shroud his wounds, his sorrows, and his indignation, from the scorn of a pitiless world, and accelerate the hour of repose.[1] Who would be born if they could help it? You would perhaps—*you may do good*—But on me, the sun shines only to mock my woes—Oh! that I had never seen the light.

'Torn by conflicting passions—wasted in anguish—life is melting fast away—A burthen to myself, a grief to those who love me, and worthless to every one. Weakened by long suspence—preyed upon, by a combination of imperi-ous feelings—I fear, I greatly fear, *the irrecoverable blow is struck!* But I blame no one—I have been entangled in error—*who is faultless?*

'While pouring itself out on paper, my tortured mind has experienced a momentary relief: If your heart be inac-cessible to tender sympathies, I have only been adding one more to my numberless mistakes!

'EMMA.'

Mr Francis visited me, and evinced for my situation the most humane and delicate consideration. He reminded me of the offer I had made him, and requested the per-

---

[1] This is the reasoning of a mind distorted by passion. Even in the moment of disappointment, our heroine judged better. See page 125.

formance of my engagement. In compliance with this request, and to beguile my melancholy thoughts, I drew up
a sketch of the events of my past life, and unfolded a
history of the sentiments of my mind (from which I have
extracted the preceding materials) reserving only any circumstance which might lead to a detection of the name
and family of the man with whom they were so intimately
blended.

CHAPTER XI

AFTER having perused my manuscript, Mr Francis returned it, at my desire, accompanied by the following
letter.

TO EMMA COURTNEY

'Your narrative leaves me full of admiration for your qualities, and compassion for your insanity.

'I entreat however your attention to the following passage, extracted from your papers. "After considering all I
have urged, you may perhaps reply, that the subject is too
nice, and too subtle, for reasoning, and that the heart is
not to be compelled. This, I think, is a mistake. There is no
topic, in fact, that may not be subjected to the laws of
investigation and reasoning. What is it we desire? pleasure,
happiness. What! the pleasure of an instant, only; or that
which is more solid and permanent? I allow, pleasure is the
supreme good! but it may be analysed. To this analysis I
now call you."

'Could I, if I had studied for years, invent a comment on
your story, more salutary to your sorrows, more immove-
able in its foundation, more clearly expressed, or more
irresistibly convincing to every rational mind?

'How few real, substantial, misfortunes there are in the
world! how few calamities, the sting of which does not
depend upon our cherishing the viper in our bosom, and
applying the aspic to our veins! The general pursuit of all
men, we are frequently told, is happiness. I have often

been tempted to think, on the contrary, that the general pursuit is misery. It is true, men do not recognize it by its genuine appellation; they content themselves with the pitiful expedient of assigning it a new denomination. But, if their professed purpose were misery, could they be more skilful and ingenious in the pursuit?

'Look through your whole life. To speak from your own description, was there ever a life, to its present period, less chequered with substantial *bona fide** misfortune? The whole force of every thing which looks like a misfortune was assiduously, unintermittedly, provided by yourself. You nursed in yourself a passion, which, taken in the degree in which you experienced it, is the unnatural and odious invention of a distempered civilization, and which in almost all instances generates an immense overbalance of excruciating misery. Your conduct will scarcely admit of any other denomination than moon-struck madness, hunting after torture. You addressed a man impenetrable as a rock, and the smallest glimpse of sober reflection, and common sense, would have taught you instantly to have given up the pursuit.

'I know you will tell me, and you will tell yourself, a great deal about constitution, early association, and the indissoluble chain of habits and sentiments. But I answer with small fear of being erroneous, "It is a mistake to suppose, that the heart is not to be compelled. There is no topic, in fact, that may not be subjected to the laws of investigation and reasoning. Pleasure, happiness, is the supreme good; and happiness is susceptible of being analysed." I grant, that the state of a human mind cannot be changed at once; but, had you worshipped at the altar of reason but half as assiduously as you have sacrificed at the shrine of illusion, your present happiness would have been as enviable, as your present distress is worthy of compassion. If men would but take the trouble to ask themselves, once every day, Why should I be miserable? how many, to whom life is a burthen, would become chearful and contented.

'Make a catalogue of all the real evils of human life;

bodily pain, compulsory solitude, severe corporal labour, in a word, all those causes which deprive us of health, or the means of spending our time in animated, various, and rational pursuits. Aye, these are real evils! But I should be ashamed of putting disappointed love into my enumeration. Evils of this sort are the brood of folly begotten upon fastidious indolence. They shrink into non-entity, when touched by the wand of truth.

'The first lesson of enlightened reason, the great fountain of heroism and virtue, the principle by which alone man can become what man is capable of being, is *independence.* May every power that is favourable to integrity, to honour, defend me from leaning upon another for support! I will use the world, I will use my fellow men, but I will not abuse these invaluable benefits of the system of nature. I will not be weak and criminal enough, to make my peace depend upon the precarious thread of another's life or another's pleasure. I will judge for myself; I will draw my support from myself—the support of my existence and the support of my happiness. The system of nature has perhaps made me dependent for the means of existence and happiness upon my fellow men taken collectively; but nothing but my own folly can make me dependent upon individuals. Will these principles prevent me from admiring, esteeming, and loving such as are worthy to excite these emotions? Can I not have a mind to understand, and a heart to feel excellence, without first parting with the fairest attribute of my nature?

'You boast of your sincerity and frankness. You have doubtless some reason for your boast—Yet all your misfortunes seem to have arisen from concealment. You brooded over your emotions, and considered them as a sacred deposit—You have written to me, I have seen you frequently, during the whole of this transaction, without ever having received the slightest hint of it, yet, if I be a fit counsellor now, I was a fit counsellor then; your folly was so gross, that, if it had been exposed to the light of day, it could not have subsisted for a moment. Even now you suppress the name of your hero: yet, unless I know how much of a hero and a model of excellence he would appear in my eyes, I can be but a very imperfect judge of the affair.

'——Francis.'

CHAPTER XII

To the remonstrance of my friend, which roused me from the languor into which I was sinking, I immediately replied—

TO MR FRANCIS

'You retort upon me my own arguments, and you have cause. I felt a ray of conviction dart upon my mind, even, while I wrote them. But what then?—"I seemed to be in a state, in which reason had no power; I felt as if I could coolly survey the several arguments of the case—perceive, that they had prudence, truth, and common sense on their side—And then answer—I am under the guidance of a director more energetic than you!"[1]* I am affected by your kindness—I am affected by your letter. I could weep over it, bitter tears of conviction and remorse. But argue with the wretch infected with the plague—will it stop the tide of blood, that is rapidly carrying its contagion to the heart? I blush! I shed burning tears! But I am still desolate and wretched! And how am I to help it? The force which you impute to my reasoning was the powerful frenzy of a high delirium.

'What does it signify whether, abstractedly considered, a misfortune be worthy of the names real and substantial, if the consequences produced are the same? That which embitters all my life, that which stops the genial current of health and peace is, whatever be its nature, a real calamity to me. There is no end to this reasoning—what individual can limit the desires of another? The necessaries of the civilized man are whimsical superfluities in the eye of the

[1] Godwin's Caleb Williams.

savage. Are we, or are we not (as you have taught me) the creatures of sensation and circumstance?

'I agree with you—and the more I look into society, the deeper I feel the soul-sickening conviction—"The general pursuit is misery"—necessarily—excruciating misery, from the source to which you justly ascribe it—"*The unnatural and odious inventions of a distempered civilization.*" I am content, you may perceive, to recognize things by their genuine appellation. I am, at least, a reasoning maniac: perhaps the most dangerous species of insanity. But while the source continues troubled, why expect the streams to run pure?

'You know I will tell you—"about the indissoluble chains of association and habit:" and you attack me again with my own weapons! Alas! while I confess their impotence, with what consistency do I accuse the flinty, impenetrable, heart, I so earnestly sought, in vain, to move? What materials does this stubborn mechanism of the mind offer to the wise and benevolent legislator!

'Had I, you tell me, "worshipped at the altar of reason, but half as assiduously as I have sacrificed at the shrine of illusion, my happiness might have been enviable." But do you not perceive, that my reason was the auxiliary of my passion, or rather my passion the generative principle of my reason? Had not these contradictions, these oppositions, roused the energy of my mind, I might have domesticated, tamely, in the lap of indolence and apathy.

'I do ask myself, every day—"Why should I be miserable?"—and I answer, "Because the strong, predominant, sentiment of my soul, close twisted with all its cherished associations, has been rudely torn away, and the blood follows from the lacerated wound." You would be ashamed of placing disappointed love in your enumeration of evils! Gray was not ashamed of this—

> "And pining love shall waste their youth,
> And jealousy, with rankling tooth,
> That inly gnaws the secret heart!

———

> These shall the stings of falsehood try,
> And hard unkindness' alter'd eye,
> That mocks the tear it forc'd to flow."*

'Is it possible that you can be insensible of all the mighty mischiefs which have been caused by this passion—of the great events and changes of society, to which it has operated as a powerful, though secret, spring? That Jupiter shrouded his glories beneath a mortal form; that he descended yet lower, and crawled as a reptile—that Hercules took the distaff, and Sampson was shorn of his strength,* are, in their spirit, no fables. Yet, these were the legends of ages less degenerate than this, and states of society less corrupt. Ask your own heart—whether some of its most exquisite sensations have not arisen from sources, which, to nine-tenths of the world, would be equally inconceivable? Mine, I believe, is *a solitary madness in the eighteenth century: it is not on the altars of love, but of gold, that men, now, come to pay their offerings.*

'Why call woman, miserable, oppressed, and impotent, woman—*crushed, and then insulted*—why call her to *independence*—which not nature, but the barbarous and accursed laws of society, have denied her? *This is mockery!* Even you, wise and benevolent as you are, can mock the child of slavery and sorrow! "Excluded, as it were, by the pride, luxury, and caprice, of the world, from expanding my sensations, and wedding my soul to society, I was constrained to bestow the strong affections, that glowed consciously within me, upon a few."[1]* Love, in minds of any elevation, cannot be generated but upon a real, or fancied, foundation of excellence. But what would be a miracle in architecture, is true in morals—the fabric can exist when the foundation has mouldered away. *Habit* daily produces this wonderful effect upon every feeling, and every principle. Is not this the theory which you have taught me?

———

[1] Godwin's *Caleb Williams.*

'Am I not sufficiently ingenuous?—I will give you a new proof of my frankness (though not the proof you require).—From the miserable consequences of wretched moral distinctions, from chastity having been considered as a sexual virtue, all these calamities have flowed. Men are thus rendered sordid and dissolute in their pleasures; their affections vitiated, and their feelings petrified; the simplicity of modest tenderness loses its charm; they become incapable of satisfying the heart of a woman of sensibility and virtue.—Half the sex, then, are the wretched, degraded, victims of brutal instinct: the remainder, if they sink not into mere frivolity and insipidity, are sublimed into a sort of—(what shall I call them?)—refined, romantic, factitious, unfortunate, beings; who, for the sake of the present moment, dare not expose themselves to complicated, inevitable, evils; evils, that will infallibly overwhelm them with misery and regret! Woe be, more especially, to those who, possessing the dangerous gifts of fancy and feeling, find it as difficult to discover a substitute for the object as for the sentiment! You, who are a philosopher, will you still controvert the principles founded in truth and nature? "Gross as is my folly," (and I do not deny it) "you may perceive I was not wholly wandering in darkness." But while the wintry sun of hope illumined the fairy frost-work with a single, slanting, ray—dazzled by the transient brightness, I dreaded the meridian fervors that should dissolve the glittering charm. Yes! it was madness—but it was the pleasurable madness which none but madmen know.

'I cannot answer your question—Pain me not by its repetition; neither seek to ensnare me to the disclosure. Unkindly, severely, as I have been treated, I will not risque, even, the possibility of injuring the man, whom I have so tenderly loved, in the esteem of any one. Were I to name him, you know him not; you could not judge of his qualities. He is not "a model of excellence." I perceive it, with pain—and if obliged to retract my judgment on some parts of his character—I retract it with agonizing reluctance! But I could trace the sources of his errors, and candour and self-abasement imperiously compel me to a mild judgment, to stifle the petulant suggestions of a wounded spirit.

'Ought not our principles, my friend, to soften the asperity of our censures?—Could I have won him to my arms, I thought I could soften, and even elevate, his mind—a mind, in which I still perceive a great proportion of good. I weep for him, as well as for myself. He will, one day, know my value, and feel my loss. Still, I am sensible, that, by my extravagance, I have given a great deal of vexation (possibly some degradation), to a being, whom I had no right to persecute, or to compel to chuse happiness through a medium of my creation. I cannot exactly tell the extent of the injury I may have done him. A long train of consequences succeed, even, our most indifferent actions.—Strong energies, though they answer not the end proposed, must yet produce correspondent effects. Morals and mechanics are here analogous. No longer, then, distress me by the repetition of a question I ought not to answer. I am content to be the victim—Oh! may I be the only victim—of my folly!

'One more observation allow me to make, before I conclude. That we can "admire, esteem, and love," an individual—(for love in the abstract, loving mankind collectively, conveys to me no idea)—which must be, in fact, depending upon that individual for a large share of our felicity, and not lament his loss, in proportion to our apprehension of his worth, appears to me a proposition, involving in itself an absurdity; therefore demonstrably false.

'Let me, my friend, see you ere long—your remonstrance has affected me—save me from myself!'

TO THE SAME
(In Continuation)

'My letter having been delayed a few days, through a mistake—I resume my pen; for, running my eye over what I had written, I perceive (confounded by the force of your expressions) I have granted you too much. My conduct was

not, altogether, so insane as I have been willing to allow. It
is certain, that could I have attained the end proposed, my
happiness had been encreased. "It is necessary for me to
love and admire, or I sink into sadness."* The behaviour of
the man, whom I sought to move, appeared to me too
inconsistent to be the result of *indifference*. To be roused
and stimulated by obstacles—obstacles admitting hope,
because obscurely seen—is no mark of weakness. Could I
have subdued, what I, *then*, conceived to be the *prejudices* of
a worthy man, I could have increased both his happiness
and my own. I deeply reasoned, and philosophized, upon
the subject. Perseverance, with little ability, has effected
wonders;—with perseverance, I felt, that, I had the power
of uniting ability—confiding in that power, I was the dupe
of my own reason. No other man, perhaps, could have
acted the part which this man has acted:—how, then, was
I to take such a part into my calculations?

   'Do not misconceive me—it is no miracle that I did not
inspire affection. On this subject, the mortification I have
suffered has humbled me, it may be, even, unduly in my
own eyes—but to the emotions of my pride, I would disdain to give words. Whatever may have been my feelings, I
am too proud to express the rage of slighted love!—Yet, I
am sensible to all the powers of those charming lines of
Pope—

> "Unequal task, a passion to resign,
> For hearts so touch'd, so pierc'd, so lost, as mine!
> Ere such a soul regains its peaceful state,
> How often must it love, how often hate;
> How often hope, despair, resent, regret,
> Conceal, disdain, *do all things but forget!*"*

'But to return. I pursued, comparatively, (as I thought) a
certain good; and when, at times, discouraged, I have
repeated to myself—What! after all these pains, shall I
relinquish my efforts, when, perhaps, on the very verge of
success?—To say nothing of the difficulty of forcing an
active mind out of its trains—if I desisted, what was to be

the result? The sensations I now feel—apathy, stagnation, abhorred vacuity!

'You cannot resist the force of my reasoning—you, who are acquainted with, who know how to paint, in colours true to nature, the human heart—you, who admire, as a proof of power, the destructive courage of an Alexander, even the fanatice fury of a Ravaillac—you, who honour the pernicious ambition of an Augustus Caesar,* as bespeaking the potent, energetic, mind!—why should *you* affect to be intolerant to a passion, though differing in nature, generated on the same principles, and by a parallel process. The capacity of perception, or of receiving sensation, is (or generates) the power; into what channel that power shall be directed, depends not on ourselves. Are we not the creatures of outward impressions? Without such impressions, should we be any thing? Are not passions and powers synonimous—or can the latter be produced without the lively interest that constitutes the former? Do you dream of annihilating the one—and will not the other be extinguished? With the apostle, Paul, permit me to say—"I am not mad, but speak the words of truth and soberness."*

'To what purpose did you read my confessions, but to trace in them a character formed, like every other human character, by the result of unavoidable impressions, and the chain of necessary events. I feel, that my arguments are incontrovertible:—I suspect that, by affecting to deny their force, you will endeavour to deceive either me or yourself.—I have acquired the power of reasoning on this subject at a dear rate—at the expence of inconceivable suffering. Attempt not to deny me the miserable, expensive, victory. I am ready to say—(ungrateful that I am)—Why did you put me upon calling forth my strong reasons?

'I perceive there is no cure for me—(apathy is, not the restoration to health, but, the morbid lethargy of the soul) but by a new train of impressions, of whatever nature, equally forcible with the past.—You will tell me, It remains with myself whether I will predetermine to resist such impressions. Is this true? Is it philosophical? Ask yourself. What!—can *even you* shrink from the consequences of your own principles?

'One word more—You accuse me of brooding in silence over my sensations—of considering them as a "sacred deposit." Concealment is particularly repugnant to my disposition—yet a thousand delicacies—a thousand nameless solicitudes, and apprehensions, sealed my lips!—He who inspired them was, alone, the depositary of my most secret thoughts!—my heart was unreservedly open before him—I covered my paper with its emotions, and transmitted it to him—like him who whispered his secret into the earth, to relieve the burden of uncommunicated thought. My secret was equally safe, and received in equal silence! Alas! he was not then ignorant of the effects it was likely to produce!

'EMMA.'

Mr Francis continued his humane and friendly attentions; and, while he opposed my sentiments, as conceiving them destructive of my tranquillity, mingled with his opposition a gentle and delicate consideration for my feelings, that sensibly affected me, and excited my grateful attachment. He judged right, that, by stimulating my mind into action, the sensations, which so heavily oppressed it, might be, in some measure, mitigated—by diverting the course of my ideas into different channels, and by that means abating their force. His kindness soothed and flattered me, and communication relieved my thoughts.

CHAPTER XIII

THE period which succeeded these events, though tedious in wearing away, marked by no vicissitude, has left little impression behind. The tenor of my days resembled the still surface of a stagnant lake, embosomed in a deep cavern, over which the refreshing breezes never sweep. Sad, vacant, inactive—the faculties both of mind and body

seemed almost suspended. I became weak, languid, enervated——my disorder was a lethargy of soul. This was
gradually succeeded by disease of body:—an inactivity, so
contrary to all the habits of my past life, generated morbid
humours, and brought on a slow, remitting, fever. I recovered, by degrees, from this attack, but remained for
some time in a debilitated, though convalescent, state. A
few weeks after my disorder returned, lasted longer, and
left me still more weakened and depressed. A third time it
assailed me, at a shorter interval; and, though less violent,
was more protracted, and more exhausting.

Mrs Denbeigh, alarmed by my situation, wrote to Mrs
Harley, expressing the apprehensions which she entertained. From this dear friend, who was herself in a declining state of health, I received a pressing invitation to visit,
once more, the village of F——; and to seek, from change
of air, change of scene, and the cordial endearments of
friendship, a restoration for my debilitated frame, and a
balm for my wounded mind.

My relation, at this period, had letters from her husband, informing her, that the term of his residence in
India was prolonged; pressing her to join him there, and
to come over in the next ship. To this request she joyfully
acceded; and, hearing that a packet was about to sail for
Bengal, secured her passage, and began immediately to
make preparations for her departure. I no longer hesitated to comply with the entreaties of my friend; besides
the tie of strong affection, which drew me to her, I had, at
present, little other resource.

After affectionately embracing Mrs Denbeigh, wishing a
happy issue to her voyage, thanking her for all her kindness, and leaving a letter of grateful acknowledgment for
Mr Francis, I quitted the metropolis, with an aching heart,
and a wasted frame. My cousin accompanied me to the
inn, from whence the vehicle set out that was to convey me
to Mrs Harley. We parted in silence—a crowd of retrospective ideas of the past, and solicitudes respecting the future,
occupied our thoughts—our sensations were too affecting
for words.

The carriage quitted London at the close of the evening, and travelled all night:—it was towards the end of the year. At midnight we passed over Hounslow and Bagshot heaths.* 'The moon,' to adopt the language of Ossian, 'looked through broken clouds, and brightened their dark-brown sides.'* A loud November blast howled over the heath, and whistled through the fern.—There was a melancholy desolation in the scene, that was in unison with my feelings, and which overwhelmed my spirits with a tide of tender recollections. I recalled to my imagination a thousand interesting images—I indulged in all the wild enthusiasm of my character. My fellow-travellers slept tranquilly, while my soul was awake to agonizing sorrow. I adopted the language of the tender Eloisa— 'Why,' said I, 'am I indebted for life to his care, whose cruelty has rendered it insupportable? Inhuman, as he is, let him fly from me for ever, and deny himself the savage pleasure of being an eye-witness to my sorrows!—But why do I rave thus?—He is not to be blamed—*I, alone, am guilty*—I, alone, am the author of my own misfortunes, and should, therefore, be the only object of anger and resentment.'[1]*

Weakened by my late indisposition, fatigued by the rough motion of the carriage, and exhausted by strong emotion, when arrived at the end of my journey, I was obliged to be lifted from the coach, and carried into the cottage of my friend. The servant led the way to the library—the door opened—Mrs Harley advanced, to receive me, with tottering steps. The ravages of grief, and the traces of sickness, were visible in her dear, affectionate, countenance. I clasped my hands, and, lifting up my eyes, beheld the portrait of Augustus—beheld again the resemblance of those features so deeply engraven on my heart! My imagination was raised—methought the lively colours of the complexion had faded, the benignant smile had vanished, and an expression of perplexity and sternness usurped its place. I uttered a faint shriek, and fell lifeless

[1] Rousseau.

into the arms of my friend. It was some time before I returned to sense and recollection, when I found myself on the bed, in the little chamber which had formerly been appropriated to my use. My friend sat beside me, holding my hand in her's, which she bathed with her tears. 'Thank God!' she exclaimed, in a rapturous accent, (as, with a deep sigh, I raised my languid eyes, and turned them mournfully towards her)—'she lives!—My Emma!—child of my affections!'—Sobs suppressed her utterance. I drew the hand, which held mine, towards me—I pressed it to my bosom———'*My mother!*'———I would have faid; but the tender appellation died away upon my lips, in inarticulate murmurs.

These severe struggles were followed by a return of my disorder. Mrs Harley would scarcely be persuaded to quit my chamber for a moment—her tenderness seemed to afford her new strength;—but these exertions accelerated the progress of an internal malady, which had for some time past been gaining ground, and gradually undermining her health.

Youth, and a good constitution, aided by the kind solicitudes of friendship, restored me, in a few weeks, to a state of convalescence. I observed the declining strength of my friend with terror—I accused myself of having, though involuntarily, added to these alarming symptoms, by the new fatigues and anxieties which I had occasioned her. Affection inspired me with those energies, that reason had vainly dictated. I struggled to subdue myself—I stifled the impetuous suggestions of my feelings, in exerting myself to fulfil the duties of humanity. My mind assumed a firmer tone—I became, once more, the cheerful companion, the tender consoler, the attentive nurse, of this excellent woman, to whose kindness I was so much indebted—and, if I stole a few moments in the day, while my friend reposed, to gaze on the resemblance of Augustus, to weep over the testimonies of his former respect and friendship, I quickly chased from my bosom, and my countenance, every trace of sadness, when summoned to attend my friend.

CHAPTER XIV

THE winter came on severe and cold. Mrs Harley was forbidden to expose herself to the frosty air, which seemed to invigorate my languid frame. I was constituted her al-moner,* to distribute to the neighbouring poor the scanty portion, which she was enabled, by a rigid œconomy, to spare from her little income: yet the value of this distri-bution had been more than redoubled, by the gentler charities of kind accents, tender sympathy, and wholesome counsels. To these indigent, but industrious, cottagers, I studied to be the worthy representative of their amiable benefactress, and found my regard in their grateful attach-ment, and the approving smiles of my friend.

By degrees, she ventured to converse with me on the subject nearest her heart—the situation of her son. He had been obliged to yield to the proofs produced of his marriage, which he had, at first, seemed desirous of evad-ing. He had written, with reserve, upon the subject to his mother; but, from the enquiries of a common friend, she had reason to apprehend, that his engagement had been of an imprudent nature. Two children were, already, the fruits of it: the mother, with a feminine helplessness of character, had a feeble constitution. The small fortune, which Augustus had originally shared with his family, was greatly reduced. His education and habits had unfitted him for those exertions which the support of an encreasing family necessarily required:—his spirits (her friend had informed her) seemed broken, and his temper soured. Some efforts had been made to serve him, which his lofty spirit had repelled with disdain.

This narration deeply affected my heart—I had resigned myself to his loss—but the idea of his suffering, I felt, was an evil infinitely severer. It was this conviction that preyed incessantly on the peace and health of his mother. My fortitude failed, when I would have tried to sustain her; and I could only afford the melancholy satisfaction of mingling my sorrows with her's.

The disorder of my friend rapidly increased—her mind became weakened, and her feelings wayward and irritable. I watched her incessantly—I strove, by every alleviating care, to soften her pains. Towards the approach of spring the symptoms grew more threatening; and it was judged, by her physician, necessary to apprize her family of her immediate danger. What a trial for my exhausted heart! I traced, with a trembling hand, a line to this melancholy purpose—addressed it to Mr Harley, and through him to his younger brother and sisters.

In a few days they arrived in the village—sending from the inn a servant, to prepare their mother for their approach. I gently intimated to her the visitants we might expect. The previous evening, a change had taken place, which indicated approaching dissolution; and her mind (not uncommon in similar cases) seemed, almost instantaneously, to have recovered a portion of its original strength. She sighed deeply, while her eyes, which were fixed wistfully on my face, were lighted with a bright, but transient, lustre.

'My dear Emma,' said she, 'this is a trying moment for us both. I shall soon close my eyes, for ever, upon all worldly cares—still cherish, in your pure and ingenuous mind, a friendship for my Augustus—the darling of my soul! He may, in future, stand in need of consolation. I had formed hopes—vain hopes!—in which you and he were equally concerned. In the happiness of this partially-favoured child—this idol of my affections—all mine was concentrated. He has disappointed me, and I have lost the desire of living—Yet, he has noble qualities? —Who, alas! is perfect? Summon your fortitude, collect your powers, my child, for this interview!'

She sunk upon her pillow—I answered her only with my tears. A servant entered—but spoke not—her look announced her tidings—It caught the eye of Mrs Harley——

'Let them enter,' said she; and she raised herself, to receive them, and assumed an aspect of composure.

I covered my face with my handkerchief—I heard the

sound of footsteps approaching the bed—I heard the murmurs of filial sorrow—The voice of Augustus, in low and interrupted accents, struck upon my ear—it thrilled through my nerves—I shuddered, involuntarily—What a moment! My friend spoke a few words, in a faint tone.

'My children,' she added, 'repay to this dear girl,' laying her hand upon mine, 'the debt of kindness I owe her—she has smoothed the pillow of death—she is an orphan—she is tender and unfortunate.'

I ventured to remove for a moment the handkerchief from my eyes—they met those of Augustus—he was kneeling by the bed-side—his countenance was wan, and every feature sunk in dejection; a shivering crept through my veins, and chilled my heart with a sensation of icy coldness—he removed his eyes, fixing them on his dying mother.

'My son,' she resumed, in still fainter accents, 'behold in Emma, your sister—*your friend!*—confide in her—she is worthy of your confidence!'—'Will you not love him, my child,'—(gazing upon me,)—'with a sisterly affection?'

I hid my face upon the pillow of my friend—I threw my arms around her—'Your request is superfluous, my friend, my more than parent, *ah, how superfluous!*'

'Forgive me, I know the tenderness of your nature—yielding, in these parting moments, to the predominant affection of my heart—I fear, I have wounded that tender nature. Farewel, my children! Love and assist each other—Augustus, where is your hand?—my sight fails me—God bless you and your little ones—*God bless you all!* My last sigh—my last prayer—is yours.'

Exhausted by these efforts, she fainted—Augustus uttered a deep groan, and raised her in his arms—but life was fled.

At the remembrance of these scenes, even at this period, my heart is melted within me.

What is there of mournful magic in the emotions of virtuous sorrow, that in retracing, in dwelling upon them, mingles with our tears a sad and sublime rapture? Nature, that has infused so much misery into the cup of human life, has kindly mixed this strange and mysterious ingredient to qualify the bitter draught.

CHAPTER XV

AFTER the performance of the last melancholy duties, this afflicted family prepared to separate. I received from them, individually, friendly offers of service, and expressions of acknowledgment, for my tender attentions to their deceased parent. I declined, for the present, their invitations, and proffered kindness, though uncertain how to dispose of myself, or which way to direct my course. Augustus behaved towards me with distant, cold, respect. I observed in his features, under a constrained appearance of composure, marks of deep and strong emotion. I recalled to my mind the injunctions of my deceased friend— I yearned to pour into his bosom the balm of sympathy, but, with an aspect bordering on severity, he repressed the expression of those ingenuous feelings which formed my character, and shunned the confidence I so earnestly sought. Unfortunate love had, in my subdued and softened mind, laid the foundation of a fervent and durable friendship—But my love, my friendship, were equally contemned! I relinquished my efforts—I shut myself in my chamber—and, in secret, indulged my sorrows.

The house of my deceased friend was sold, and the effects disposed of. On the day previous to their removal, and the departure of the family for London, I stole into the library, at the close of the evening, to view, for *the last time*, the scene of so many delightful, so many afflicting, emotions. A mysterious and sacred enchantment is spread over every circumftance, even every inanimate object, connected with the affections. To those who are strangers to these delicate, yet powerful sympathies, this may appear ridiculous—but the sensations are not the less genuine, nor the less in nature. I will not attempt to analyse them; it is a subject upon which the language of philosophy would appear frigid, and on which I feel myself every moment on the verge of fanaticism. Yet, affections like these are not so much weakness, as strength perhaps badly exerted. Rousseau was, right, when he asserted, that, 'Common men know nothing of violent sorrows, nor do great passions ever break out in weak minds. Energy of sentiment is the characteristic of a noble soul.'*

I gazed from the windows on the shrubbery, where I had so often wandered with my friends—where I had fondly cherished so many flattering, so many visionary, prospects. Every spot, every tree, was associated with some past pleasure, some tender recollection. The last rays of the setting sun, struggling from beneath a louring cloud, streamed through its dark bosom, illumined its edges, played on the window in which I was standing, and gilding the opposite side of the wainscot, against which the picture of Augustus still hung, shed a soft and mellow lustre over the features. I turned almost unconsciously, and contemplated it with a long and deep regard. It seemed to smile benignly—it wore no traces of the cold austerity, the gloomy and inflexible reserve, which now clouded the aspect of the original. I called to my remembrance a thousand interesting conversations—when

'Tuned to happy unison of soul, a fairer world of which the vulgar never had a glimpse, displayed, its charms.'*

Absorbed in thought, the crimson reflection from the western clouds gradually faded, while the deep shades of the evening, thickened by the appearance of a gathering tempest, involved in obscurity the object on which, without distinctly perceiving it, I still continued to gaze.

I was roused from this reverie by the sudden opening of the door. Some person, whom the uncertain light prevented me from distinguishing, walked across the room, with a slow and solemn pace, and, after taking several turns backwards and forwards, reclined on the sopha, remaining for some time perfectly still. A tremor shook my nerves—unable either to speak, or to move, I continued silent and trembling—my heart felt oppressed, almost to suffocation—at length, a deep, convulsive sigh, forced its way.

'My God!' exclaimed the person, whose meditations I had interrupted, 'what is that?'

It was the voice of Mr Harley, he spoke in a stern tone, though with some degree of trepidation, and advanced hastily towards the window against which I leaned.

The clouds had for some hours been gathering dark and gloomy. Just as Augustus had reached the place where I stood, a flash of lightning, pale, yet vivid, glanced suddenly across my startled sight, and discovered to him the object which had alarmed him.

'Emma,' said he, in a softened accent, taking my trembling and almost lifeless hand, 'how came you here, which way did you enter?'

I answered not—Another flash of lightning, still brighter, blue and sulphurous, illuminated the room, succeeded by a loud and long peal of thunder. Again the heavens seemed to rend asunder and discover a sheet of livid flame—a crash of thunder, sudden, loud, short, immediately followed, bespeaking the tempest near. I started with a kind of convulsive terror. Augustus led me from the window, and endeavoured, in vain, to find the door of the library—the temporary flashes, and total darkness by which they were succeeded, dazzled and confounded the sight. I stumbled over some furniture, which stood in the middle of the room, and unable to recover my feet, which refused any longer to sustain me, sunk into the arms of Augustus, suffering him to lift me to the sopha. He seated himself beside me, the storm continued; the clouds, every moment parting with a horrible noise, discovered an abyss of fire, while the rain descended in a deluge. We silently contemplated this sublime and terrible scene. Augustus supported me with one arm, while my trembling hand remained in his. The tempest soon exhausted itself by its violence—the lightning became less fierce, gleaming at intervals—the thunder rolled off to a distance—its protracted sound, lengthened by the echoes, faintly died away; while the rain continued to fall in a still, though copious, shower.

My spirits grew calmer, I gently withdrew my hand from

that of Mr Harley. He once more enquired, but in a tone
of greater reserve, how I had entered the room without his
knowledge? I explained, briefly and frankly, my situation,
and the tender motives by which I had been influenced.

'It was not possible,' added I, 'to take leave of this house
for ever, without recalling a variety of affecting and melancholy ideas—I feel, that I have lost *my only friend*.'

'This world,' said he, 'may not unaptly be compared to
the rapids on the American rivers—We are hurried, in a
frail bark, down the stream—It is in vain to resist its
course—happy are those whose voyage is ended!'

'My friend,' replied I in a faultering voice, 'I could teach
my heart to bear your loss—though, God knows, the lesson
has been sufficiently severe—but I know not how, with
fortitude, to see you suffer.'

'Suffering is the common lot of humanity—but, pardon
me, when I say, your conduct has not tended to lessen my
vexations!'

'My errors have been the errors of *affection*—Do they
deserve this rigor?'

'Their source is not important, their consequences have
been the same—you make not the allowances you claim.'

'Dear, and severe, friend!—Be not unjust—the confidence which I sought, and merited, would have
obviated'—

'I know what you would alledge—that confidence, you
had reason to judge, was of a painful nature—it ought not
to have been extorted.'

'If I have been wrong, my faults have been severely
expiated—if the error has been *only mine*, surely my
sufferings have been in proportion; seduced by the fervor
of my feelings; ignorant of your situation, if I wildly sought
to oblige you to chuse happiness through a medium of my
creation—yet, to have assured *yours*, was I not willing to
risque all my own? I perceive my extravagance, my views
were equally false and romantic—dare I to say—they were
the ardent excesses of a generous mind? Yes! my wildest
mistakes had in them a dignified mixture of virtue. While
the institutions of society war against nature and happi-

ness, the mind of energy, struggling to emancipate itself, will entangle itself in error'—

'Permit me to ask you,' interrupted Augustus, 'whether, absorbed in your own sensations, you allowed yourself to remember, and to respect, the feelings of others?'

I could no longer restrain my tears, I wept for some moments in silence—Augustus breathed a half-suppressed sigh, and turned from me his face.

'The pangs which have rent my heart,' resumed I, in low and broken accents, 'have, I confess, been but too poignant! That lacerated heart still bleeds—we have neither of us been guiltless—*Alas! who is?* Yet in my bosom, severe feelings are not more painful than transient—already have I lost sight of your unkindness, (God knows how little I merited it!) in stronger sympathy for your sorrows—whatever be their nature! We have both erred—why should we not exchange mutual forgiveness? Why should we afflict each other? Friendship, like charity, should suffer all things and be kind!'

'My mind,' replied he coldly, 'is differently constituted.'

'*Unpitying man!* It would be hard for us, if we were all to be judged at so severe a tribunal—you have been a *lover*,' added I, in a softer tone, 'and can you not forgive the faults of *love*?'

He arose, visibly agitated—I also stood up—my bosom deeply wounded, and, unknowing what I did, took his hand and pressed it to my lips.

'You have rudely thrown from you a heart of exquisite sensibility—you have contemned my love, and you disdain my friendship—is it brave, is it manly,' added I wildly—almost unconscious of what I said—forgetting at the moment his situation and my own—'thus to triumph over a spirit, subdued by its affections into unresisting meekness?'

He broke from me, and precipitately quitted the room.

I threw myself upon the floor, and, resting my head on the seat which Augustus had so lately occupied, passed the night in cruel conflict—a tempest more terrible than that which had recently spent its force, shook my soul! The

morning dawned, ere I had power to remove myself from
the fatal spot, where the measure of my afflictions seemed
filled up.—Virtue may conquer weakness, but who can
bear to be despised by those they love. The sun darted its
beams full upon me, but its splendour appeared mockery—hope and joy were for ever excluded from my benighted spirit. The contempt of the world, the scoffs of
ignorance, the contumely of the proud, I could have
borne without shrinking—but to find myself rejected, contemned, scorned, by him with whom, of all mankind, my
heart claimed kindred; by him for whom my youth, my
health, my powers, were consuming in silent anguish—
who, instead of pouring balm into the wound he had
inflicted, administered only corrosives!—*It was too painful.*
I felt, that I had been a lavish prodigal—that I had become
a wretched bankrupt; that there was but *one way* to make
me happy and *a thousand* to make me miserable! Enfeebled and exhausted, I crawled to my apartment, and,
throwing myself on the bed, gave a loose to the agony of
my soul.

CHAPTER XVI

UNDER pretence of indisposition, I refused to meet the
family. I heard them depart. Too proud to accept of obligation, I had not confided to them my plans, if plans they
could be called, where no distinct end was in view.

A few hours after their departure, I once more seated
myself in a stage coach, in which I had previously secured
a place, and took the road to London, I perceived, on
entering the carriage, only one passenger, who had placed
himself in the opposite corner, and in whom, to my great
surprise, I immediately recognized Mr Montague. We had
not met since the visit he had paid me at Mrs Harley's, the
result of which I have already related: since that period, it
had been reported in the village, that he addressed Sarah
Morton, and that they were about to be united. Montague
manifested equal surprise at our meeting: the intelligence

of my friend's death (at which he expressed real concern) had not reached him, neither was he acquainted with my being in that part of the country. He had not lately been at Mr Morton's, he informed me, but had just left his father's, and was going to London to complete his medical studies.

After these explanations, absorbed in painful contemplation, I for some time made little other return to his repeated civilities, than by cold monosyllables: till at length, his cordial sympathy, his gentle accents, and humane attentions, awakened me from my reverie. Ever accessible to the soothings of kindness, I endeavoured to exert myself, to prove the sense I felt of his humanity. Gratified by having succeeded in attracting my attention, he redoubled his efforts to cheer and amuse me. My dejected and languid appearance had touched his feelings, and, towards the end of our journey, his unaffected zeal to alleviate the anxiety under which I evidently appeared to labour, soothed my mind and inspired me with confidence.

He respectfully requested to know in what part of the town I resided, and hoped to be permitted to pay his respects to me, and to enquire after my welfare? This question awakened in my bosom so many complicated and painful sensations, that, after remaining silent for a few minutes, I burst into a flood of tears.

'I have no home;' said I, in a voice choked with sobs— 'I am an alien in the world—and alone in the universe.'

His eyes glistened, his countenance expressed the most lively, and tender, commiseration, while, in a timid and respectful voice, he made me offers of service, and entreated me to permit him to be useful to me.

'I then mentioned, in brief, my present unprotected situation, and hinted, that as my fortune was small, I could wish to procure a humble, but decent, apartment in a reputable family, till I had consulted one friend, who, I yet flattered myself, was interested in my concerns, or till I could fix on a more eligible method of providing for myself.'

He informed me—'That he had a distant relation in town, a decent, careful, woman, who kept a boarding house, and whose terms were very reasonable. He was assured, would I permit him to introduce me to her, she would be happy, should her accommodation suit me, to pay me every attention in her power.'

In my forlorn situation, I confided, without hesitation, in his recommendation, and gratefully acceded to the proposal.

Mr Montague introduced me to this lady in the most flattering terms, she received me with civility, but, I fancied, not without a slight mixture of distrust. I agreed with her for a neat chamber, with a sitting room adjoining, on the second floor, and settled for the terms of my board, more than the whole amount of the interest of my little fortune.

CHAPTER XVII

I took an early opportunity of addressing a few lines to Mr Francis, informing him of my situation, and entreating his counsel. I waited a week, impatiently, for his reply, but in vain: well acquainted with his punctuality, and alarmed by this silence, I mentioned the step I had taken, and my apprehensions, to Montague, who immediately repaired, himself, to the house of Mr Francis; and, finding it shut up, was informed by the neighbours, that Mr Francis had quitted England, a short time before, in company with a friend, intending to make a continental tour.

This intelligence was a new shock to me. I called on some of my former acquaintance, mentioning to them my wish of procuring pupils, or of engaging in any other occupation fitted to my talents. I was received by some with civility, by others with coldness, but every one appeared too much engrossed by his own affairs to give himself the trouble of making any great exertion for others.

I returned dispirited—I walked through the crowded city, and observed the anxious and busy faces of all around me. In the midst of my fellow beings, occupied in various pursuits, I seemed, as if in an immense desart, a solitary outcast from society. Active, industrious, willing to employ my faculties in any way, by which I might procure an honest independence, I beheld no path open to me, but that to which my spirit could not submit—the degradation of servitude. Hapless woman!—crushed by the iron hand of barbarous despotism, pampered into weakness, and trained the slave of meretricious folly!—what wonder, that, shrinking from the chill blasts of penury (which the pernicious habits of thy education have little fitted thy tender frame to encounter) thou listenest to the honied accents of the spoiler; and, to escape the galling chain of servile dependence, rushest into the career of infamy, from whence the false and cruel morality of the world forbids thy return, and perpetuates thy disgrace and misery! When will mankind be aware of the uniformity, of the importance, of truth? When will they cease to confound, by sexual, by political, by theological, distinctions, those immutable principles, which form the true basis of virtue and happiness? The paltry expedients of combating error with error, and prejudice with prejudice, in one invariable and melancholy circle, have already been sufficiently tried, have already been demonstrated futile:—they have armed man against man, and filled the world with crimes, and with blood.—How has the benign and gentle nature of Reform been mistated! 'One false idea,' justly says an acute and philosophic writer,[1] 'united with others, produces such as are necessarily false; which, combining again with all those the memory retains, give to all a tinge of falsehood. One error, alone, is sufficient to infect the whole mass of the mind, and produce an infinity of capricious, monstrous, notions.—Every vice is the error of the understanding; crimes and prejudices are brothers; truth and virtue sisters. These things, known to the wise, are hid from fools!'*

Without a sufficiently interesting pursuit, a fatal torpor

---

[1] Helvetius.

stole over my spirits—my blood circulated languidly through my veins. Montague, in the intervals from business and amusement, continued to visit me. He brought me books, read to me, chatted with me, pressed me to accompany him to places of public entertainment, which (determined to incur no pecuniary obligation) I invariably refused.

I received his civilities with the less scruple, from the information I had received of his engagement with Miss Morton; which, with his knowledge of my unhappy attachment, I thought, precluded every idea of a renewal of those sentiments he had formerly professed for me.

In return for his friendship, I tried to smile, and exerted my spirits, to prove my grateful sensibility of his kindness: but, while he appeared to take a lively interest in my sorrows, he carefully avoided a repetition of the language in which he had once addressed me; yet, at times, his tender concern seemed sliding into a sentiment still softer, which obliged me to practise more reserve: he was not insensible of this, and was frequently betrayed into transient bursts of passion and resentment, which, on my repelling with firmness, he would struggle to repress, and afterwards absent himself for a time.

Unable to devise any method of increasing my income, and experiencing the pressure of some daily wants and inconveniencies, I determined, at length, on selling the sum vested, in my name, in the funds, and purchasing a life annuity.

Recollecting the name of a banker, with whom my uncle, the friend of my infancy, had formerly kept cash, I learned his residence, and, waiting upon him, made myself known as the niece of an old and worthy friend; at the same time acquainting him with my intentions.—He offered to transact the affair for me immediately, the funds being, then, in a very favourable position; and to preserve the money in his hands till an opportunity should offer of laying it out to advantage. I gave him proper credentials for the accomplishing of this business, and returned to my apartment with a heart somewhat lightened. This scheme had never before occurred to me. The banker, who was a man of commercial reputation, had assured me, that my fortune might now be sold out with little loss; and that, by purchasing an annuity, on proper security, at seven or eight per cent, I might, with œconomy, be enabled to support myself decently, with comfort and independence.

CHAPTER XVIII

SOME weeks elapsed, and I heard no more from my banker. A slight indisposition confined me to the house. One evening, Mr Montague, coming to my apartment to enquire after my health, brought with him a newspaper (as was his frequent custom), and, finding me unwell, and dispirited, began to read some parts from it aloud, in the hope of amusing me. Among the articles of home-intelligence, a paragraph stated—'The failure of a considerable mercantile house, which had created an alarm upon the Exchange, as, it was apprehended, some important consequences would follow in the commercial world. A great banking-house, it was hinted, not many miles from——, was likely to be affected, by some rumours, in connection with this business, which had occasioned a considerable run upon it for the last two or three days.'

My attention was roused—I eagerly held out my hand for the paper, and perused this alarming paragraph, again and again, without observing the surprize expressed in the countenance of Montague, who was at a loss to conceive why this intelligence should be affecting to me.—I sat, for some minutes, involved in thought, till a question from my companion, several times repeated, occasioned me to start. I immediately recollected myself, and tried to reason away my fears, as vague and groundless. I was about to explain the nature of them to my friend—secretly accusing myself for not having done so sooner, and availed myself of his advice, when a servant, entering, put a letter into his hand.

Looking upon the seal and superscription, he changed colour, and opened it hastily. Strong emotion was painted in his features while he perused it. I regarded him with anxiety. He rose from his seat, walked up and down the room with a disordered pace—opened the door, as if with an intention of going out—shut it—returned back again—threw himself into a chair—covered his face with his hand-kerchief—appeared in great agitation—and burst into tears. I arose, went to him, and took his hand—'*My friend!*' said I——I would have added something more—but, unable to proceed, I sunk into a seat beside him, and wept in sympathy. He pressed my hand to his lips—folded me wildly in his arms, and attempted to speak—but his voice was lost in convulsive fobs. I gently withdrew myself, and waited, in silence, till the violence of his emotions should subside. He held out to me the letter he had received. I perused it. It contained an account of the sudden death of his father, and a summons for his immediate return to the country, to settle the affairs, and to take upon him his father's professional employment.

'You leave me, then!' said I—'I lose my only remaining friend!'

'*Never!*'—he replied, emphatically.

I blushed for having uttered so improper, so selfish, a remark; and endeavoured to atone for it by forgetting the perils of my own situation, in attention to that of this ardent, but affectionate, young man.—His sufferings were acute and violent for some days, during which he quitted me only at the hours of repose—I devoted myself to sooth* and console him. I felt, that I had been greatly indebted to his friendship and kindness, and I endeavoured to repay the obligation. He appeared fully sensible of my cares, and mingled with his acknowledgments expressions of a tenderness, so lively, and unequivocal, as obliged me, once more, to be more guarded in my behaviour.

In consideration for the situation of Mr Montague—I had forgotten the paragraph in the paper, till an accidental intelligence of the bankruptcy of the house, in which my little fortune was entrusted, confirmed to me the certainty of this terrible blow. Montague was sitting with me when I received the unwelcome news.

'Gracious God!' I exclaimed, clasping my hands, and raising my eyes to heaven—'What is to become of me now?—The measure of my sorrows is filled up!'

It was some time before I had power to explain the circumstances to my companion.

'Do not distress yourself, my lovely Emma,' said he; 'I will be your friend—your guardian—' (and he added, in a low, yet fervent, accent)—'*your husband!*'

'No—no—no!' answered I, shaking my head, 'that must not, cannot, be! I would perish, rather than take advantage of a generosity like yours. I will go to service—I will work for my bread—and, if I cannot procure a wretched sustenance—*I can but die!* Life, to me, has long been worthless!'

My countenance, my voice, my manner, but too forcibly expressed the keen anguish of my soul. I seemed to be marked out for the victim of a merciless destiny—*for the child of sorrow!** The susceptible temper of Montague, softened by his own affliction, was moved by my distress. He repeated, and enforced, his proposal, with all the ardour of a youthful, a warm, an uncorrupted, mind.

'You add to my distress,' replied I. 'I have not a heart to bestow—I lavished mine upon one, who scorned and contemned it. Its sensibility is now exhausted. Shall I reward a faithful and generous tenderness, like yours, with a cold, a worthless, an alienated, mind? No, no!—Seek an object more worthy of you, and leave me to my fate.'

At that moment, I had forgotten the report of his engagement with Miss Morton; but, on his persisting, vehemently, to urge his suit, I recollected, and immediately mentioned, it, to him. He confessed—

'That, stung by my rejection, and preference of Mr Harley, he had, at one period, entertained a thought of that nature; but that he had fallen out with the family, in adjusting the settlements. Mrs Morton had persuaded her husband to make, what he conceived to be, ungenerous requisitions. Miss Morton had discovered much artifice, but little sensibility, on the occasion. Disgusted with the apathy of the father, the insolence of the mother, and the low cunning of the daughter, he had abruptly quitted them, and broken off all intercourse with the family.'

It is not necessary to enlarge on this part of my narrative. Suffice it to say, that, after a long contest, my desolate situation, added to the persevering affection of this enthusiastic young man, prevailed over my objections. His happiness, he told me, entirely depended on my decision. I would not deceive him:—I related to him, with simplicity and truth, all the circumstances of my past conduct towards Mr Harley. He listened to me with evident emotion—interrupted me, at times, with execrations; and, once or twice, vowing vengeance on Augustus, appeared on the verge of outrage. But I at length reasoned him into greater moderation, and obliged him to do justice to the merit and honour of Mr Harley. He acquiesced reluctantly, and with an ill grace, yet, with a lover-like partiality, attributed his conduct to causes, of which I had discerned no traces. He assured himself, that the affections of a heart, tender as mine, would be secured by kindness and assiduity—and I at last yielded to his importunity. We were united in a short time, and I accompanied my husband to the town of ——, in the county of ——, the residence of his late father.

CHAPTER XIX

MR MONTAGUE presented me to his relations and friends, by whom I was received with a flattering distinction. My wearied spirits began now to find repose. My husband was much occupied in the duties of his profession. We had a respectable circle of acquaintance. In the intervals of social engagement, and domestic employment, ever thirsting after knowledge, I occasionally applied myself to the study of physic, anatomy, and surgery, with the various branches of science connected with them; by which means I frequently rendered myself essentially

serviceable to my friend; and, by exercising my understanding and humanity, strengthened my mind, and stilled
the importunate suggestions of a heart too exquisitely
sensible.

The manners of Mr Montague were kind and affectionate, though subject, at times, to inequalities and starts of
passion; he confided in me, as his best and truest friend—
and I deserved his confidence:—yet, I frequently observed
the restlessness and impetuosity of his disposition with
apprehension.

I felt for my husband a rational esteem, and a grateful
affection:—but those romantic, high-wrought, frenzied,
emotions, that had rent my heart during its first attachment—that enthusiasm, that fanaticism, to which opposition had given force, the bare recollection of which still
shook my soul with anguish, no longer existed. Montague
was but too sensible of this difference, which naturally
resulted from the change of circumstances, and was unreasonable enough to complain of what secured our
tranquillity. If a cloud, at times, hung over my brow—if
I relapsed, for a short period, into a too habitual
melancholy, he would grow captious, and complain.

'You esteem me, Emma: I confide in your principles,
and I glory in your friendship—but, you have never *loved*
me!'

'Why will you be so unjust, both to me, and to yourself?'

'Tell me, then, sincerely—I know you will not deceive
me—Have you ever felt for me those sentiments with
which Augustus Harley inspired you?'

'Certainly not—I do not pretend to it—neither ought
you to wish it. My first attachment was the morbid excess of
a distempered imagination. Liberty, reason, virtue, usefulness, were the offerings I carried to its shrine. It preyed
incessantly upon my heart, it drank up its vital spirit, it
became a vice from its excess—it was a pernicious, though
a sublime, enthusiasm—its ravages are scarcely to be remembered without shuddering—all the strength, the dignity, the powers, of my mind, melted before it! Do you wish
again to see me the slave of my passions—do you regret,

that I am restored to reason? To you I owe every thing—
life, and its comforts, rational enjoyment, and the opportunity of usefulness. I feel for you all the affection that a
reasonable and a virtuous mind ought to feel—that affection which is compatible with the fulfilling of other duties.
We are guilty of vice and selfishness when we yield ourselves up to unbounded desires, and suffer our hearts to be
wholly absorbed by one object, however meritorious that
object may be.'

'Ah! how calmly you reason,—while I listen to you I
cannot help loving and admiring you, but I must ever hate
that accursed Harley—No! *I am not satisfied*—and I sometimes regret that I ever beheld you.'

Many months glided away with but little interruption to
our tranquillity.—A remembrance of the past would at
times obtrude itself, like the broken recollections of a
feverish vision. To banish these painful retrospections, I
hastened to employ myself; every hour was devoted to
active usefulness, or to social and rational recreation.

I became a mother; in performing the duties of a nurse,
my affections were awakened to new and sweet emotions.—The father of my child appeared more respectable
in my eyes, became more dear to me: the engaging smiles
of my little Emma repayed me for every pain and every
anxiety. While I beheld my husband caress his infant, I
tasted a pure, a chaste, an ineffable pleasure.

CHAPTER XX

About six weeks after my recovery from childbed, some
affairs of importance called Mr Montague to London.
Three days after he had quitted me, as, bending over the
cradle of my babe, I contemplated in silence its tranquil
slumbers, I was alarmed by an uncommon confusion in
the lower part of the house. Hastening down stairs, to
enquire into the cause, I was informed—that a gentleman,
in passing through the town, had been thrown from his
horse, that he was taken up senseless, and, as was custom-

ary in cases of accident, had been brought into our house, that he might receive assistance.

Mr Montague was from home, a young gentleman who resided with us, and assisted my husband in his profession, was also absent, visiting a patient. Having myself acquired some knowledge of surgery, I went immediately into the hall to give the necessary directions on the occasion. The gentleman was lying on the floor, without any signs of life. I desired the people to withdraw, who, crowding round with sincere, but useless sympathy, obstructed the circulation of air. Approaching the unfortunate man, I instantly recognised the well-known features, though much altered, wan and sunk, of *Augustus Harley*. Staggering a few paces backward—a death-like sickness overspread my heart—a crowd of confused and terrible emotions rushed through my mind.—But a momentary reflection recalled my scattered thoughts. Once before, I had saved from death an object so fatal to my repose. I exerted all my powers, his hair was clotted, and his face disfigured with blood; I ordered the servants to raise and carry him to an adjoining apartment, wherein was a large, low sopha, on which they laid him. Carefully washing the blood from the wound, I found he had received a dangerous contusion in his head, but that the scull, as I had at first apprehended, was not fractured. I cut the hair from the wounded part, and applied a proper bandage. I did more—no other assistance being at hand, I ventured to open a vein:* the blood presently flowed freely, and he began to revive. I bathed his temples, and sprinkled the room with vinegar, opened the windows to let the air pass freely through, raised his head with the pillows of the sopha, and sprinkled his face and breast with cold water. I held his hand in mine—I felt the languid and wavering pulse quicken—I fixed my eyes upon his face—at that moment every thing else was forgotten, and my nerves seemed firmly braced by my exertions.

He at length opened his eyes, gazed upon me with a vacant look, and vainly attempted, for some time, to speak. At last, he uttered a few incoherent words, but I perceived his senses were wandering, and I conjectured, too truly, that his brain had received a concussion. He made an effort to rise, but sunk down again.

'Where am I,' said he, 'every object appears to me double.'

He shut his eyes, and remained silent. I mixed for him a cordial and composing medicine, and entreating him to take it, he once more raised himself, and looked up.—Our eyes met, his were wild and unsettled.

'That voice,'—said he, in a low tone,—'that countenance—Oh God! where am I?'

A strong, but transient, emotion passed over his features. With a trembling hand he seized and swallowed the medicine I had offered, and again relapsed into a kind of lethargic stupor. I then gave orders for a bed to be prepared, into which I had him conveyed. I darkened the room, and desired, that he might be kept perfectly quiet.

I retired to my apartment, my confinement was yet but recent, and I had not perfectly recovered my strength. Exhausted by the strong efforts I had made, and the stronger agitation of my mind, I sunk into a fainting fit, (to which I was by no means subject) and remained for some time in a state of perfect insensibility. On my recovery, I learnt that Mr Lucas, the assistant of my husband, had returned, and was in the chamber of the stranger; I sent for him on his quitting the apartment, and eagerly interrogated him respecting the state of the patient. He shook his head—I related to him the methods I had taken, and enquired whether I had erred? He smiled—

'You are an excellent surgeon,' said he, 'you acted very properly, but,' observing my pallid looks, 'I wish your little nursery may not suffer from your humanity'—

'I lay no claim,' replied I with emotion—'to extraordinary humanity—I would have done the same for the poorest of my fellow creatures—but this gentleman is an old acquaintance, *a friend*, whom, in the early periods of my life, I greatly respected.'

'I am sorry for it, for I dare not conceal from you, that I think him in a dangerous condition.'

I changed countenance—'There is no fracture, no bones are broken.'—

'No, but the brain has received an alarming concussion—he is also, otherwise, much bruised, and, I fear, has suffered some internal injury.'

'You distress and terrify me,' said I, gasping for breath—'What is to be done—shall we call in further advice?'

'I think so; in the mean time, if you are acquainted with his friends, you would do well to apprize them of what has happened.'

'I know little of them, I know not where to address them—Oh! save him,' continued I, clasping my hands with encreased emotion, unconscious what I did, 'for God's sake save him, if you would preserve me from dis—'

A look penetrating and curious from Lucas, recalled me to reason. Commending his patient to my care, he quitted me, and rode to the next town to procure the aid of a skilful and experienced Physician. I walked up and down the room for some time in a state of distraction.

'He will die'—exclaimed I—'die in my house—fatal accident! Oh, Augustus! *too tenderly beloved*, thou wert fated to be the ruin of my peace! But, whatever may be the consequences, I will perform, for thee, the last tender offices.— I will not desert my duty!'

The nurse brought to me my infant, it smiled in my face—I pressed it to my bosom—I wept over it.—How could I, from that agitated bosom, give it a pernicious sustenance?

CHAPTER XXI

IN the evening, I repaired to the chamber of Mr Harley, I sat by his bed-side, I gazed mournfully on his flushed, but vacant countenance—I took his hand—it was dry and burning—the pulse beat rapidly, but irregularly, beneath my trembling fingers. His lips moved, he seemed to speak, though inarticulately—but sometimes raising his voice, I could distinguish a few incoherent sentences. In casting

my eyes round the room, I observed the scattered articles
of his dress, his cloaths were black, and in his hat, which lay
on the ground, I discovered a crape hatband. I continued
to hold his burning hand in mine.

'She died,'—said he—'and my unkindness killed her—
unhappy Emma—thy heart was too tender!'—I shuddered'—No, no,'—continued he, after a few minutes
pause, 'she is not married—she dared not give her hand
without her heart, *and that heart was only mine*!' he added
something more, in a lower tone, which I was unable to
distinguish.

Overcome by a variety of sensations, I sunk into a chair,
and, throwing my handkerchief over my face, indulged my
tears.

Sometimes he mentioned his wife, sometimes his
mother.—At length, speaking rapidly, in a raised voice—
'My son,'—said he,—'thou hast no mother—but Emma
will be a mother to thee—she will love thee—*she loved thy
father*—her heart was the residence of gentle affections—
yet, I pierced that heart!'

I suspected, that a confused recollection of having seen
me on recovering from the state of insensibility, in which
he had been brought, after the accident, into our house,
had probably recalled the associations formerly connected
with this idea. The scene became too affecting: I rushed
from the apartment. All the past impressions seemed to
revive in my mind—my thoughts, with fatal mechanism,
ran back into their old and accustomed channels.—For a
moment, conjugal, maternal, duties, every consideration
but for one object faded from before me!

In a few hours, Mr Lucas returned with the physician;—
I attended them to the chamber, heedfully watching their
looks. The fever still continued very high, accompanied
with a labouring, unsteady pulse, a difficult respiration,
and strong palpitations of the heart. The doctor said little,
but I discovered his apprehensions in his countenance.
The patient appeared particularly restless and uneasy, and
the delirium still continued. On quitting the apartment, I
earnestly conjured the gentlemen to tell me their opinion

of the case. They both expressed an apprehension of internal injury.

'But a short time,' they added, 'would determine it; in the mean while he must be kept perfectly still.'

I turned from them, and walked to the window—I raised my eyes to heaven—I breathed an involuntary ejaculation—I felt that the crisis of my fate was approaching, and I endeavoured to steel my nerves—to prepare my mind for the arduous duties which awaited me.

Mr Lucas approached me, the physician having quitted the room.—'*Mrs Montague*,' said he, in an emphatic tone—' in your sympathy for a *stranger*, do not forget other relations.'

'I do not need, sir, to be reminded by you of my duties; were not the sufferings of a fellow being a sufficient claim upon our humanity, this gentleman has *more affecting claims*—I am neither a stranger to him, nor to his virtues.'

'So I perceive, madam,' said he, with an air a little sarcastic, 'I wish, Mr Montague were here to participate your cares.'

I wish he were, sir, his generous nature would not disallow them.' I spoke haughtily, and abruptly left him.

I took a turn in the garden, endeavouring to compose my spirits, and, after visiting the nursery, returned to the chamber of Mr Harley. I there found Mr Lucas, and in a steady tone, declared my intention of watching his patient through the night.

'As you please, madam,' said he coldly.

I seated myself in an easy chair, reclining my head on my hand. The bed curtains were undrawn on the side next me. Augustus frequently started, as from broken slumbers; his respiration grew, every moment, more difficult and laborious, and, sometimes, he groaned heavily, as if in great pain. Once he suddenly raised himself in the bed, and, gazing wildly round the room, exclaimed in a distinct, but hurried tone—

'Why dost thou persecute me with thy ill-fated tenderness? A fathomless gulf separates us!—Emma!' added he, in a plaintive voice, '*dost thou, indeed, still love me?*' and, heaving a convulsive sigh, sunk again on his pillow.

Mr Lucas, who stood at the feet of the bed, turned his eye on me. I met his glance with the steady aspect of conscious rectitude. About midnight, our patient grew worse, and, after strong agonies, was seized with a vomiting of blood. The fears of the physician were but too well verified, he had again ruptured the blood-vessel, once before broken.

Mr Lucas had but just retired, I ordered him to be instantly recalled, and, stifling every feeling, that might incapacitate me for active exertion, I rendered him all the assistance in my power—I neither trembled, nor shed a tear—I banished the *woman* from my heart—I acquitted myself with a firmness that would not have disgraced the most experienced, and veteran surgeon. My services were materially useful, my solicitude vanquished every shrinking sensibility, *affection had converted me into a heroine!* The haemorrhage continued, at intervals, all the next day: I passed once or twice from the chamber to the nursery, and immediately returned. We called in a consultation, but little hope was afforded.

The next night, Mr Lucas and myself continued to watch—towards morning our exhausted patient sunk into an apparently tranquil slumber. Mr Lucas intreated me to retire and take some repose, on my refusal, he availed himself of the opportunity, and went to his apartment, desiring to be called if any change should take place. The nurse slept soundly in her chair, I alone remained watching—I felt neither fatigue nor languor—my strength seemed preserved as by a miracle, so omnipotent is the operation of moral causes!

Silence reigned throughout the house; I hung over the object of my tender cares—his features were serene—but his cheeks and lips were pale and bloodless. From time to time I took his lifeless hand—a low, fluttering, pulse, sometimes seeming to stop, and then to vibrate with a tremulous motion, but too plainly justified my fears—his breath, though less laborious, was quick and short—a cold

dew hung upon his temples—I gently wiped them with my
handkerchief, and pressed my lips to his forehead. Yet, at
that moment, that solemn moment—while I beheld the
object of my virgin affections—whom I had loved with
a tenderness, 'passing the love of woman'*— expiring
before my eyes—I forgot not that I was a wife and
a mother.—The purity of my feelings sanctified their
enthusiasm!

The day had far advanced, though the house still remained quiet, when Augustus, after a deep drawn sigh,
opened his eyes. The loss of blood had calmed the delirium, and though he regarded me attentively, and with
evident surprize, the wildness of his eyes and countenance
had given place to their accustomed steady expression. He
spoke in a faint voice.

'Where am I, how came I here?'

I drew nearer to him—'An unfortunate accident has
thrown you into the care of kind friends—you have been
very ill—it is not proper that you should exert yourself—
rely on those to whom your safety is precious.'

He looked at me as I spoke—his eyes glistened—he
breathed a half-smothered sigh, but attempted not to reply. He continued to doze at intervals throughout the day,
but evidently grew weaker every hour—I quitted him not
for a moment, even my nursery was forgotten. I sat, or
knelt, at the bed's head, and, between his short and
broken slumbers, administered cordial medicines. He
seemed to take them with pleasure from my hand, and a
mournful tenderness at times beamed in his eyes. I neither
spake nor wept—my strength appeared equal to every trial.

In the evening, starting from a troubled sleep, he fell
into convulsions—I kept my station—our efforts were successful—he again revived. I supported the pillows on
which his head reclined, sprinkled the bed-cloaths, and
bathed his temples, with hungary water,* while I wiped
from them the damps of death. A few tears at length
forced their way, they fell upon his hand, which rested on
the pillow—he kissed them off, and raised to mine his
languid eyes, in which death was already painted.

The blood forsaking the extremities, rushed wildly to my heart, a strong palpitation seized it, my fortitude had well nigh forsaken me. But I had been habituated to subdue my feelings, and should I suffer them to disturb the last moments of him, *who had taught me this painful lesson?* He made a sign for a cordial, an attendant offering one—he waved his hand and turned from her his face—I took it—held it to his lips, and he instantly drank it. Another strong emotion shook my nerves—once more I struggled and gained the victory. He spoke in feeble and interrupted periods—kneeling down, scarce daring to breathe, I listened.

'I have a son'—said he,—'I am dying—he will have no longer a parent—transfer to him a portion of—'

'I comprehend you—say no more—*he is mine*—I adopt him—where shall I find——?'

He pointed to his cloaths—'a pocket book'—said he, in accents still fainter.

'Enough!—I swear, in this awful moment, never to forsake him.'

He raised my hand to his lips—a tender smile illumined his countenance—'Surely,' said he, 'I have sufficiently fulfilled the dictates of a rigid honour!—In these last moments—when every earthly tie is dissolving—when human institutions fade before my sight—I may, without a crime, tell you—*that I have loved you.*—Your tenderness early penetrated my heart—aware of its weakness—I sought to shun you—I imposed on myself those severe laws of which you causelessly complained.—Had my conduct been less rigid, I had been lost—I had been unjust to the bonds which I had voluntarily contracted; and which, therefore, had on me indispensible claims. I acted from good motives, but no doubt, was guilty of some errors—yet, my conflicts were, even, more cruel than yours—I had not only to contend against my own sensibility, but against yours also.—The fire which is pent up burns the fiercest!'—

He ceased to speak—a transient glow, which had lighted up his countenance, faded—exhausted, by the strong effort he had made, he sunk back—his eyes grew dim—they closed—*their last light beamed on me!*—I caught him in my arms—and—*he awoke no more.* The spirits, that had hitherto supported me, suddenly subsided. I uttered a piercing shriek, and sunk upon the body.

CHAPTER XXII

MANY weeks passed of which I have no remembrance, they were a blank in my life—a long life of sorrow! When restored to recollection, I found myself in my own chamber, my husband attending me. It was a long time before I could clearly retrace the images of the past. I learned——

'That I had been seized with a nervous fever, in consequence of having exerted myself beyond my strength; that my head had been disordered; that Mr Montague on his return, finding me in this situation, of which Mr Lucas had explained the causes, had been absorbed in deep affliction; that, inattentive to every other concern, he had scarcely quitted my apartment; that my child had been sent out to nurse; and that my recovery had been despaired of.'

My constitution was impaired by these repeated shocks. I continued several months in a low and debilitated state.—With returning reason, I recalled to my remembrance the charge which Augustus had consigned to me in his last moments. I enquired earnestly for the pocket-book he had mentioned, and was informed, that, after his decease, it had been found, and its contents examined, which were a bank note of fifty pounds, some letters, and memorandums. Among the letters was one from his brother, by which means they had learned his address, and had been enabled to transmit to him an account of the melancholy catastrophe, and to request his orders respecting the disposal of the body. On the receipt of this intelligence, the younger Mr Harley had come immediately into ——shire, had received his brother's effects, and had his remains decently and respectfully interred in the town where the fatal accident had taken place, through which he was passing in his way to visit a friend.

As soon as I had strength to hold a pen, I wrote to this gentleman, mentioning the tender office which had been consigned to me; and requesting that the child, or children, of Mr Augustus Harley might be consigned to my care. To this letter I received an answer, in a few days, hinting—

'That the marriage of my deceased friend had not been more imprudent than unfortunate; that he had struggled with great difficulties and many sorrows; that his wife had been dead near a twelvemonth; that he had lost two of his children, about the same period, with the small-pox, one only surviving, the younger, a son, a year and a half old; that it was, at present, at nurse, under his (his brother's) protection; that his respect for me, and knowledge of my friendship for their family, added to his wish of complying with every request of his deceased brother, prevented him from hesitating a moment respecting the propriety of yielding the child to my care; that it should be delivered to any person whom I should commission for the purpose; and that I might draw upon him for the necessary charges towards the support and education of his nephew.'

I mentioned to Mr Montague these particulars, with a desire of availing myself of his counsel and assistance on the occasion.

'You are free, madam,' he replied, with a cold and distant air, 'to act as you shall think proper; but you must excuse me from making myself responsible in the affair.'

I sighed deeply. I perceived, but too plainly, that *a mortal blow was given to my tranquillity*; but I determined to persevere in what I considered to be my duty. On the retrospect of my conduct, my heart acquitted me; and I endeavoured to submit, without repining, to my fate.

I was, at this period, informed by a faithful servant, who attended me during my illness, of what I had before but too truly conjectured—That in my delirium I had incessantly called upon the name of Augustus Harley, and

repeated, at intervals, in broken language, the circumstances of our last tender and fatal interview; this, with
some particulars related by Mr Lucas to Mr Montague on
his return, had, it seems, at the time, inflamed the irascible
passions of my husband, almost to madness. His transports
had subsided, by degrees, into gloomy reserve: he had
watched me, till my recovery, with unremitting attention;
since which his confidence and affection became, every
day, more visibly alienated. Self-respect suppressed my
complaints—conscious of deserving, even more than ever,
his esteem, I bore his caprice with patience, trusting that
time, and my conduct, would restore him to reason, and
awaken in his heart a sense of justice.

I sent for my babe from the house of the nurse, to whose
care it had been confided during my illness, and placed
the little Augustus in its stead. 'It is unnecessary, my friend,
to say, that you were that lovely and interesting child.—
Oh! with what emotion did I receive, and press, you to my
care-worn bosom; retracing in your smiling countenance
the features of your unfortunate father! Adopting you for
my own, I divided my affection between you and my
Emma. Scarce a day passed that I did not visit the cottage
of your nurse. I taught you to call me by the endearing
name of *mother*! I delighted to see you caress my infant with
fraternal tenderness—I endeavoured to cherish this growing affection, and found a sweet relief from my sorrows in
these tender, maternal, cares.'

CHAPTER XXIII

MY health being considerably injured, I had taken a
young woman into my house, to assist me in the nursery,
and in other domestic offices. She was in her eighteenth
year—simple, modest, and innocent. This girl had resided
with me for some months. I had been kind to her, and she
seemed attached to me. One morning, going suddenly
into Mr Montague's dressing-room, I surprised Rachel sitting on a sopha with her master:—he held her hand in his,

while his arm was thrown round her waist; and they appeared to be engaged in earnest conversation. They both started, on my entrance.—Unwilling to encrease their confusion, I quitted the room.

Montague, on our meeting at dinner, affected an air of unconcern; but there was an apparent constraint in his behaviour. I preserved towards him my accustomed manner, till the servants had withdrawn. I then mildly expostulated with him on the impropriety of his behaviour. His replies were not more unkind than ungenerous—they pierced my heart.

'It is well, sir, I am inured to suffering; but it is not of *myself* that I would speak. I have not deserved to lose your confidence—this is my consolation;—yet, I submit to it:—but I cannot see you act in a manner, that will probably involve you in vexation, and intail upon you remorse, without warning you of your danger. Should you corrupt the innocence of this girl, she is emphatically *ruined*. It is the strong mind only, that, firmly resting on its own powers, can sustain and recover itself amidst the world's scorn and injustice. The morality of an uncultivated understanding, is that of *custom*, not of reason:—break down the feeble barrier, and there is nothing to supply its place—you open the flood-gates of infamy and wretchedness. Who can say where the evil may stop?'

'You are at liberty to discharge your servant, when you please, madam.'

'I think it my duty to do so, Mr Montague—not on my own, but on *her*, account. If I have no claim upon your affection and principles, I would disdain to watch your conduct. But I feel myself attached to this young woman, and would wish to preserve her from destruction!'

'You are very generous; but as you thought fit to bestow on me your *hand*, when your *heart* was devoted to another——'

'It is enough, sir!—To your justice, only, in your cooler moments, would I appeal!'

I procured for Rachel a reputable place, in a distant part of the county.—Before she quitted me, I seriously, and affectionately, remonstrated with her on the consequences of her behaviour. She answered me only with tears and blushes.

In vain I tried to rectify the principles, and subdue the cruel prejudices, of my husband. I endeavoured to shew him every mark of affection and confidence. I frequently expostulated with him, upon his conduct, with tears—urged him to respect himself and me—strove to convince him of the false principles upon which he acted—of the senseless and barbarous manner in which he was sacrificing my peace, and his own, to a romantic chimera. Sometimes he would appear, for a moment, melted with my tender and fervent entreaties.

'Would to God!' he would say, with emotion, 'the last six months of my life could be obliterated for ever from my remembrance!'

He was no longer active, and chearful: he would sit, for hours, involved in deep and gloomy silence. When I brought the little Emma, to soften, by her engaging caresses, the anxieties by which his spirits appeared to be overwhelmed, he would gaze wildly upon her—snatch her to his breast—and then, suddenly throwing her from him, rush out of the house; and, inattentive to the duties of his profession, absent himself for days and nights together:—his temper grew, every hour, more furious and unequal.

He by accident, one evening, met the little Augustus, as his nurse was carrying him from my apartment; and, breaking rudely into the room, overwhelmed me with a torrent of abuse and reproaches. I submitted to his injustice with silent grief—my spirits were utterly broken. At times, he would seem to be sensible of the impropriety of his conduct—would execrate himself, and entreat my forgiveness;—but quickly relapsed into his accustomed paroxysms, which, from having been indulged, were now become habitual, and uncontroulable. These agitations seemed daily to encrease—all my efforts to regain his confidence—my patient, unremitted, attentions—were fruitless. He shunned me—he appeared, even, to regard me

with horror. I wept in silence. The hours which I passed
with my children afforded me my only consolation—they
became painfully dear to me. Attending to their little
sports, and innocent gambols, I forgot, for a moment, my
griefs.

CHAPTER XXIV

SOME months thus passed away, with little variation in my
situation. Returning home one morning, early, from the
nurse's, where I had left my Emma with Augustus (whom
I never, now, permitted to be brought to my own house) as
I entered, Mr Montague shot suddenly by me, and rushed
up stairs towards his apartment. I saw him but transiently,
as he passed; but his haggard countenance, and furious
gestures, filled me with dismay. He had been from home
the preceding night; but to these absences I had lately
been too much accustomed to regard them as any thing
extraordinary. I hesitated a few moments, whether I
should follow him. I feared, lest I might exasperate him by
so doing; yet, the unusual disorder of his appearance gave
me a thousand terrible and nameless apprehensions. I
crept towards the door of his apartment—listened attentively, and heard him walking up and down the room, with
hasty steps—sometimes he appeared to stop, and groaned
heavily:—once I heard him throw up the sash, and shut it
again with violence.

I attempted to open the door, but, finding it locked, my
terror increased.—I knocked gently, but could not attract
his attention. At length I recollected another door, that
led to this apartment, through my own chamber, which
was fastened on the outside, and seldom opened. With
trembling steps I hurried round, and, on entering the
room, beheld him sitting at a table, a pen in his hand, and
paper before him. On the table lay his pistols—his hair was
dishevelled—his dress disordered—his features distorted
with emotion—while in his countenance was painted the
extreme of horror and despair.

I uttered a faint shriek, and sunk into a chair. He started from his seat, and, advancing towards me with hurried and tremulous steps, sternly demanded, Why I intruded on his retirement? I threw myself at his feet,—I folded my arms round him—I wept—I deprecated his anger—I entreated to be heard—I said all that humanity, all that the most tender and lively sympathy could suggest, to inspire him with confidence—to induce him to relieve, by communication, the burthen which oppressed his heart.—He struggled to free himself from me—my apprehensions gave me strength—I held him with a strenuous grasp—he raved—he stamped—he tore his hair—his passion became frenzy! At length, forcibly bursting from me, I fell on the floor, and the blood gushed from my nose and lips. He shuddered convulsively—stood a few moments, as if irresolute—and, then, throwing himself beside me, raised me from the ground; and, clasping me to his heart, which throbbed tumultuously, burst into a flood of tears.

'I will not be thy *murderer*, Emma!' said he, in a voice of agony, interrupted by heart-rending sobs—'I have had enough of blood!'

I tried to sooth him—I assured him I was not hurt—I besought him to confide his sorrows to the faithful bosom of his wife! He appeared softened—his tears flowed without controul.

'Unhappy woman!—you know not what you ask! To be ingenuous, belongs to purity like yours!—Guilt, black as hell!—conscious, aggravated, damnable, guilt!—*Your fatal attachment*—my accursed jealousy!—Ah! Emma! I have injured you—but you are, indeed, revenged!'

Every feature seemed to work—seemed pregnant with dreadful meaning—he was relapsing into frenzy.

'Be calm, my friend—be not unjust to yourself—you can have committed no injury that I shall not willingly forgive—you are incapable of persisting in guilt. The ingenuous mind, that avows, has already made half the reparation. Suffer me to learn the source of your inquietude! I may find much to extenuate—I may be able to convince you, that you are too severe to yourself.'

'Never, never, never!—nothing can extenuate—*the expiation must be made!*—Excellent, admirable, woman!—Remember, without hating, the wretch who has been unworthy of you—who could not conceive, who knew not how to estimate, your virtues!—Oh! do not—do not'—straining me to his bosom—'curse my memory!'

He started from the ground, and, in a moment, was out of sight.

I raised myself with difficulty—faint, tottering, gasping for breath, I attempted to descend the stairs. I had scarcely reached the landing-place, when a violent knocking at the door shook my whole frame. I stood still, clinging to the balustrade, unable to proceed. I heard a chaise draw up—a servant opening the door—a plain-looking countryman alighted, and desired instantly to speak to the lady of the house—his business was, he said, of life and death! I advanced towards him, pale and trembling!

'What is the matter, my friend—whence came you?'

'I cannot stop, lady, to explain myself—you must come with me—I will tell you more as we go along.'

'Do you come,' enquired I, in a voice scarcely articulate, 'from my husband?'

'No—no—I come from a person who is dying, who has somewhat of consequence to impart to you—Hasten, lady—there is no time to lose!'

'Lead, then, I follow you.'

He helped me into the chaise, and we drove off with the rapidity of lightning.

CHAPTER XXV

I ASKED no more questions on the road, but attempted to fortify my mind for the scenes which, I foreboded, were approaching. After about an hour's ride, we stopped at a small, neat, cottage, embosomed in trees, standing alone, at a considerable distance from the high-road. A decent-looking, elderly, woman, came to the door, at the sound of the carriage, and assisted me to alight. In her countenance were evident marks of perturbation and horror. I asked for a glass of water; and, having drank it, followed the woman, at her request, up stairs. She seemed inclined to talk, but I gave her no encouragement—I knew not what awaited me, nor what exertions might be requisite—I determined not to exhaust my spirits unnecessarily.

On entering a small chamber, I observed a bed, with the curtains closely drawn. I advanced towards it, and, unfolding them, beheld the unhappy Rachel lying in a state of apparent insensibility.

'She is dying,' whispered the woman, she has been in strong convulsions; but she could not die in peace without seeing Madam Montague, and obtaining her forgiveness.'

I approached the unfortunate girl, and took her lifeless hand.—A feeble pulse still trembled—I gazed upon her, for some moments, in silence.—She heaved a deep sigh—her lips moved, inarticulately. She, at length, opened her eyes, and, fixing them upon me, the blood seemed to rush through her languid frame—reanimating it. She sprung up in the bed, and, clasping her hands together, uttered a few incoherent words.

'Be pacified, my dear—I am not angry with you—I feel only pity.'

She looked wildly. 'Ah! my dear lady, I am a wicked girl—but not—Oh, no!—*not a murderer!* I did not——indeed, I did not——murder my child!'

A cold tremor seized me—I turned heart-sick—a sensation of horror thrilled through my veins!

'My dear, my kind mistress,' resumed the wretched girl, 'can you forgive me?——Oh! that cruel, barbarous, man!—It was *he* who did it—indeed, it was *he* who did it!' distraction glared in her eyes.

'I do forgive you,' said I, in broken accents. 'I will take care of you—but you must be calm.'

'I will—I will'—replied she, in a rapid tone of voice—'but do not send me to prison—*I did not murder it!*—Oh! my child, my child!' continued she, in a screaming tone of frantic violence, and was again seized with strong convulsions.

We administered all the assistance in our power. I endeavoured, with success, to stifle my emotions in the active duties of humanity. Rachel once more revived. After earnestly recommending her to the care of the good woman of the house, and promising to send medicines and nourishment proper for her situation, and to reward their attentions—desiring that she might be kept perfectly still, and not be suffered to talk on subjects that agitated her—I quitted the place, presaging but too much, and not having, at that time, the courage to make further enquiries.

CHAPTER XXVI

ON entering my own house my heart misgave me. I enquired, with trepidation, for my husband, and was informed—'That he had returned soon after my departure, and had shut himself in his apartment; that, on being followed by Mr Lucas, he had turned fiercely upon him, commanding him, in an imperious tone, instantly to leave him; adding, he had affairs of importance to transact; and should any one dare to intrude on him, it would be at the peril of their lives.' All the family appeared in consternation, but no one had presumed to disobey the orders of their master.—They expressed their satisfaction at my return—Alas! I was impotent to relieve the apprehensions which, I too plainly perceived, had taken possession of their minds.

I retired to my chamber, and, with a trembling hand, traced, and addressed to my husband, a few incoherent lines—briefly hinting my suspicions respecting the late transactions—exhorting him to provide for his safety, and offering to be the companion of his flight. I added—'Let us reap wisdom from these tragical consequences of *indulged passion!* It is not to atone for the past error, by cutting off the prospect of future usefulness—Repentance for what can never be recalled, is absurd and vain, but as it affords a lesson for the time to come—do not let us wilfully forfeit the fruits of our dear-bought experience! I will never reproach you! Virtuous resolution, and time, may yet heal these aggravated wounds. Dear Montague, be no longer the slave of error; inflict not on my tortured mind new, and more insupportable, terrors! I await your directions—let us fly—let us summon our fortitude—let us at length, bravely stem the tide of passion—let us beware of the criminal pusillanimity of despair!'

With faultering steps, I sought the apartment of my husband. I listened a moment at the door—and hearing him in motion, while profound sighs burst every instant from his bosom, I slid my paper under the door, unfolded, that it might be the more likely to attract his attention. Presently, I had the satisfaction of hearing him take it up. After some minutes, a slip of paper was returned, by the same method which I had adopted, in which was written, in characters blotted, and scarcely legible, the following words—

'Leave me, one half hour, to my reflections: at the end of that period, be assured, I will see, or write, to you.'

I knew him to be incapable of falsehood—my heart palpitated with hope. I went to my chamber, and passed the interval in a thousand cruel reflections, and vague plans for our sudden departure. Near an hour had elapsed, when the bell rang. I started, breathless, from my seat. A servant passed my door, to take his master's orders. He returned instantly, and, meeting me in the passage, delivered to me a letter. I heard Montague again lock the door.—Disappointed, I reentered my chamber. In my haste to get at the contents of the paper, I almost tore it in pieces—the words swam before my sight. I held it for some moments in my hand, incapable of decyphering the fatal characters. I breathed with difficulty—all the powers of life seemed suspended—when the report of a pistol roused me to a sense of confused horror.—Rushing forward, I burst, with preternatural strength, into the apartment of my husband——What a spectacle!—Assistance was vain!——

Montague—the impetuous, ill-fated, Montague—*was no more—was a mangled corpse!*—Rash, unfortunate, young, man!

But, why should I harrow up your susceptible mind, by dwelling on these cruel scenes? *Ah! suffer me to spread a veil over this fearful catastrophe!* Some time elapsed ere I had fortitude to examine the paper addressed to me by me unfortunate husband. Its contents, which were as follows, affected me with deep and mingled emotions.

TO MRS MONTAGUE

'Amidst the reflections which press, by turns, upon my burning brain, an obscure consciousness of the prejudices upon which my character has been formed, is not the least torturing—because I feel *the inveterate force of habit*—I feel, that my convictions come too late!

'I have destroyed myself, and you, dearest, most generous, and most unfortunate, of women! I am a monster— I have seduced innocence, and embrued my hands in blood!——Oh, God!—Oh, God!——*'Tis there distraction lies!*—I would, circumstantially, retrace my errors; but my disordered mind, and quivering hand, refuse the cruel task—yet, it is necessary that I should attempt a brief sketch.

'After the cruel accident, which destroyed our tranquillity, I nourished my senseless jealousies (the sources of which I need not, now, recapitulate), till I persuaded myself—injurious wretch that I was!—that I had been perfidiously and ungenerously treated. Stung by false pride, I tried to harden my heart, and foolishly thirsted for revenge. Your meekness, and magnanimity, disappointed me.—I would willingly have seen you, not only suffer the PANGS, but express the *rage*, of a slighted wife. The simple victim of my baseness, by the artless affection she expressed for me, gained an ascendency over my mind; and, when you removed her from your house, we still contrived, at times, to meet. The consequences of our intercourse could not long be concealed. It was, then, that I first began to open my eyes on my conduct, and to be seized with remorse!—Rachel, now, wept incessantly. Her father, she told me, was a stern and severe man; and should he hear of her misconduct, would, she was certain, be her destruction. I procured for her an obscure retreat, to which I removed the unhappy girl (Oh, how degrading is vice!), under false pretences. I exhorted her to conceal her situation—to pretend, that her health was in a declining state—and I visited her, from time to time, as in my profession.

'This poor young creature continued to bewail the disgrace she anticipated—her lamentations pierced my soul! I recalled to my remembrance your emphatic caution. I foresaw that, with the loss of her character, this simple girl's misfortune and degradation would be irretrievable; and I could, now, plainly distinguish the morality of *rule* from that of *principle*. Pursuing this train of reasoning, I entangled myself, for my views were not yet sufficiently clear and comprehensible! Bewildered, amidst contending principles—distracted by a variety of emotions—in seeking a remedy for one vice, I plunged (as is but too common), into others of a more scarlet dye. With shame and horror, I confess, I repeatedly tried, by medical drugs, to procure an abortive birth: the strength and vigour of Rachel's constitution defeated this diabolical purpose. Foiled in these attempts, I became hardened, desperate, and barbarous!

'Six weeks before the allotted period, the infant saw the light—for a moment—to close its eyes on it for ever! I, only, was with the unhappy mother. I had formed no deliberate purpose—I had not yet arrived at the acme of guilt—but, perceiving, from the babe's premature birth, and the consequences of the pernicious potions which had been administered to the mother, that the vital flame played but feebly—that life was but as a quivering, uncertain, spark—a sudden and terrible thought darted through my mind. I know not whether my emotion betrayed me to the ear of Rachel—but, suddenly throwing back the curtain of the bed, she beheld me grasp—with savage ferocity—*with murderous hands!*—Springing from the bed, and throwing herself upon me—her piercing shrieks—

'*I can no more*—of the rest you seem, from whatever means, but too well informed!

'I need not say—protect, if she survive, the miserable mother!—To you, whose heavenly goodness I have so ill requited, it would be injurious as unnecessary! I read, too late, the heart I have insulted!

'I have settled the disposal of my effects—I have commanded my feelings to give you this last, sad, proof of my confidence.—*Kneeling*, I entreat your forgiveness for the sufferings I have caused you! I found your heart wounded—and into those festering wounds I infused a deadly venom—curse not my memory—*We meet no more*.

'Farewell! first, and last, and only, beloved of women!— a long—a long farewell!

'MONTAGUE.'

These are the consequences of confused systems of morals—and thus it is, that minds of the highest hope, and fairest prospect, are blasted!

CHAPTER XXVII

THE unhappy Rachel recovered her health by slow degrees. I had determined, when my affairs were settled, to leave a spot, that had been the scene of so many tragical events. I proposed to the poor girl to take her again into my family, to which she acceded with rapture. She has never since quitted me, and her faithful services, and humble, grateful attachment, have repaid my protection an hundred fold.

Mr Montague left ten thousand pounds, the half of which was settled on his daughter, the remainder left to my disposal. This determined me to adopt you wholly for my son. I wrote to your uncle to that purport, taking upon myself the entire charge of your education, and entreating, that you might never know, unless informed by myself, to whom you owed your birth. That you should continue to think me *your mother*, flattered my tenderness, nor was my Emma, herself, more dear to me.

I retired in a few months to my present residence, sharing my heart and my attentions between my children, who grew up under my fostering care, lovely and beloved.

> 'While every day, soft as it roll'd along,
> Shew'd some new charm.'*

I observed your affection for each other with a flattering presage. With the features of your father, you inherited his intrepidity, and manly virtues—even, at times, I thought I perceived the seeds of his inflexible spirit: but the caresses of my Emma, more fortunate than her mother—yet, with all her mother's sensibility—could, in an instant, soften you to tenderness, and melt you into infantine sweetness.

I endeavoured to form your young minds to every active virtue, to every generous sentiment.—You received, from the same masters, the same lessons, till you attained your twelfth year; and my Emma emulated, and sometimes outstripped your progress. I observed, with a mixture of hope and solicitude, her lively capacity—her enthusiastic affections; while I laboured to moderate and regulate them.

It now became necessary that your educations should take a somewhat different direction; I wished to fit you for a commercial line of life; but the ardor you discovered for science and literature occasioned me some perplexity, as I feared it might unfit you for application to trade, in the pursuit of which so many talents are swallowed up, and powers wasted. Yet, to the professions my objections were still more serious.—The study of law, is the study of chicanery.—The church, the school of hypocrisy and usurpation! You could only enter the universities by a moral degradation, that must check the freedom, and contaminate the purity, of the mind, and, entangling it in an inexplicable maze of error and contradiction, *poison virtue at its source*, and lay the foundation for a duplicity of character and a perversion of reason, destructive of every manly principle of integrity. For the science of physic you expressed a disinclination. A neighbouring gentleman, a surveyor, a man high in his profession, and of liberal manners, to whose friendship I was indebted, offered to take you. You were delighted with this proposal, (to which I had no particular objection) as you had a taste for drawing and architecture.

Our separation, though you were to reside in the same town, cost us many tears—I loved you with more than a mother's fondness—and my Emma clung round the neck of her beloved brother, her Augustus, her playfellow, and sobbed on his bosom. It was with difficulty that you could disentangle yourself from our embraces. Every moment of leisure you flew to us—my Emma learned from you to draw plans, and to study the laws of proportion. Every little exuberance in your disposition, which, generated by a noble pride, sometimes wore the features of asperity, was soothed into peace by her gentleness and affection: while she delighted to emulate your fortitude, and to rise superior to the feebleness fostered in her sex, under the specious name of delicacy. Your mutual attachment encreased with your years, I renewed my existence in my children, and anticipated their more perfect union.

Ah! my son, need I proceed? Must I continually blot the page with the tale of sorrow? Can I tear open again, can I cause to bleed afresh, in your heart and my own, wounds scarcely closed? In her fourteenth year, in the spring of life, your Emma and mine, lovely and fragile blossom, was blighted by a killing frost—After a few days illness, she drooped, faded, languished, and died!

It was now that I felt—'That no agonies were like the agonies of a mother.'* My broken spirits, from these repeated sorrows, sunk into habitual, hopeless, dejection. Prospects, that I had meditated with ineffable delight, were for ever veiled in darkness. Every earthly tie was broken, except that which bound you to my desolated heart with a still stronger cord of affection. You wept, in my arms, the loss of her whom you, yet, fondly believed your sister.—I cherished the illusion lest, by dissolving it, I should weaken your confidence in my maternal love, weaken that tenderness which was now my only consolation.

TO AUGUSTUS HARLEY

My Augustus, *my more than son*, around whom my spirit, longing for dissolution, still continues to flutter! I have unfolded the errors of my past life—I have traced them to their source—I have laid bare my mind before you, that the experiments which have been made upon it may be beneficial to yours! It has been a painful, and a humiliating recital—the retrospection has been marked with anguish. As the enthusiasm—as the passions of my youth—have passed in review before me, long forgotten emotions have been revived in my lacerated heart—it has been again torn with *the pangs of contemned love*—the disappointment of rational plans of usefulness—the dissolution of the darling hopes of maternal pride and fondness. The frost of a premature age sheds its snows upon my temples, the ravages of a sickly mind shake my tottering frame. The morning dawns, the evening closes upon me, the seasons revolve, without hope; the sun shines, the spring returns, but, to me, it is mockery.

And is this all of human life—this, that passes like a tale that is told? Alas! it is a tragical tale! Friendship was the star, whose cheering influence I courted to beam upon my benighted course. The social affections were necessary to my existence, but they have been only inlets to sorrow—*yet, still, I bind them to my heart!*

Hitherto there seems to have been something strangely wrong in the constitutions of society—a lurking poison that spreads its contagion far and wide—a canker at the root of private virtue and private happiness—a principle of deception, that sanctifies error—a Circean cup* that lulls into a fatal intoxication. But men begin to think and reason; reformation dawns, though the advance is tardy. Moral martyrdom may possibly be the fate of those who press forward, yet, their generous efforts will not be lost.— Posterity will plant the olive and the laurel, and consecrate their mingled branches to the memory of such, who, daring to trace, to their springs, errors the most hoary, and prejudices the most venerated, emancipate the human mind from the trammels of superstition, and teach it, *that its true dignity and virtue, consist in being free.*

Ere I sink into the grave, let me behold *the son of my affections*, the living image of him, whose destiny involved mine, who gave an early, but a mortal blow, to all my worldly expectations—let me behold my Augustus, escaped from the tyranny of the passions, restored to reason, to the vigor of his mind, to self-controul, to the dignity of active, intrepid, virtue!

The dawn of my life glowed with the promise of a fair and bright day; before its noon, thick clouds gathered; its mid-day was gloomy and tempestuous.—It remains with thee, my friend, to gild with a mild radiance the closing evening; before the scene shuts, and veils the prospect in impenetrable darkness.

FINIS

EXPLANATORY NOTES

1 *The perceptions of persons in retirement . . . who spend their lives in solitude*: Jean-Jacques Rousseau (1712–78), [La Nouvelle Héloïse] *Eloisa: Or, A Series of Original Letters* (4 vols., new edn. transl. William Kendrick, London, T. Becket, 1776), vol. i, p. xxviii. This translation reads: 'their imaginations *constantly* imprest by the same objects'.

3 *The most interesting, and the most useful, fictions . . . learn the springs which set it in motion*: Hays is influenced by the French philosopher Claude Adrien Helvétius (1715–71) who states that 'the principal merit' of romances 'depends on the exactness with which . . . the virtues and vices, the passions, customs, and follies of a nation are painted', *De L'esprit: or, Essays on the Mind, and its Several Faculties* (London, 1759), 89. Helvétius argues that 'strong passions' are the 'germ productive of genius, and the powerful spring that carries men to great actions', ibid. 150.

Understanding, and talents . . . desires, and particular situations: Helvétius, *A Treatise on Man, His Intellectual Faculties and His Education*, transl. W. Hooper (2 vols., London, B. Law; G. Robinson, 1777) ii. 396. This translation reads: 'being *never anything more*'. Helvétius cites Henry IV as an example of one whose talents are the product of his desires and situation.

Mrs Radcliffe: Ann Radcliffe (1764–1823), author of Gothic novels such as *A Sicilian Romance* (1790), *Romance of the Forest* (1791), *The Mysteries of Udolpho* (1794), and *The Italian* (1797). Her romances are known for arousing terror and curiosity by events apparently supernatural.

Caleb Williams: in William Godwin's (1756–1836) *Things As They Are; or, The Adventures of Caleb Williams* (1794), ed. David McCracken (London, Oxford Univ. Press, 1970), the hero, Caleb Williams, says, 'The spring of action which, perhaps more than any other, characterized the whole train of my life was curiosity' (p. 4). Caleb has an uncontrollable desire to find out the secrets of his master, Mr Falkland, for whom 'reputation has been the idol, the jewel' of his life (p. 102).

3 *a more universal sentiment*: i.e., love, a common subject of sentimental novels.

business of fiction . . . a sort of ideal perfection: perhaps a reference to Samuel Johnson (1709–84) who, in his *Rambler* essay of 31 March 1750, suggested that writers should exhibit 'the most perfect idea of virtue' in fiction rather than representing lives which are 'discoloured by passion, or deformed by wickedness'.

4 *'Do men gather figs of thorns, or grapes of thistles?'*: a version of: 'Are grapes gathered from thorns, or figs from thistles?', Matt. 7: 16; or 'For figs are not gathered from thorns, nor are grapes picked from a bramble bush', Luke 6: 44.

links of the chain: William Godwin's doctrine of necessity suggests that the universe is 'a body of events in systematical arrangement', and that 'in the life of every human being there is a chain of events, generated in the lapse of ages which preceded his birth.' He argues that the 'mind is a real principle, an indispensable link in the great chain of the universe', *Enquiry Concerning Political Justice* (1793), (Harmondsworth, Penguin, 1978), pp. 351–2. Similarly, in *Caleb Williams*, Falkland says: 'All are but links of one chain' (p. 135).

a simple story: title of a novel published in 1791 by Elizabeth Inchbald (1753–1821), actress, playwright, and novelist who was a friend of Thomas Holcroft (1745–1809) and William Godwin. See *A Simple Story*, ed. J. M. S. Tompkins (Oxford, World's Classics, 1988). Hays knew of Inchbald as she quotes from Inchbald's second novel, *Nature and Art* (1796) in a letter to William Godwin dated 1 Mar. 1796.

5 *late popular novel—'That an author . . . a thousand mortifications'*: Matthew G. Lewis's (1775–1818) *Ambrosio, or The Monk* (3 vols., 4th edn., London, J. Bell, 1798) ii. 134. Hays added the parenthetical 'frequently'. The novel was first published anonymously in 1796.

7 *harrows up my soul*: 'I could a tale unfold whose lightest word | Would harrow up thy soul, freeze thy young blood.' Shakespeare, *Hamlet, Prince of Denmark*, I. v. 15–16.

8 *Rouse the nobler energies . . . eradicating them*: both Godwin and Helvétius believed that passions were necessary to the human spirit. In *Enquiry Concerning Political Justice*, Godwin writes: 'the passions ought to be purified, but not to be

eradicated' (p. 136). In *De L'esprit*, Helvétius writes: 'Passions indeed are the celestial fire which vivifies the moral world, it is to the passions that the arts and sciences owe their discoveries, and the soul its elevation', p. 160.

Sensation generates . . . determine the future character: this passage describing the importance of sensations on the formation of character is largely based on Helvétius's and Godwin's philosophies. According to Helvétius in *A Treatise on Man*, 'the character of a man is the immediate effect of his passions, and his passions are often the immediate effects of his situations', i. 27. He argues that 'all the operations of the mind are reducible to sensation', i. 94. Godwin echoes these ideas in *Enquiry Concerning Political Justice*: 'the actions and dispositions of men are not the offspring of any original bias that they bring into the world in favour of one sentiment or character rather than another, but flow entirely from the operation of circumstances and events acting upon a faculty of receiving sensible impressions' (p. 98). Again he writes, 'All our knowledge, all our ideas, everything we possess as intelligent beings, comes from impression' (p. 146). At one point in *Caleb Williams*, a character says: 'you did not make yourself; you are just what circumstances irresistibly compelled you to be' (p. 310).

9 *The term metaphysics . . . the first principles of arts and sciences*: Helvétius, *Treatise on Man*, i. 239: 'By metaphysics, I do not mean that jargon transmitted by the Egyptian priests to Pythagoras, by him to Plato, and by Plato to us, and which is still taught in some schools: but I mean, with Bacon, the knowledge of the first principles of any art or science whatever.'

11 *an Orlando, or an Oroondates*: legendary adventurous heroes. Orlando was one of twelve paladins and nephew of Charlemagne. Oroondates, Prince of Scythia, is a leading character in Gauthier de Costes de La Calprenède's *Cassandra: the fam'd Romance* (1652). He was adorned with every perfection of mind and body, and seems to have typified the romance hero for many eighteenth-century English writers.

a ship in the West India trade: in the eighteenth century, the West Indies supplied Britain with sugar, coffee, cotton, mahogany, logwood, and indigo. In 1795 the West Indies trade was sufficiently lucrative to warrant the construction of a new dock in London which opened in August 1802.

11 *Pope and Bolingbroke*: Alexander Pope (1688-1744), ac-
    claimed poet and translator of Homer. Pope dedicated his
    philosophical *Essay on Man* (1733–4) to his friend and
    patron Lord Bolingbroke (1678–1751), Tory minister in
    the last years of Queen Anne's reign, whose *The Spirit of
    Patriotism* (1749) argued that government and liberty must
    support each other.

12 *Thomson's charming description . . . nature pressing on the heart!*:
    James Thomson (1700–48), *The Seasons* (1730), from
    'Spring', i, ll. 1076–7.

    the counting house: a building, chamber, or room appropri-
    ated to the keeping of accounts.

13 *an equipage*: a carriage and horses, with the attendant
    servants.

    war time: France declared war on England, Holland, and
    Spain in early 1793 when it was also involved in the First
    War of the Coalition (1792–7) against Austria. Britain and
    other European powers intervened in 1793 because of the
    threat to the European balance of power.

    Portsmouth: a large port on the south coast, west of Brighton;
    the closest town to the Isle of Wight.

    nurse: a woman employed to breastfeed a child; a wet nurse.
    Many criticized this custom of handing over children, pri-
    marily of women of fashion, to nurses of the lower classes
    because it tended to promote disease and illness; and by the
    end of the century, more women were beginning to nurse
    their own children.

14 *stories . . . of like marvellous import*: 'Eastern' or 'Oriental'
    tales were extremely popular in the eighteenth century.
    Antoine Galland's translation of *Arabian Nights Entertain-
    ment: Consisting of One Thousand and One Stories*, published
    in English in the first decade of the century, went into at
    least ten editions. Seyhzade (or Checzade), *Turkish Tales;
    Consisting of Several Extraordinary Adventures: With the History
    of the Sultaness of Persia, and the Visiers*, trans. from the French
    version of François Pétis de la Croix (London, Jacob
    Tonson, 1708).

    Pope's Homer, and Thomson's Seasons: Alexander Pope, transl.
    The Iliad of Homer (London, 1715–20); James Thomson, *The
    Seasons, A Hymn, a Poem to the Memory of Sir Isaac Newton, and
    Britannia, a Poem* (London, Millar, 1730).

15 *I ran like the hind . . . sang like the lark*: Hays's description of
childhood idyll is similar to William Wordsworth's: 'like a
roe | I bounded o'er the mountains, by the sides | Of the
deep rivers,' 'Lines Composed a Few Miles Above Tintern
Abbey', ll. 67–9. Both conceive of childhood as a period of
unfettered, animal-like innocence.

sent to boarding school: in Elizabeth Inchbald's *A Simple Story*
(1791), Miss Milner's lack of a proper education is attributed in part to her 'Protestant boarding-school, from
whence she was sent with merely such sentiments of religion, as young ladies of fashion mostly imbibe. Her little
heart employed in all the endless pursuits of personal accomplishments, had left her mind without one ornament,
except those which nature gave, and even they were not
wholly preserved from the ravages made by its rival, *Art*'
(Oxford, World's Classics, 1988), pp. 4–5.

needle-work: Mary Wollstonecraft (1759–97) was similarly
against forcing girls to do needlework. In *A Vindication of the
Rights of Woman* (1792) she says that society's idea of female
education is that 'young girls ought to dedicate great part of
their time to needle-work; yet, this employment contracts
their faculties more than any other that could have been
chosen for them, by confining their thoughts to their persons' (New York, Norton Critical Edition, 1988), p. 75.

16 *verses from the French testament*: probably the New Testament
in French. A more unlikely possibility is François Villon's
(1431–?) *Le Grand Testament*, written in 1461 though not
published until 1489, a work of 2,023 lines written in the
form of a mock will. The author envisages his death and
looks back on his life and sufferings with bitterness and
humour.

18 *'His death was the serene evening of a beautiful day!'*: in his
Treatise on Man Helvétius quotes this line, explaining: 'It was
not in the tomb of Croesus, but on that of Baucis, this
epitaph was engraved,' ii. 156. Hays had added the word
'serene'.

a circulating library: a library of which the books are circulated among subscribers.

19 *Berkley-square*: Berkeley Square is a 'spacious square of ir-
regular houses, situated at the west end of Bruton St. from
New Bond St., to the south end of Davies St. from Oxford St.

and at the north end of Berkeley St. going from Piccadilly', James Elmes, *A Topographical Dictionary of London and its Environs* (London, Whittaker, Treacher and Arnot, 1831), 55. Some notable people who lived in Berkeley Square in the eighteenth century include the Marquis of Lansdowne (formerly the Earl of Shelburne); Colley Cibber, dramatist and Poet Laureate; Horace Walpole, letter writer and novelist; and Mary Robinson, poet, actress, and novelist, who is satirized in a work called 'The Vis-à-Vis of Berkley-Square' (London, Murray, Bowen, & Southerne, 1783).

21 *hauteur*: pride, haughtiness.

mistake my valet for a prince . . . my house for a haunted castle: in Gothic romances, such as those by Ann Radcliffe, the heroine often imagines terrors as described by Mr Courtney. Jane Austen parodies the heroines of novels like these in *Northanger Abbey* (1817).

the lives of Plutarch: Plutarch's *Vitae Parallelae* (*c.*100 AD) was available in English in several editions in the seventeenth and eighteenth centuries. In Mary Shelley's *Frankenstein* (1818), the creature learns 'high thoughts' from Plutarch: 'this book developed new and mightier scenes of action . . . I felt the greatest ardour for virtue rise within me, and abhorrence for vice', ch. 15.

22 *Venice Preserved*: according to John Genest's *Some Account of the English Stage from the Restoration in 1660 to 1830* (10 vols., Bath, H. E. Carrington, 1832), Thomas Otway's *Venice Preserved* was first performed in Dorset Garden Theatre in 1682. The performance that Hays alludes to is probably the one which opened at Drury Lane on 21 Oct. 1795. Genest records that 'After the third night this play was obliged to be laid aside on account of the improper application of some of the political passages—when Pierre said, "Curs'd be your Senate—curs'd your Constitution," he was rapturously applauded', vii. 229.

Aristides the just: Athenian statesman (530?–468 BC) who was known for his strict observance of equity and justice. He was entrusted by members of the Delian Confederacy with fixing assessments of states in the confederacy, and remained influential in Athenian politics until his death.

23 *knowledge and learning . . . their true empire*: these sentiments are expressed by Rousseau in *Emilius; or, An Essay on Educa-*

tion, transl. Mr Nugent (2 vols., London, J. Nourse & P. Vaillant, 1763), ii. 229: 'An inquiry into abstract and speculative truths, into the principles and axioms of sciences, and everything that tends to render our ideas more general, is not the province of women. Their studies ought to be all practical.' He stresses that woman's violence increases her charms: 'The female empire is that of softness, address, and complacency; their orders are caresses, their menaces tears' (ii. 270). Both Hays and Wollstonecraft disagreed with Rousseau's views on women and on female intellectual capabilities. Wollstonecraft says, 'My own sex, I hope, will excuse me, if I treat them like rational creatures, instead of flattering their *fascinating graces*, and viewing them as if they were in a state of perpetual childhood, unable to stand alone', *A Vindication of the Rights of Woman*, Introduction, 9.

'Loveliest . . . engaging man': James Thomson, *The Seasons*, 'Autumn', 583–5.

Charlemagne: Carolus Magnus, Charles I, the Great (742–814), King of the Franks 768–814, crowned Emperor of the West 800–14.

25 *My early associations rendered theology an interesting subject*: Emma, like Hays, is fascinated with philosophy and theology. In the early 1780s Mary Hays began a correspondence with Robert Robinson on various topics, including deism. In 1791 she debated with Gilbert Wakefield on the necessity and benefits of public worship in her *Cursory Remarks on an Enquiry into the Expediency and Propriety of Public or Social Worship*.

writings of Descartes: René Descartes (1596–1650), French scientist, mathematician, and philosopher, was the first to liberate philosophical thought from Scholasticism in favour of dualistic or Cartesian philosophy that distinguished between mind and body. He focused attention on the problem of how we know, and believed that a single method of reasoning could apply to all natural sciences, providing a unified body of knowledge. His writings include *Discourse on Method* (1637) and *Meditations* (1641).

the Heloise of Rousseau: Jean-Jacques Rousseau's *La Nouvelle Héloïse* (1761) was available in a number of English editions shortly after it was published in France. It is an adaptation of the story of two famous twelfth-century lovers, Abelard and

Eloisa. An epistolary novel, it tells the story of a young girl
who falls passionately in love with her tutor, but who acqui-
esces to her father and marries the 50-year old Wolmar,
chosen by her father.

25 *the sorrows of the tender St Preux*: the young tutor of Héloïse
who is forced to separate from her in Rousseau's novel.

30 *dose*: doze.

32 *magic circle*: Mary Wollstonecraft uses this term to refer to
romantic imagination in her *Letters Written During a Short
Residence in Sweden, Norway, and Denmark*, letter 10, p. 100: 'I
must fly from thought, and find refuge from sorrow in a
strong imagination—the only solace for a feeling heart.
Phantoms of bliss! ideal forms of excellence! again inclose
me in your magic circle, and wipe clear from my remembrance the disappointments which render the sympathy
painful.' Hays uses the term here and i. ch. 26 to refer to
constraints which society imposes on women, but she later
uses the term to refer to an illusory romance: 'I felt guarded
as by a talisman, encompassed in magic circle, through
which neither danger could assail nor sorrow pierce me',
The Victim of Prejudice (Peterborough, Ont., Broadview,
1994), p. 122).

33 *'Had I beheld . . . my heart had broke'*: *Douglas; A Tragedy* was a
popular play set in medieval Scotland, written by the Minis-
ter of Athelstaneford, John Home (1722–1808), first performed in Edinburgh in Dec. 1756. The unhappily married
Lady Randolph says: 'Had some good angel op'd to me the
book | Of Providence, and let me read my life, | My heart
had broke, when I beheld the sum | Of ills, which one by one
I have endur'd' (Edinburgh, John Beugo, 1792), i. 261–4.
wave: waive.

severally: separately, each in turn.

34 *Mr Francis, the elder, was in his fortieth year*: Mr Francis is
modelled after William Godwin, who was 40 in 1796.

39 *the world appears to me a thorny and a pathless wilderness*: not a
direct quotation, but the metaphor of the world as a wilderness is common; e.g., 'As I walk'd through the wilderness of
this world,' John Bunyan, *The Pilgrim's Progress* (1678), pt. I.

The character . . . is modified by circumstances: this is one of
Godwin's central arguments in *Enquiry Concerning Political
Justice*: 'the actions and dispositions of mankind are the

offspring of circumstances and events, and not of any original determination that they bring into the world' (p. 97). Hays adapts Godwin's ideas for feminist purposes.

41 *'Parting is such sweet sorrow!'*: William Shakespeare, *Romeo and Juliet*, v. iii. 185.

47 *what have those to do . . . that which passeth shew?*: William Shakespeare, *Hamlet*, I. ii. 76–86, esp. ll. 83–6: 'These, indeed, seem; | For they are actions that a man might play; | But I have that within which passes show— | These but the trappings and the suits of woe.'

48 *The growth of reason is slow . . . the increase of virtue and happiness*: in *Enquiry Concerning Political Justice*, Book IV, ch. 5, 'Of the Cultivation of Truth', Godwin speaks of the benefits of the discovery and knowledge of truth: 'Abstractedly considered, it conduces to the happiness and virtue of the individual, as well as to the improvement of our social institutions' (p. 298).

49 *We may trace . . . political institutions*: Godwin came to the conclusion that governments counteract the improvement of the individual mind. In *Enquiry Concerning Political Justice*, he says: 'Government was intended to suppress injustice, but its effect has been to embody and perpetuate it', Summary of Principles, section II, p. 76. 'The injuries to a nation depend for their nature, for the most part, upon their permanency' (p. 264). Towards the latter part of the book he writes, 'With what delight must every well informed friend of mankind look forward to the auspicious period, the dissolution of political government, of that brute engine which has been the only perennial cause of the vices of mankind, and which, as has abundantly appeared in the progress of the present work, has mischiefs of various sorts incorporated with its substance, and no otherwise removable than by its utter annihilation!' (p. 554).

50 *Obedience, is a word, which ought never to have had existence . . . we quench the principle of action, of virtue, of reason*: Godwin is against tyranny and obedience, but his discussion is more forgiving than Hays's expostulation here. 'As long as a man is held in the trammels of obedience, and habituated to look to some foreign guidance for the direction of his conduct, his understanding and the vigour of his mind will sleep', *Political Justice*, p. 692.

50 *The hordes of barbarians, which overwhelmed ancient Rome*: the Barbarian migrations occurred between AD 375 and 568. Hays is not entirely right in saying that they 'adopted at length' the Roman religion, because these east Germanic Ostrogoths and Visigoths had already been converted to the Arian form of Christianity by the Goth Wulfila (*c.*310–80). Rome was sacked by Alaric the Goth in AD 410.

the grain of mustard seed, growing up into a large tree, shelters the fowls of heaven in its branches: this parable is told several times in the Gospels; see Matt. 13: 31–2; Mark 4: 30–2, and Luke 13: 18–19.

51 *Our duties . . . to lead them to habits of goodness and greatness*: Godwin believed that it was possible to overcome vices and moral weaknesses: 'Man is perfectible or in other words susceptible of perpetual improvement', *Political Justice*, p. 140. He writes, 'I am bound to employ my talents, my understanding, my strength and my time, for the production of the greatest quantity of general good', p. 175; and 'Duty is that mode of action on the part of an individual which constitutes the best possible application of his capacity to the general benefit', p. 190.

52 *having neglected to make a will, a freehold estate . . . devolved of course to his eldest son*: Referring mainly to the seventeenth century, Alan Macfarlane, in 'The Myth of the Peasantry: Family and Economy in a Northern Parish', *Land, Kinship and Life-Cycle*, ed. Richard M. Smith (Cambridge, Cambridge Univ. Press, 1984), 341, notes: 'If we look more closely at both Common Law as it applied to freehold estates and manorial customs . . . the principle that a "living man has no heirs", that children had no inalienable rights in a family estate, appears to have been present. Thus, a father could totally disinherit a son if he so wished; primogeniture merely meant that an eldest male heir would inherit if no will or transfer before death had been made to the contrary. It did not mean that a son would automatically inherit.' By 1724 the enforcement of the custom of London, which was impartible inheritance or primogeniture, was abolished. But the custom still applied in cases of intestacy, according to J. P. Cooper, in 'Inheritance and Settlement by Great Landowners', in Jack Goody, Joan Thirsk, E. P. Thompson (eds.), *Family and Inheritance: Rural Society in Western Europe,*

1200–1800 (Cambridge, Cambridge Univ. Press, 1976), 226.

55 *desert*: dessert.

59 *the St Preux, the Emilius*: Emma projects onto Augustus Harley the qualities of Rousseau's heroes from *La Nouvelle Héloïse* and *Emile*.

61 *'People, in general,' says Rousseau . . . till the day of their deaths.'*: Rousseau anticipates that some readers might find the 'simple narrative' of the innocent loves of Emile and Sophia 'trifling, and unworthy of notice', but suggests that 'such a judgment' is 'mistaken': 'They do not sufficiently consider the influence which the first connexion between man and woman hath over the remainder of their lives. They do not perceive that an impression, so strong and so lively as that of love, is productive of a long chain of effects, which pass unobserved in a course of years, and nevertheless continue to operate till the day of their deaths.' *Emilius; or, An Essay on Education*, p. 285.

'melted into thin air': Shakespeare, *The Tempest*, IV. i. 148–50: 'These our actors, | As I foretold you, were all spirits, and | Are melted into air, into thin air.'

'The more desires I have . . . all our desires within one point.': Helvétius, *A Treatise on Man*, ii. 42. He argues that 'it is not the number, but the strength of the passions' which is important.

62 *a chaise*: a light, open carriage drawn by four horses. In the eighteenth century, it was probably the quickest mode of travel.

65 *litter*: a light bed or couch with a frame covered by curtains, capable of being carried on men's shoulders or placed on some steady vehicle drawn by animals; a slow mode of travel.

69 *an express*: a dispatch, sent with speed; 'a message sent on purpose', Samuel Johnson, *A Dictionary of the English Language* (London, 1755).

delicious poison: this term, used by Emma here and in the next chapter, echoes that of Alexander Pope and Rousseau. In Pope's poem, Eloisa tells Abelard her wishes, to 'still drink delicious poison from thy eye, | Pant on thy lip, and to thy heart be prest' (ll. 122–3). Rousseau uses the same language in *La Nouvelle Héloïse* and *Emile*: 'The very first day we met, I imbibed the poison which now infects my senses and my reason', *Eloisa: Or, A Series of Original Letters*, i. 14; 'Then it was that the irresistible charms of that heavenly person rushed like a torrent, and overpowered Emilius's heart: then did he begin to suck in the delicious poison, which lulled his reason asleep', *Emilius*, p. 284.

71 *'While truths divine came mended from his tongue'*: 'And truths divine came mended from that tongue,' Alexander Pope, 'Eloisa to Abelard', l. 66.

'The feast of reason, and the flow of souls': Alexander Pope, 'The First Satire of the Second Book of Horace, Imitated', l. 128.

72 *'the spot of azure in the cloudy sky'*: John Scott (1730–83), 'Elegy Written at Amwell, 1768': 'O Human Life! how mutable, how vain! | How thy wide sorrows circumscribe thy joy— | A sunny island in a stormy main, | A spot of azure in a cloudy sky!' *The Poetical Works of John Scott Esq.* (London, J. Buckland, 1782), 54.

79 *'pity melted the soul to love!'*: 'For Pity melts the Mind to Love,' John Dryden (1631–1700), 'Alexander's Feast; or The Power of Musique. An Ode, in Honour of St. Cecilia's Day' (1697) l. 96.

80 *'the strength of an affection is generally in the same proportion, as the character of the species, in the object beloved, is lost in that of the individual'*: this is Wollstonecraft's note to a comment about 'individuality of character, the only fastener of the affections', *Vindication of the Rights of Woman*, p. 70.

81 *'a shade that follows wealth and fame'*: 'And what is friendship but a name, | A charm that lulls to sleep: | A shade that follows wealth and fame, | But leaves the wretch to weep?' Oliver Goldsmith (*c.*1730–74), 'Edwin and Angelina. A Ballad' (1765 or 1766), ll. 73–6.

'Shall those by heaven's own influence join'd, . . . of the sky?': Mary Robinson (1758—1800), 'Anselmo, the Hermit of the Alps', *Poetical Works of the Late Mrs. Mary Robinson* (3 vols., London, Richard Phillips, 1806), 34–5. 'Anselmo' is a narrative poem about a hermit who discovers 'that absence cannot conquer love'. He resolves too late to rebel against 'tyrant pow'r', 'insatiate pride', and 'the spells of paltry gold' because they separated him from his 'peerless maid' Rosa.

'The hope-flush'd enterer on the stage of life': John Scott, 'Elegy IV: Written at the Approach of Winter': 'Who dreams of Nature, free from Nature's strife? | Who dreams of constant happiness below? | The hope-flush'd ent'rer on the stage of life; | The youth to knowledge unchastis'd by woe,' ll. 37–40, *The Poetical Works of John Scott Esq.* (London, 1782), 43.

82 *'the body charms, because the mind is seen'*: Edward Young (1683–1765), 'Love of Fame, The Universal Passion. In Seven Characteristical Satires', *Edward Young: The Complete Works, Poetry and Prose*, ed. James Nichols (2 vols., Hildesheim, Georg Olms, 1968), i. 393, ll. 150–4: 'And yet the case is clear; | What's female beauty, but an air divine, | Through which the mind's all-gentle graces shine? | They, like the sun, irradiate all between; | The body charms because the soul is seen.'

83 *'Oh! what a world is this! . . . be misconstrued into something too degrading for expression?'*: Thomas Holcroft, *Anna St. Ives* (1792), ed. Peter Faulkner (London, Oxford Univ. Press, 1970), vol. iii, letter 44, p. 146. This letter was written by Anna to her friend Louisa after her efforts to reform Clifton are met with romantic advances by him.

confident: confidante.

84 *'That such things were, and were the most dear'*: an echo of William Shakespeare's *Macbeth*, iv. iii. 222–3: 'I cannot but remember such things were | That were most precious to me.'

85 *'hanging drapery on a smooth block'*: Mary Wollstonecraft, *A Vindication of the Rights of Woman*. Hays uses this same quote in a letter to William Godwin dated 28 July 1795, Pforzheimer Collection.

86 *What are passions, but another name for powers?*: Helvétius, in *De L'esprit*, expresses a similar opinion about passions: 'It is therefore to strong passions that we owe the invention and wonders of arts; and consequently they are to be considered as the germ productive of genius, and the powerful spring that carries men to great actions' (p. 150).

'They make the impossibility they fear!' 'They conquer difficulties, by daring to attempt them': Nicholas Rowe, *The Ambitious Stepmother. A Tragedy* (1700), i. i: 'The wise and active conquer difficulties | By daring to attempt them. Sloth and folly | Shiver and shrink at sight of toil and hazard, | And make th'impossibility they fear.' This passage is also quoted by

Richardson's *Clarissa* (Harmondsworth, Penguin, 1985), p. 552.

87 *ignis fatuus*: a will-o'-the-wisp, a delusive hope, an apparition.

89 '*The voice of nature is too strong to be silenced by artificial precepts*': source not found.

'*The thousand . . . in the gross*': source not found.

the vehicular state, and . . . the sentient language: Edward Search's *The Light of Nature Pursued* (5 vols., London, T. Jones, 1768) is a work which deals with various philosophical topics such as human nature, the faculties of the mind, necessity, etc. In a chapter called 'Vehicular State', vol. ii. p. 2, ch. 21, the author surmises that after a person dies, the spirit leaves the body in a vehicle 'extremely small so that the nicest eye may not discern it when going', p. 13. This vehicle is like a muscle and fibre, 'tough and strong but extremely flexible and obedient to the will', p. 19. In a visionary state, Ned Search meets the spirit of John Locke, who teaches him about sentient language which is distinguished from the vocal. Of this language the fictional Locke says: 'this is carried on by applying our vehicles close to one another and raising certain figures or motions on our outsides which communicate the like to our neighbour and thereby excite in him the same ideas that gave rise to them in ourselves, making him as it were feel our thoughts. This is a much completer way of conversing, being not liable to misapprehension provided the recipient takes care to remove all his own ideas that none of them may confound or interfere with those delivered: but to do that effectually requires great dexterity and long practice' (pp. 135–6).

'*Something, than beauty dearer*': James Thomson, *The Seasons*, 'Something than beauty dearer, should they look', 'Spring', l. 1141.

90 *The shame of being singular . . . requires strong principles, and much native firmness of temper, to surmount*: John Aiken, MD, *Letters from A Father To his Son, On Various Topics, Relative to Literature and the Conduct of Life. Written in the Years 1792 and 1793* (London, J. Johnson, 1793), letter 2, p. 9: 'On retracing my own feelings, I find that the first and principal cause of juvenile weakness is false shame. The shame of being singular,—the shame of lying under restraints from which others are free,—the shame of appearing ungenteel,—are

all acutely felt by young persons in general, and require strong principle or much native firmness of temper to surmount.'

'*put to sea upon a shattered plank, and placed my trust in miracles for safety*': Edward Yound, *The Revenge, The Complete Works Poetry and Prose*, ed. James Nichols (Hildesheim, Georg Olms, 1968), p. 228; Leonora: 'Why did I leave my tender father's wing, | And venture into love? That maid that loves, | Goes out to sea upon a shatter'd plank, | And puts her trust in miracles for safety.'

'*Truth and good are one, | And beauty dwells with them*': Mark Akenside (1721–70), *The Pleasures of Imagination. A Poem in Three Books*, in *The Poetical Works of Mark Akenside*, with a Preface and Life by Alexander Dyce (London, 1845; facsimile repr. New York, AMS Press, 1969). 'Thus was Beauty sent from heaven, | The lovely ministress of Truth and Good | In this dark world: for Truth and Good are one, | And Beauty dwells in them, and they in her, | With like participation,' i. 96, ll. 372–6; first published in 1744, and revised as *The Pleasures of the Imagination*, 1757.

the palace of Truth: Stephanie Felicité Brulart de Genlis (1746–1830), *Tales of the Castle: Or, Stories of Instruction and Delight*, transl. Thomas Holcroft (5 vols., London, G. Robinson, 1785) contains a tale called 'The Palace of Truth', v. 139–286). In this moral tale, the hero asks the Sovereign of the Genii to build a palace in which, 'by a charm, everyone who entered it, should be obliged to declare their secret thoughts whenever they spoke', 167.

91   *the Book of Fate*: Alexander Pope, 'An Essay on Man', Epistle I, l. 77: 'Heaven from all creatures hides the book of fate.'

in the East India Service: at this time, India was a colony which was largely under the control of the East India Company, originally chartered in 1600 as a trading company, but by the mid-eighteenth century granted joint sovereignty of India with the Crown. An officer in the East India Service would most likely have a career in territorial administration.

94   *like Hamlet, you had spoke daggers*: 'I will speak daggers to her, but use none,' *Hamlet*, III. ii. 386. In the same play, the Queen says, 'O, speak to me no more! | These words like daggers enter in my ears,' III. iv. 95.

95 *confident*: confidant.

96 *India House*: the East India House, also called 'India House', located at the north-west corner of Lime St., extending to Leadenhall Market, was the offices of the East India Company.

98 *adopt the sentiment of Plato . . . esteemed by one whom I so sincerely regard.*': Plato (428–348 BC), Greek philosopher whose ideas, along with those of Socrates and Aristotle, have laid the philosophical foundations of Western culture.

'the shakes and agues of his fragile nature': in Thomas Holcroft's *Anna St. Ives*, Frank Henley writes, 'Oliver, I am a man, and subject to the shakes and agues of his fragile nature!' vol. iii, letter 42, p. 139.

'Let not the coldly wise exult, that their heads were never led astray by their hearts': source not found.

99 *'The ideas, the associations, the circumstances . . . a precise, general rule'*: William Godwin, *Enquiry Concerning Political Justice*: 'The ideas, associations and circumstances of each man are properly his own; and it is a pernicious system that would lead us to require all men, however different their circumstances, to act by a precise general rule' (p. 758).

'That there may exist . . . daughter of an executioner': Nugent's translation reads: 'I affirm, that the influence of natural relations is so superior to the other, that it is this alone which decides the fate of humanity; and that there is such an agreement of tastes, humour, sentiments, and tempers, as should engage a prudent father, were he a prince, or a great monarch, to marry his son, without the least hesitation, to the damsel that had all those fitnesses or agreements, were she even sprung from a base ignoble family, were she even the daughter of a common executioner', Jean-Jacques Rousseau, *Emilius, Or, An Essay on Education*, p. 267.

101 *In fine*: to conclude, in short.

a restless, an insatiable, curiosity: Emma's overdeveloped sense of curiosity is like Caleb Williams's desire to find out the truth at all cost in Godwin's novel.

102 *ignis fatuus of false hope*: in Thomas Holcroft's *Anna St. Ives*, Frank Henley similarly writes, 'Impossibility must be made more impossible!—'Tis that, Oliver, which kills me, that ignis fatuus of false hope', vol. iv, letter 73, p. 243.

a question of utility: Helvétius, *De L'esprit*: '[Public utility] is the principle on which all human virtues are founded, and the basis of all legislations' (p. 41). Utility is a notion to which William Godwin returns many times in *Enquiry Concerning Political Justice*. For example, 'Morality is that system of conduct which is determined by a consideration of the greatest general good... governed by views of benevolence, and made subservient to public utility', pp. 165–6.

a sentiment of Richardson's Clarissa... I will reveal them': Samuel Richardson, *Clarissa, or The History of a Young Lady* (1747–8): 'You seem to think me faulty: I should be glad that all the world knew my heart. Let my enemies sit in judgement upon my actions: fairly scanned, I fear not the result. Let them even ask me my most secret thoughts, and, whether they make for me or against me, I will reveal them' (Penguin, 1985), p. 822. The passage is spoken by Clarissa to Captain Tomlinson.

104 *desart*: desert.

'*The affections (truly says Sterne) must be exercised on something... when they rejoiced, I would rejoice with them*': the first sentence of the passage is not Sterne's, but may be Hays's own. In a letter to William Godwin dated 20 November 1795, she writes: 'The source of all my pleasures and of all my improvements has been in my attachments—I love to find excellence, and to admire, and to emulate, it—when I lose this ardour I shall sink into apathy and lassitude' (Letter in Carl Pforzheimer Library, New York). The passage from Sterne begins: 'I declare, ... that was I in a desart', and ends 'I would rejoice along with them', Laurence Sterne, *A Sentimental Journey* (1768; London, Oxford Univ. Press, 1968), p. 28.

108 *Bedford square*: built in 1775–80, Bedford Square is located in what is now called the Bloomsbury area of London, north of High Holborn, with Gower Street to its east and Tottenham Court Road to its west. Henry Cavendish, the scientist, lived at No. 11 from 1796 to 1810, Lord Loughborough, the Lord Chancellor, at No. 6 in 1787–96, and Thomas Leverton at No. 13 in 1796–1824. Hays visited Mary Wollstonecraft, who lived in Store St., Bedford Square, in 1792.

109 *'Pride, pomp, and circumstance of glorious war!'*: William Shakespeare, *Othello*, III. iii. 358.

111 *nice*: not obvious or readily apprehended, difficult to decide or settle, demanding close consideration or thought.

112 *A blow on the right cheek . . . turn the left, also*: 'whosoever shall smite thee on thy right cheek, turn to him the other also', Matt. 5: 39; see also Luke 6: 29.

the Slave Trade: towards the end of the eighteenth century, there was increasing agitation for an end to the slave trade. The poet Helen Maria Williams (1761–1827) published a poem called 'On the Bill . . . for Regulating the Slave-Trade' in 1788. In 1792 the 'Antisaccharites' called for abstention from slave-produced sugar, tobacco, and rum, while Charles James Fox persuaded the House of Commons to approve a motion to consider the measures necessary for the abolition of the slave trade. However, Britain did not declare an end to the slave trade until March 1807, and slavery itself was not abolished until 1833.

'with more than selfish vanity': source not found.

113 *to be treated like ideots . . . the weak beings they helped to form*: this sentiment is similar to Mary Wollstonecraft's: 'I wish to persuade women to endeavour to acquire strength, both of mind and body, and to convince them that the soft phrases, susceptibility of heart, delicacy of sentiment, and refinement of taste, are almost synonymous with epithets of weakness, and that those beings who are only the objects of pity and that kind of love, which has been termed its sister, will soon become objects of contempt', *Vindication of the Rights of Woman*, Introduction, 9.

115 *'That one channel . . . of all connection'*: Emma is trying to analyse her feelings in Helvétius's terms. For Helvétius, having only one strong passion was more dangerous than having many: 'Great crimes are not always the effects of the multitude of our desires', *A Treatise on Man*, ii. 42. See note to p. 61 above.

116 *Individual happiness . . . the only true end of existence*: these ideas are echoes of Godwin's notions of happiness in *Enquiry Concerning Political Justice*: 'The true object of moral and political disquisition is pleasure or happiness', Summary of Principles, 75. Godwin argues that 'virtue consists in a desire of the happiness of the species' (p. 304), and that

men 'will find the highest gratification in promoting and contemplating the general happiness' (p. 743).

the grand end of life—general utility: Godwin discusses general utility several times in *Enquiry Concerning Political Justice*. For example, 'if only the criterion of justice be general utility, the inevitable consequence is that the more we have of justice, the more we shall have of truth, virtue and happiness' (p. 689).

117 *Rousseau's Julia*: Emma identifies herself with the young Julia, rather than the mature woman who renounces her first love in obedience to her father. In the prefatory 'Dialogue Between a Man of Letters and Mr. J. J. Rousseau, on the Subject of Romances', Rousseau writes, 'Love is nothing more than an illusion . . . it is surrounded with objects which have no existence but in imagination . . . When it is arrived at its greatest height, its objects appears in a state of perfection, and then becomes its idol, it is placed in the heavens', vol. i. p. xxxi.

120 *'Where the imagination is vivid . . . to attain its end'*: Hays has rearranged the order of the sentences slightly. In Holcroft's *Anna St. Ives*, the quotations are in two paragraphs as follows: 'Our imaginations are vivid, our feelings strong, our views and desires not bounded by common rules. In such minds, passions, if not subdued, become ungovernable, and fatal. . . . My mind is no less ardent than yours, though education and habit may have given it a different turn. It glows with equal zeal to attain its end. Where there is much warmth, much enthusiasm, I suspect there is much danger', vol. iii, letter 53, p. 171.

123 *palsey*: to affect with palsy or to paralyse; to render powerless.

124 *too nice*: punctilious, sensitive, scrupulous, strict in matters of reputation or conduct.

a long chain of events: see explanatory note to the Preface, p. 4.

127 *'Oh! with what difficulty is an active mind . . . as hopeless!'*: Godwin, *Caleb Williams*, p. 199: 'An active mind, which has once been forced into any particular train, can scarcely be persuaded to desert it as hopeless.'

129 *'The rose . . . a blister there.'*: *Hamlet*, III. iv. 42–4: 'takes off the rose | From the fair forehead of an innocent love, | And sets a blister there.'

131 *'There, where the human heart most exquisitely feels!'*: source not found.

132 *'The world might call my plans . . . the customs of the world?'*: Hays has amalgamated two passages from Holcroft's *Anna St. Ives* here. 'The world perhaps would call my views extravagant, my pretensions impertinent, and my plans absurd', written by Anna to Clifton, vol. iv, letter 79, p. 264; 'Was I or was I not guilty of any crime, when in the very acme of the passions, I so totally disregarded the customs of the world?' written by Anna to her friend Louisa Clifton after she takes the initiative and kisses Frank Henley in spite of the difference in their backgrounds, vol. iii, letter 41, p. 138.

133 *'Man cometh forth . . . and continueth not!'*: Job 14: 2, 'He cometh forth like a flower, and is cut down: he fleeth also as a shadow, and continueth not.'

       'What, in fact,' says a philosophic writer . . . of a strong passion': exact quotation not found, but Helvétius does assert that 'the more lively our passions are, the greater are the effects produced by them. Thus success, as all history proves, constantly attends the people who are animated by strong passions', *De L'esprit*, 216.

137 *solitary wanderer*: an echo of Rousseau's *Les Rêveries du Promeneur Solitaire* (1776–8).

139 *bona fide*: in good faith; with sincerity; without any intention to deceive or defraud.

141 *'I seemed to be in a state, in which reason had no power . . . I am under the guidance of a director more energetic than you!'*: Godwin, *Caleb Williams*, ii. 154.

143 *'And pining love . . . forc'd to flow.'*: Thomas Gray, 'Ode on a Distant Prospect of Eton College' (1747): 'Or pining Love shall waste their youth, | Or Jealousy with rankling tooth, | That inly gnaws the secret heart,' ll. 65–7. 'The stings of Falsehood these shall try, | And hard Unkindness' altered eye, | That mocks the tear it forced to flow,' ll. 75–7.

       Jupiter shrouded . . . shorn of his strength: in Roman mythology, Jupiter is the sky god. He became identified with the sky god of the Greeks, Zeus, who transformed himself into various forms in order to seduce women: he made love to Leda in the form of a swan; changed himself into a cuckoo to seduce his wife, Hera; and entered Danae's chamber in the form of a shower of gold. Hercules is the Roman form of Heracles. The son of Jupiter, Hercules is one of the strongest and most celebrated heroes. At one point, he became a slave of Omphale, Queen of Lydia, in whose service he wore the dress of a woman and was employed in spinning. Delilah in the Bible betrayed Samson to the Philistines by shaving off the locks of his head and thereby depriving him of his strength: see Judges 16.

'*Excluded, as it were . . . within me, upon a few*': exact quotation not found in *Caleb Williams*. The closest passage is as follows: 'Excluded as I was from all intercourse with my species in general, I found pleasure in the occasional exchange of a few words with this inoffensive and good-humoured creature, who was already of an age to preclude scandal', iii. 257.

146 '*It is necessary for me to love and admire, or I sink into sadness*': a misquotation of Mary Wollstonecraft's sentiment, 'I must love and admire with warmth, or I sink into sadness', *Letters Written During a Short Residence in Sweden, Norway, and Denmark*, ed. Carol H. Poston (1796; Lincoln, Univ. of Nebraska Press, 1976), 74.

'*Unequal task . . . do all things but forget!*': Pope, 'Eloisa to Abelard' (1717), ll. 195–200.

147 *courage of an Alexander, . . . Augustus Caesar*: Alexander III, the Great (356–323 BC), King of Macedon and legendary conqueror of Egypt and Persia; François Ravaillac (1578–1610), the murderer of King Henry IV of France; Gaius Julius Caesar (101–44 BC), Roman statesman and general who joined Pompey and Crassus to form the first Triumvirate in 60 BC. In *Enquiry Concerning Political Justice* Godwin writes, 'The conquests of Alexander cost innumerable lives, and the immortality of Caesar is computed to have been purchased by the death of one million two hundred thousand men' (p. 84). Godwin also mentions Ravaillac: 'The most determined political assassins, Clement, Ravaillac, Damiens, and Gerard, seem to have been deeply penetrated with anxiety for the eternal welfare of mankind' (p. 188).

With the apostle, Paul, permit me to say—'I am not mad, but speak the words of truth and soberness': in response to Festus's accusation that he is beside himself, Paul says, 'I am not mad, most noble Festus; but speak forth the words of truth and soberness', Acts 26: 25.

150 *Hounslow and Bagshot heaths*: open tracts of land near Hounslow, a district chapelry in the county of Middlesex, $9\frac{1}{2}$ miles west-south-west from London; and Bagshot, a chapelry in Surrey 26 miles west-south-west from London on the great West road.

'*The moon . . . dark-brown sides.*': Hays has joined two lines from two separate pieces by Ossian. The first is from 'Carthon', ll. 11–14: 'Age is dark and unlovely; it is like the glimmering light of the moon, when it shines through broken clouds, and the mist is on the hills; the blast of north is on the plain, the traveller shrinks in the midst of his journey.' The other is from 'Dar-Thula: A Poem', ll. 3–4: 'The clouds rejoice in thy presence, O moon, and brighten their dark-brown sides.' Ossian, *Fingal; An Ancient Epic Poem in Six Books: Together with Several Other Poems composed by Ossian, the son of Fingal*, transl. James Macpherson (London, T. Becket & P. A. De Hondt, 1762).

the language of the tender Eloisa . . . the only object of anger and resentment': in a letter to Clara written just after the loss of her virginity, Eloisa writes of St. Preux: 'What evil genius could inspire you to invite him to return; him, alas! who is now the cruel author of my disgrace? And am I indebted to his care for a life, which he has since made insupportable by his cruelty?' *Eloisa: Or, A Series of Original Letters*, i. 97.

152 *almoner*: an official distributor of the alms of another.

156 *Rousseau was right . . . a noble soul*': exact quotation from Rousseau not found. However, in *Emilius*, the narrator tells Emile to think carefully when he considers his choice of a spouse: 'Not that the people of the lowest class are more vicious than those of the highest, but they have very few ideas of beauty and virtue, . . . They who spend their whole lives in working for a livelihood, have no other idea but that of their labour or their interest, and their sense and understanding seem to be seated in their hands', *Emilius; or, an Essay on Education*, transl. Mr Nugent (2 vols., London, J. Nourse & P. Vaillant, 1763), ii. 270–1.

'*Tuned to happy . . . displayed, its charms.*': James Thomson, *The Seasons*: 'Attuned to happy unison of soul; | To whose exalting eye a fairer world, | Of which the vulgar never had a glimpse, | Displays its charms,' 'Summer', ll. 1385–8.

163 *'One false idea . . . These things, known to the wise, are hid from fools!'*: Hays has condensed two paragraphs from Helvétius here. The original passages in ch. 13, 'Of the Evils Produced by an Indifference for the Truth' read: 'If [a man] adopts a false idea, that, united with others, produces such as are necessarily false, which combining again with all those his memory contains, give to all of them a greater or less tinge of falshood. Theologic errors are a proof of this: one of them is alone sufficient to infect the whole mass of a man's ideas, and produce an infinity of capricious, monstrous, and always unexpected ideas; for the birth of monsters can never be predicted before their delivery . . . Every vice, say the philosophers, is an error of the understanding. Crimes and prejudices are brothers; truth and virtue are sisters. But who are the parents of truth? Contradiction and dispute', *A Treatise on Man*, ii. 325.

166 *sooth*: soothe.

167 *the child of sorrow*: Mary Robinson, in *Walsingham; Or, The Pupil of Nature* (1797), also uses this term. 'I am the child of sorrow, the victim of deception. . . . Mine have been the errors of a too vivid imagination; the miseries of sensibility, acute, but not indiscriminate' (London, T. N. Longman; facsimile repr. New York, Garland, 1974), i. 7. Robinson had read *Emma Courtney*, and made comments to Mary Wollstonecraft about its ending (see Introduction).

171 *I ventured to open a vein*: Emma is performing what we would call bleeding, phlebotomy, or venesection. The most common technique for bleeding was to tie a bandage around the arm so the veins of the forearm would swell up and then to open the exposed vein with a sharp knife. Bloodletting was a long-established medical practice which lasted until the middle of the nineteenth century. In the eighteenth century there was some debate as to the efficacy of bleeding as a cure for fevers, but by the 1830s and 1840s the antiphlogistic system of treatment recommended copious bleeding, violent purgatives, and poor liquid diet for almost every kind of illness or malfunction.

177 *'passing the love of woman'*: an echo of 2 Samuel 1: 26, 'I am distressed for thee, my brother Jonathan: very pleasant hast thou been unto me: thy love to me was wonderful, passing the love of women.'

177   *hungary water*: a distilled water, named after the Queen of
      Hungary, for whose use it was first prepared, made of rose-
      mary flowers infused in rectified spirit of wine and then
      distilled.

193   '*While every day . . . new charm*': Thomson, *The Seasons*, 'The
      human blossom blows; and every day | Soft as it rolls along,
      shows some new charm,' 'Spring', ll. 1147–8.

194   '*That no agonies were like the agonies of a mother*': source not
      found.

195   *a Circean cup*: in Book 10 of Homer's *Odyssey*, Odysseus
      and his men land on the island of Aeaea where the darkly
      beautiful witch goddess, Circe, daughter of Helios, offers
      them food and wine. When they eat and drink, the men all
      turn into pigs. Odysseus is able to resist the spell because he
      is given a herb by Hermes.

	Women's Writing 1778–1838
WILLIAM BECKFORD	**Vathek**
JAMES BOSWELL	**Life of Johnson**
FRANCES BURNEY	**Camilla**
	Cecilia
	Evelina
	The Wanderer
LORD CHESTERFIELD	**Lord Chesterfield's Letters**
JOHN CLELAND	**Memoirs of a Woman of Pleasure**
DANIEL DEFOE	**A Journal of the Plague Year**
	Moll Flanders
	Robinson Crusoe
	Roxana
HENRY FIELDING	**Joseph Andrews and Shamela**
	A Journey from This World to the Next and The Journal of a Voyage to Lisbon
	Tom Jones
WILLIAM GODWIN	**Caleb Williams**
OLIVER GOLDSMITH	**The Vicar of Wakefield**
MARY HAYS	**Memoirs of Emma Courtney**
ELIZABETH HAYWOOD	**The History of Miss Betsy Thoughtless**
ELIZABETH INCHBALD	**A Simple Story**
SAMUEL JOHNSON	**The History of Rasselas**
	The Major Works
CHARLOTTE LENNOX	**The Female Quixote**
MATTHEW LEWIS	**Journal of a West India Proprietor**
	The Monk
HENRY MACKENZIE	**The Man of Feeling**
ALEXANDER POPE	**Selected Poetry**